APOSTLE *to the* PLAINS

The Life of Father Nicola Yanney

THE SAINT RAPHAEL CLERGY BROTHERHOOD

ANCIENT FAITH PUBLISHING
CHESTERTON, INDIANA

Apostle to the Plains: The Life of Father Nicola Yanney

Published by:
Ancient Faith Publishing
A Division of Ancient Faith Ministries
P.O. Box 748
Chesterton, IN 46304

ISBN: 978-1-944967-65-9

Printed in the United States of America

Contents

Preface & Acknowledgments

The Reverend Nicola Yanney was the first priest to be ordained by Saint Raphael of Brooklyn after his own consecration to the episcopacy during Great Lent of 1904. Thus, Father Nicola was the first man to be ordained by the first Orthodox bishop consecrated in the Western Hemisphere.

Immediately after his ordination, Father Nicola returned to his home in central Nebraska, where he was tasked with continuing Saint Raphael's missionary labors across the Great Plains, thereby freeing the holy bishop to focus his pastoral efforts in other areas of his newly formed diocese. Father Nicola pastored thousands of Orthodox Christians within his missionary territory and remained a circuit-riding priest until the end of his earthly life. However, due to historical circumstances, his incredible ministry has remained little known to Orthodox Christians in North America. It is hoped that this book will contribute to a greater knowledge and appreciation of this faithful servant of God.

To begin with, this book was not a book. Though some research into the life of Father Nicola Yanney had previously taken place, much of what you will read in these pages was found—or rather rediscovered—beginning in 2007. In preparation for a diocesan pilgrimage held in Kearney, Nebraska, in 2008 in honor of the ninetieth anniversary of Father Nicola's repose, members of the Saint Raphael Clergy Brotherhood began searching for additional information about the missionary priest. This research soon turned into a project tracing Father Nicola's personal and cultural background, as well as focusing on his priestly ministry.

During this time, Father Nicola's handwritten sacramental record books were rediscovered. As these records were slowly translated from Arabic into English, the full scope of Father Nicola's ministry came to light. Notes from the many baptisms, weddings, and funerals that he performed made it possible to reconstruct his extensive missionary journeys. Concurrently, the search for articles about Father Nicola that had begun with local newspapers was expanded to include periodicals printed in the many far-flung communities he regularly visited.

As this much greater pool of information accumulated, the story of Father Nicola's incredible life emerged. What originally began as a brief study had unexpectedly yielded enough material for a full-fledged biography. As is evident from the extensive bibliography, this research could have been presented in a more academic format. However, a decision was made to write this book as the story of a man's life in order to appeal to a wider audience.

It is our hope that in learning about Father Nicola Yanney, you will experience the same feelings of inspiration and gratitude the compilers of this biography felt during the years of research that led to this book. It has been a collaborative effort involving many individuals to whom are due special thanks.

First and foremost, we offer our thanks to Bishop Basil (Essey) of Wichita and Mid-America for his continued prayers and support of this project and for writing the foreword to this book. Through his eloquent words and personal interest, Bishop Basil has kept the memory of Father Nicola Yanney before the hearts and minds of the clergy and faithful of his diocese, leading to this present biography.

Thanks to Archbishop Michael (Dahulich) of New York and New Jersey and the Very Reverend Alexey Karlgut for translating several of Saint Raphael's missionary journal entries from Russian into English and providing us with the wonderful details of Saint Raphael and Father Nicola's very first meeting.

The years of combined research from the Hieromonk Philip (Vreeland), the Very Reverend Paul Hodge, the Very Reverend Christopher Morris, and Andrew Walker into the life of Father Nicola proved invaluable in compiling this biography. Our heartfelt thanks to each of you.

The Very Reverend Gabriel Karam graciously offered his time on several occasions to translate Arabic sources and search for information concerning Father Nicola in the al-Kalemat magazine.

Nizar Wehbi provided translations of correspondence from Lebanon and numerous Yanney family letters. He also discovered one of the eulogies included in this biography. We thank Nizar for his kind and valuable help.

Thanks to Rafaat Saba of Tripoli, Lebanon, who graciously provided important historical information about the Yanney family and the village of Fi'eh al-Koura. We also offer our thanks to Georges Karam for sharing his photos of the ancestral Yanney home, the village of Fi'eh, and the church of Saint Simeon.

We offer our gratitude to Doctor Diane Beauchemin of Queen's University in Kingston, Ontario, who confirmed an important detail about Father Nicola's pocket watch and chain through her forensic research.

During the years of research, many others offered valuable

information and helpful leads. Among them are the Very Reverend Andrew Damick, the Very Reverend Timothy Ferguson, Murrish Yanney of blessed memory, Michael Yanney, Lisa (Yanney) Roskens, Milly (Yanney) Shada of blessed memory, Norma Deeb, Wayne Yanney, Nicholas Shada, Irene (Yanney) Blomquist of blessed memory, Marci Duryea, Michael Kacere, Tom Salem, the volunteers at Buffalo County Trails and Rails Museum, the children of Moses Yanney, and the children and grandchildren of Elias Khoury Yanney. Thanks to all of you, and others who remain unnamed, who proved crucial to this project.

Special thanks are due to Orthodox historian Matthew Namee for his continued interest and help, as well as his research tips and constant encouragement. Matthew repeatedly showed his great love and admiration for Father Nicola by providing us with a wider ecclesiastical context for the missionary priest's life as well as many personal and historical insights. We especially thank Matthew for writing the afterword to this book.

Special thanks are also due to Rocky Steinbrink, great-grandson of Father Nicola, for his enthusiasm for this project and for providing most of the photos and primary sources for our research. Thank you, Rocky, for helping complete the work that your mother, Minnette, began so many years ago.

We offer our deepest thanks to Virginia Suleiman. Without Virginia's inestimable help, this biography would not have been possible. Virginia spent many hours reading and translating most of the Arabic sources into English—including Father Nicola's sacramental records, notes from the Yanney family Bible, Arabic newspaper articles, and volumes of the al-Kalemat magazine. Because of Virginia's work, we now know where and when Father Nicola traveled in his ministry, as well as many personal details about his life. We are greatly indebted to her for completing the translation work begun by her beloved and dearly departed husband Bob. May God richly reward Virginia for her selfless labors.

The work to compile and preserve Father Nicola's story first began with Minnette Steinbrink of blessed memory, paternal granddaughter of Father Nicola, with the help of Bob Suleiman of blessed memory. Their work provided the foundation upon which this biography was completed. May their memory be eternal!

Finally, thanks are due to Sarah Fothergill, Anastasia Morris, and Amy Hadley, who offered many helpful suggestions and corrections during earlier drafts of this biography, to Katherine Hyde for her tremendous editorial help, and to Ancient Faith Ministries for making this book available to a wide readership.

Whoever reads this record and finds any mistake in it,
please correct it in God's name, and God will correct
his life in this world and in the life to come,
because no one is perfect except God,
who has no mistakes.

Foreword

Blessed is he whom Thou hast chosen and taken to Thyself; he shall dwell in Thy courts. (Psalm 64:5)

July 1, 1987, was my first day as proistamenos at St. George Church (now Cathedral) in Wichita, Kansas. Shortly thereafter I was called upon to visit an elderly parishioner who was nearing death. After I prayed with the gentleman, he gave me a photo of a black-bearded priest surrounded by several of his young sons, saying, "This is the priest who baptized me and several of my siblings here in Wichita many decades ago. He baptized many children here, but since he was a visiting priest I do not recall his name." Later, after returning to my office, I noticed an embossed seal on the lower right corner of the sepia-colored photo, giving the name of the photographic studio and its location—Kearney, Nebraska.

I wrote to Father (now Hieromonk) Philip Vreeland, proistamenos at St. George Church in Kearney, and sent along a copy of the photo, asking if by chance he might know the name of the priest. Evidently he passed my inquiry on to Minnette Yanney-Steinbrink, because shortly thereafter this now-departed faithful woman (may God give her Paradise!) began what would become an extended and extensive correspondence with me about the priest in the old photograph—her paternal grandfather, Father Nicola Yanney.

Since then, we have come to know and admire much about Father Nicola (may the Lord God remember his priesthood in His kingdom always!), whose final resting place in Kearney Cemetery has been the site of two diocese-wide pilgrimages (in 2008 and 2018). On December 15, 2004, I spoke the following words in my homily upon being enthroned at St. George Cathedral in Wichita, Kansas, as the first bishop of the newly created Diocese of Wichita and Mid-America:

> That which we celebrate this evening is something much bigger and of greater importance than me or any one person. It is much bigger and of greater importance than this Cathedral or any one holy temple, this City of Wichita or any one town, this State of Kansas or any one state. That which is the cause of our great rejoicing and the reason for this festive celebration is the establishment, by the Will of God, of the Diocese of Wichita and Mid-America—a recognition that the pleroma, the fullness, of the Church of Christ lives and breathes right here in America's Heartland. Shortly after his consecration to the sacred episcopacy a century ago—on March 13, 1904—St. Raphael of Brooklyn performed his first priestly ordination, the ordinand being a young widower, Nicola Yanney, a native of the tiny village of Fi'eh in north Lebanon, living with his children on a farm in Gibbon, Nebraska. Father Nicola was ordained for what was then the westernmost parish of St. Raphael's Diocese, St. George Church in Kearney, Nebraska, but he was given pastoral responsibility for an area that is nearly identical to the boundaries of our newly created Diocese

of Mid-America. Father Nicola's parish stretched from the Canadian border in the north, to the Mexican border in the south, and from the Mississippi River in the east, to the Rocky Mountains in the west. It is Father Nicola who, as a circuit-riding priest headquartered in Kearney, followed the example of his Father in Christ, St. Raphael, and visited Orthodox Christians in the scattered towns, villages and isolated farmlands throughout America's Heartland.

Could Father Nicola, the sole priest serving a parish as large as the Great Plains, have imagined that the seeds he planted would bear fruit this day as we witness the birth of a Diocese comprised of fifty congregations and served by a Bishop and dozens of priests and deacons? Could any among those immigrants gathered with him at Divine Liturgy in a crowded living room on the west side of Wichita have imagined that exactly one century later there would be in this All-American city (named for a local tribe of Native Americans and which counts among its founders Catherine McCarty, the mother of Billy the Kid) a Diocesan Cathedral? "Come and see the works of the Lord, how awesome He is in His counsels, more than the sons of men" (Ps. 65:4). We bless the memory of Father Nicola and his brothers in the sacred priesthood who came after him to minister to Christ's flock in Mid-America, and we bless the memory of their wives and children and of all the sons and daughters of the Church who first brought Holy Orthodoxy to the Great Plains and witnessed to its Truth by their very lives. God grant that we be found worthy of their sacrifice.

The members of the St. Raphael Clergy Brotherhood of the Diocese of Wichita and Mid-America are pleased to offer for your edification, dear reader, this volume about the life and ministry of our predecessor here in the Great Plains Father Nicola Yanney, and pray that it may be soul-profiting to you. May this book be blessed to the glory of the All-holy Trinity and the upbuilding of Holy Orthodoxy.

+BASIL
Bishop of Wichita and Mid-America
Antiochian Orthodox Christian Archdiocese
of North America

CHAPTER ONE

Leaving Koura

DECEMBER 1892

NICOLA YANNEY LINGERED AT THE edge of the pier and stared at the ship that lay anchored in the open waters beyond the harbor. It was an awesome sight. The massive hull stretched a hundred meters from bow to stern. Two spindly masts sprung from its deck, but no sails hung from the rigging. As he watched, a wisp of black smoke rose from the towering chimney and disappeared against the brightening sky. The ship was a steamer. Within a month, it would bear him to the other side of the world, where a promised land and a new life awaited.

A cold wind blowing from the sea nipped at Nicola's lean face and ruffled his dark brown hair. Pulling his coat tighter around his wiry frame, he searched the harbor again and spied a string of dinghies moving across the water. The first passengers were being ferried out to the steamer. Their tiny forms blurred together as each oar stroke carried them farther from shore. Soon, Nicola would join them.

The exodus had begun a decade earlier. At first, it had been a slow trickle, with only a handful leaving Nicola's homeland. With each successive year, however, their numbers grew. A steady stream of a few thousand was now departing for the New World each year. Though it would still be another two decades before the emigration reached its peak, every villager in the land already knew someone who had made for America.

Nicola's older sister had been the first from their family to leave. She had married at fourteen; two years after their wedding her husband had left to work in Pennsylvania. Opportunities abounded there, and, deciding to stay, he sent for his wife a year later. The parting was hard on Nicola. Born only ten months apart, he and his sister had been particularly close, especially since the death of their mother.

Nicola's best friend, John Shada, was the next to leave. His departure came unexpectedly. One morning, Nicola woke up to find that John, along with two of his older brothers, had disappeared from the village. News quickly spread that their mother had sworn them to secrecy, then stolen away with them while their father was far from home on business. By the time her unsuspecting husband had returned from his trip, she and her sons were halfway around the world.

John eventually came home. More than a year later, the three brothers strolled back into the village as unexpectedly as they had left. They instantly became local celebrities, regaling their friends with tales of the vast country they had crisscrossed by hopping freight cars. As Nicola and the others listened eagerly, they heard of sprawling cities and powerful steam engines that pulled long trains across endless prairies. Although there were no rumored streets of gold to be found, the money with which John and his brothers had returned was compelling enough.

Soon, another of Nicola's close friends sailed away, making for a town in Michigan where a few others from their village were working as peddlers. The biggest surprise, however, came when Nicola's two younger brothers decided to leave for New York together. The youngest was only fifteen and, sadly, the boys' journey took an unexpected turn that ended with each of them arriving on different continents.

Nicola had always been sad to see his loved ones leave without him. He, too, had long thought of going to America. Letters from his friends and siblings urged him to follow. Nicola, however, had chosen to stay. He did not fear the long passage or the miserable conditions aboard the steamers. Nor did his brothers' mishap dissuade him. Even his love for his homeland was not enough to hold him there. Only two things kept Nicola from leaving home. One was a young woman named Martha. The other was his father.

Martha al-Baik was a petite young woman with dark eyes and brown hair. Only a few months older than Nicola, she lived with her parents and siblings in a neighboring village. Like the Yanneys, her family was devout and well respected. Because the two families were known to each other, arrangements had been made for Nicola and Martha to marry when they came of age. Almost twenty years old, Martha was older than many of the girls in her village who had already married.

Though they had never been alone together, Nicola had seen Martha frequently during his youth. He often passed through her village of Qilhat on the way to the nearby Balamand monastery. Like many villagers, the Yanneys were close to the monks and often went to the monastery on feast days. Sometimes, Nicola saw Martha and her family praying in the monastery church. He had also attended a school run by the monks in Martha's village.

There, he had learned to read and write and had been educated in his Orthodox Christian faith.

Nicola also passed through Qilhat whenever he went to visit his mother's grave. His mother had died when he was only thirteen years old, and was buried in Balamand's cemetery, near one of his older brothers who had died a year earlier. While visiting their graves, Nicola also stopped to see his orphaned nephew who was attending the school and living at the monastery.

As the time drew closer for him to marry Martha, Nicola grew worried, wondering how he would provide for a family. With so few opportunities in the village, he once again thought of America. From his talks with John, Nicola knew that in America he could make more money than he had ever dreamed possible. Many of his fellow countrymen held the same hope. After working for a few years in the New World, they dreamed of returning home with enough wealth to help their families and live comfortably for the rest of their lives.

With the wedding only a few months away, the decision whether to stay or go grew more urgent. If he decided to go, Nicola could get married, then leave for America alone—as his brother-in-law and almost all of the married men did—with the promise that he would return to Martha as soon as he could. Nicola might also delay their wedding and go to America as a single man, as his best friend John had done, and, like John, promise to return home in a few short years.

Neither option appealed to Nicola. Though the married men always promised to return, very few ever did. Instead, after long years of separation, they inevitably sent money to their wives and children, along with instructions on how to make the crossing to join them in the New World. Nicola could not imagine leaving Martha to make the harrowing journey by herself years later if he decided to stay in America. The single men, too, rarely came back, and almost every one that did soon changed his mind. Even his friend John was already thinking of returning to America.

Besides Martha, Nicola had an even greater concern. With the departure of his younger brothers, he was the only child left at home. Nicola's parents, Elias and Katherine, had seven children. Along with his younger brothers, Nicola had two older brothers and two older sisters. With one brother dead and a sister living in Pennsylvania, only Nicola's oldest brother and oldest sister remained. His oldest brother, who was something of a wanderer and liked to travel abroad, was living far to the south in Beirut. Nicola's oldest sister lived nearby; she was married, however, and busy raising children of her own. With their mother gone, Nicola was the only one at home with his aged father.

Though Nicola's father was still in good health, at seventy-five, Elias Yanney was too old to make the crossing. Besides maintaining the family home, the Yanneys farmed several scattered plots of land some distance from their village. When Nicola's siblings first began to leave, they had still hoped to come back one day. Someone had to stay behind to help his father tend the family's properties until everyone returned, or so Nicola had once believed. Sadly, the same conditions that had compelled his loved ones and so many others to leave weighed just as heavily on him. Life in the village had always been difficult, but in recent years, it had become almost unbearable.

Those who left had done so reluctantly, so deeply did they love their home. A small land nestled between Mount Lebanon and the Mediterranean Sea, its inhabitants called it Koura. In between the weathered foothills that rose from the rocky coastline and the majestic mountains that lay further inland, the country opened into rolling plains. Olive orchards covered the plains, and groves of fruit trees grew on the weathered hilltops and up the terraced hillsides. Dozens of villages dotted the countryside, clusters of small limestone homes set against the rich greens and browns of the hills and the deep blues of the sea.

Koura's inhabitants proudly traced their lineage to the Phoenician traders who had once built their civilization along its shores. Their ancestors had seen other great empires rise and fall. Assyrians, Persians, and Romans had all laid claim to their land, only to disappear with time. Travelers from the Far East had passed through with their heavy-laden caravans during the days of the Silk Road. Prophets and apostles had walked along their roads and preached the Good News in their towns. Invading Crusaders had raised battlements on their hills, which the residents later rebuilt into churches and monasteries.

Nicola's village sat atop the highest hill in Koura and commanded the most splendid view in all the land. Its name was Fi'eh. Though only thirty or forty extended families lived there, the larger port city of Tripoli lay a day's walk to the north. Beirut and Damascus were a week's journey to the south.

After laboring all day, the villagers of Fi'eh gathered in their homes for a large evening meal, then went from house to house,

The village of Fi'eh in Koura, Lebanon

visiting friends and relatives. In the evenings, they watched as the sun set the Mediterranean ablaze, its fiery glow reflected on the snow-covered peaks in the east. On many nights, the villagers slept outside beneath the stars. Though Nicola and his loved ones felt that their home was the most beautiful place on earth, sadly, their lives there had become a misery.

Two decades earlier, their economy had begun to collapse, together with a burgeoning cottage industry that had promised to bring prosperity from Beirut all the way to Tripoli. Silk had become the region's greatest export, and every family who owned a piece of land planted mulberry trees and began raising the worms that spun the precious thread. The Suez Canal, however, opened a trade route between the Far East and the Europeans who had once eagerly bought the villagers' silk by the ton. The new canal made the formidable trip to the Orient far easier, and cheap silk from China and Japan soon flooded the market. Prices plummeted, and many in Nicola's homeland were driven back into poverty.

Like most villagers, the Yanneys had returned to farming. In the hilly countryside around the village, however, good land was scarce. Nicola's family—whose ancestors had fled to Koura from Cyprus two centuries earlier—had less land than many whose families who had lived in Fi'eh much longer. Over the years, Nicola's family had acquired several plots that they passed down from father to son. On these, they raised olive and fruit trees and grew whatever produce they could.

With few tools, Koura's farmers relied on methods dating back to biblical times. The arduous, time-consuming work had hardened and calloused Nicola's large hands. Every day, he would trek to the family's plots to tend their trees and vegetables, carry water for irrigation, or haul soil to build up terraces on the uneven ground. Even in good years, the harvest was humble.

Not everyone in Fi'eh relied on farming. Several villagers ran small shops. A few worked as stone masons, cutting the white limestone from the hillsides and shaping it into the blocks from which Koura's homes and churches were fashioned. The family of Nicola's best friend made their living as caravaners, driving pack camels over the mountains back and forth to Damascus. The poorest wandered from village to village, peddling goods wherever they could. Regardless of the profession, surviving grew harder with each passing year.

The oppression they faced was even worse than their poverty. For centuries, Nicola's people had suffered under the cruel reign of the Turks. Though every village in Koura was Orthodox Christian, Koura was only a small region in Greater Syria,[1] itself a province in the Ottomans' vast empire. Nicola and his loved ones were second-class citizens who were forced to pay a heavy price for their faith.

Bands of armed soldiers regularly swept through the villages on horseback to collect the exorbitant taxes required of the Christians. Taking more than their law demanded, the Turks left Nicola's people with little on which to live. The roving gangs mistreated anyone they suspected of hiding money. Even the elderly were sometimes beaten, and the young women were afraid to leave home alone for fear of being robbed and raped.

More and more frequently, people talked about the bad times. Nicola could not remember them—they had happened before he was born. Many of the villagers, however, had lived through the great wave of violence that had swept over the entire land. By the time the Massacre of 1860 was over, tens of thousands lay

1 Greater Syria included the territories of Syria, Lebanon, Palestine, and Jordan.

slaughtered, and hundreds of churches and villages were burned to the ground. Ever since, there had been a tenuous peace, but many believed that the terrible days were bound to return.

Amid the growing fears and the crushing poverty, Nicola finally realized that he, too, must leave. The family obligations that had once convinced him to stay were now compelling him to go. He would soon be married, and he wanted Martha and their children to live in safety and peace. Sadly, Nicola realized that his siblings, too, were never coming back and that he could do far more for his father in America than by remaining at his side. In America, he could make a new home not only for himself and Martha but also for his brothers. If they all worked together, Nicola could send enough money to make sure that their father would live the rest of his days in comfort, cared for by loved ones who would remain in their village. To do this, however, Nicola himself would have to leave home.

Once he had made his decision, Nicola was swept up in a whirlwind of activity. First, he had to break the news to Martha and her family and convince her to go with him. Then, he had to make arrangements for their passage. The tickets would be expensive. Because Nicola had few items that could be sold for cash, most of the money would have to be borrowed and paid back once he found work in America. Fortunately, his friend John knew a businessman in Nebraska—himself once an émigré from Koura—who could help him.

A date also had to be picked for their wedding. Nicola wanted to leave soon after the ceremony, so he and Martha chose a day before the beginning of the upcoming Christmas fast. Since the betrothal had taken place in Qilhat, the wedding would take place in Fi'eh. Nicola was happy because theirs would be one of the first weddings in the village's new church.

For most of his youth, Nicola had worked with his father and brothers alongside the other villagers building the stone church. It was dedicated to the village's patron saint, Simeon the Stylite. Ever since a miracle associated with the saint had occurred in the village many years earlier, Saint Simeon had become Fi'eh's beloved protector. Every year, they celebrated his feast day with a great festival to which all the surrounding villages were invited. Nicola remembered the most recent one vividly. On the day of the Orthodox New Year, September 1, the church that he had helped to build was finally consecrated. Martha and her family had been in the crowd. Now, only a few months later, he and Martha would be married there.

When the time for the wedding came, there was a weeklong celebration. On the Feast of the Archangels, November 8, a priest from Martha's village joined the priest from Nicola's village for the ceremony. Nicola's friend John stood by his side as his best man. According to the custom, John was to be godfather to their children, though Nicola wondered how that would ever be possible since he and Martha were soon to leave.

Too quickly the festivities were over, and Nicola and Martha made their final preparations to depart. Nicola bought their tickets, and Martha cooked food to bring with them on their long voyage. They visited their extended family and friends and went to the monastery for the last time. They also went to confession and received Holy Communion, not knowing when they would again see an Orthodox priest or partake of the Sacrament.

The hardest farewells came when Nicola and Martha said goodbye to their parents. Nicola had received his father's blessing to go, and they embraced tearfully, doubtful that they would ever see each other again. Other family members and friends wept and prayed over the young couple, asking God to bless their journey. A few of his younger relatives even dreamed of following Nicola someday and hoped to meet him again on the other side of the world.

After the sad parting, Nicola walked through his beloved village for the last time. He knew each rock and tree in Fi'eh, and he knew every family that lived in each house he passed. The long walk from the Yanney home to the harbor had taken him down through the hills and past Martha's village, where she wept as she said goodbye to her family, leaving behind everything she had ever known.

The young couple made their way to the village next to the harbor. One of Nicola's ancestors had been the priest there long ago. Nicola and Martha found the steamship agents' office, and the next morning they made their way to the harbor to board the steamer. The pier was crowded with excited and apprehensive passengers, almost all of them young men. An even larger crowd of women and children gathered along the shoreline, come to say goodbye and watch the ship as it sailed away.

One of the few women on the pier, Martha stood next to her husband, hidden beneath the heavy layers she wore to protect her from the winter air and the steamer's cold compartments. She looked to Nicola nervously. Though her village was only ten miles away, she was already farther from home than she had ever been.

As Martha watched him, Nicola scanned the harbor, then he peered back up into the hills toward his home. At nineteen years old, he was the same age as many of those on the pier. Yet, despite the touch of boyishness that still lingered in his face, he had a thoughtful air. His deep-set eyes were often inscrutable. A few weeks earlier Nicola and Martha had been almost strangers. Now, they were leaving for the New World together.

The passengers began to move again toward the empty

dinghies at the end of the pier. A few harried steamship agents wound their way through the crowd, checking their manifests and shouting directions at the anxious passengers. All clutched their tickets. Even with their departure so near, some still feared the worst. The Ottoman officials who might bar their escape, however, had been bribed by the steamship agents earlier and were nowhere to be seen.

The crowd moved again, and the couple found themselves looking down into one of the small boats. The moment had finally come. As hard as it was for Nicola to leave, for Martha it was terrifying. She feared the large ship, the long voyage, and the unknown world that waited at its end. She was making the journey with a man she barely knew. In this, however, Martha was comforted. While the other married men on the pier were craning their necks to catch a last glimpse of their wives and children along the shore, Nicola was unique. Not wanting to be parted, he had convinced Martha to join him. Though desperately frightened, she had found the faith and the courage to come.

Nicola climbed down into the boat and reached up to help Martha. She settled uncomfortably at her husband's side. After the last passenger had taken his seat, the rowers untied the dinghy and cast out into the harbor. The crowd on the shoreline grew small while the great ship loomed before them. Martha and Nicola stared in awe. It was even more massive than it had appeared from the pier.

Arriving at the steamer's hull, the young couple climbed up a ladder onto the deck high above. A uniformed steward met them. Nicola presented their tickets, and they were waved through a doorway in the bulkhead. The blue skies and the bright sunlight disappeared as the Yanneys stepped through the hatch and followed the other passengers down the steep stairs. Remembering what his best friend had told him, Nicola steeled himself for what he and Martha might find.

Naked lightbulbs strung from the ceiling dimly lit their way as they descended deeper into the bowels of the ship. Far below deck, Nicola and Martha were overcome by the stench as they filed into a dingy compartment. The large room smelled of vomit and sweat, mixed with the scent of the seawater that had been used to mop the filthy floors.

Rows of narrow bunks filled the room and lined the walls. Nicola and Martha chose two berths and laid out their bedding and few belongings on the rough mattresses. The narrow beds would be their only haven for the next two weeks. Along with the extra layers they each wore, they carried a few eating utensils and the food that Martha had made for their journey. The money for the rest of their trip remained hidden in their clothing.

After settling in their bunks, Nicola and Martha waited as the compartment continued to fill. In a short time, the passengers were called back on deck for an examination before the ship's departure. Routine inspections were required by the immigration authorities, especially by those in America. Any number of illnesses might cause the emigrants to be turned away.

The very first exam had taken place onshore when Nicola had purchased their tickets. After the agents had filled out Nicola's and Martha's manifests, a man had checked their mouths, ears, and eyes, and looked for any signs of disease or deformity. On deck, the process was repeated once more. The stewards hurriedly lined up the passengers as a man walked quickly down the rows. He glanced at the emigrants' general appearance and briefly looked at their eyes. The exam was cursory, done to meet regulations more than to weed out the sick.

After the inspection, they waited on deck for the last supplies to be loaded. In the meantime, Nicola and Martha mingled with their fellow passengers. They soon found others they knew from neighboring villages who were also going to America, and they all began excitedly sharing details about where they were going and what they hoped awaited them at the end of the journey.

Within a few hours, the ship was made ready to sail. With a loud blast and a belch of smoke from the chimney high above, the ship began to move. Shouts of joy went up with cries of sorrow on the crowded deck. Looking east, the Yanneys gazed at their home for the last time. As he looked to the foothills rising up to his village and the snowy peaks beyond, the decision to leave still grieved Nicola. He loved the mountains, the hills, the sea, the monks, and the old stone churches scattered throughout the countryside. Most of all, he loved his family and friends in Fi'eh.

Nicola knew that history was repeating itself. His distant ancestor—the first Yanney to come to their land—had once fled his own home in Cyprus because of religious persecution and overwhelming poverty. His forebear had made his way to Koura to find a new home. He had married and raised his family there, eventually becoming a priest in the small village next to the harbor. Now it was Nicola's turn to sail away. He wondered if his family would also find a welcome home in a foreign land so far away.

Neither he nor Martha would ever set foot in Koura again, and their hearts would ache for the rest of their lives for the homeland they had to leave behind. As their ship pulled out to sea, the village next to the harbor shrank, and the pier was soon gone from sight. The hills faded and the mountains became a faint blur. Nicola and Martha watched until Koura became a thin line on the horizon, then finally disappeared. The newlyweds turned west and faced the open sea.

CHAPTER TWO

New World

JANUARY TO NOVEMBER 1893

WEARY FROM THEIR LONG JOURNEY, Nicola and Martha climbed onto the deck of the steamship for the last time. It was even more crowded than usual. Throughout their journey—both the trip from Syria to France and again from France to America—the decks of the ships had been their refuge. Whenever they could, the newlyweds fled there, driven back down below only by heavy rains and rough seas. Together with their steerage mates, they had endured plenty of both, especially during the Atlantic crossing.

The trip from the harbor near Tripoli had taken two weeks. Little had Nicola known that what appeared to him a massive ship anchored off the port of al-Mina was only a midsize freighter. Over the course of its trip, the freighter had made many stops along the Mediterranean coast. Cargo and livestock were loaded and unloaded at each port. Most of the passengers, however, had remained onboard, bound for France, and from there, hoping to make for North or South America. New travelers boarded at each stop, cramming themselves into any spare berth or empty corner they could find.

At first, Nicola's excitement had bolstered him against the miserable conditions, and he had encouraged Martha as best he could. Huddling with a small group of newfound friends, the couple sang folk songs from Koura or shared stories about their friend John and his brothers or their other loved ones who had already made their way to America. Seasickness, however, struck quickly. Nicola comforted Martha when she fell ill, reminding her of the wonders waiting for them in the New World. When not confined to their bunks with nausea, the Yanneys escaped to the deck, enduring the cold and wind for the sake of the fresh air.

Finally, their ship had arrived in France. With prayers of thanksgiving, Nicola and Martha stepped onto dry land. For days afterward, they felt the ground swell beneath their feet as if they were still on the sea. With the help of some fellow Syrians[2] who worked for the steamship line, the Yanneys found a hostel in which to stay until the next ship for America departed. Martha was especially happy to be out of the cramped, smelly freighter. Nicola, however, was anxious to continue their journey. While they waited, they replenished their supplies for the next leg of the journey and enjoyed a short respite, eating fresh food and sleeping in clean beds.

Word soon came of a steamer bound for New York. Before leaving the hostel, the couple had to undergo another medical examination by the steamship officials, this time more thorough than the one they had received on the freighter. Seeing that Nicola and Martha were in good health, the officials escorted them back to the bustling port where they had arrived several days before.

---

2 During the Yanneys' lifetimes, the modern state of Lebanon did not yet exist. Because immigrants from Greater Syria identified themselves as "Syrian" at this time, the term is used throughout the book.

The port of Le Havre was the very place where Nicola's younger brothers, George and John, had been separated a year earlier. Lost among the throng of people and the many ships, each had heard a cry for a departure to America and raced to a nearby ship, hoping to find the other brother already aboard. It was only after his ship was out to sea that John realized his mistake. Though he searched for George, he was nowhere to be found. Too late, John found out that his steamer was bound for South America. George, in the meantime, had gotten on their intended ship sailing for New York.

Sadly, the brothers never saw each other again. John would live the rest of his days in Brazil working on a plantation, while George arrived in America alone. Once there, the lonely teenager wandered the city streets for a day until he was taken in by a Syrian family. After peddling for a short time, George had made his way to Canada, where he found work as a farmhand.

Standing amid the hubbub, Nicola now understood how his younger brothers had gotten separated and confused and ended up on different ships. Nicola held Martha's hand tightly as they navigated through the crowd, searching for their steamer.

Arriving at the pier, Nicola and Martha stared in amazement. An enormous passenger liner stood before them, tethered directly to the dock. Its hull rose like a sheer cliff from the water, stretching twice as long as the freighter that had brought them to Le Havre. Twin masts and double smokestacks soared high above. More than a thousand people could fit inside the behemoth. Gripping their tickets, Nicola and Martha followed a swarm of passengers up the gangplank and were once again herded down into the belly of a ship. The steam liner was newer than the freighter and had better steerage compartments. They were nonetheless damp and poorly lit, and Martha noticed the all-too-familiar stench of seasickness that the recent mopping could not hide.

The newlyweds followed other married couples and families into the center compartments, while the single men were taken to a forward room and the single women to the aft. Though much larger, the passenger liner's steerage was arranged like the freighter had been, with bunks along each wall and stacked in rows in the middle of the room. The Yanneys found two berths, stowed their belongings, and returned to the deck.

Another inspection soon took place, with a bona fide ship's doctor examining the steerage passengers. The physician peered into Martha's and Nicola's eyes, searching for the dreaded trachoma, an eye disease that had turned many would-be immigrants back at the very threshold of America. A second physician followed and vaccinated all the passengers to help keep them from contracting a disease during the voyage. Over the next few hours, the first- and second-class passengers boarded, and the steamship soon left Le Havre.

If possible, the second leg of their journey was even worse than the first. The ship's stewards shouted impatiently, treating Nicola and Martha and the other steerage passengers little better than cattle. The ship's food—delivered by the stewards in pails—was plentiful, though barely edible, and their quarters were especially cramped during mealtimes as the hungry crowds scrambled to be served. The Yanneys mostly ate the food they had brought with them and retired to the deck whenever they could. As their voyage progressed, however, eating became nearly impossible.

Though the living conditions were less deplorable than those on the freighter and the route to New York took only half the time, the seas were much rougher. Without knowing, the Yanneys had chosen the worst season to cross the Atlantic. In the open ocean, many of the passengers were afflicted with terrible seasickness, unable to rise from their bunks for days at a time. The steerage floor became slick with vomit, and the stench was overwhelming. No stewards came to clean the mess. In the poorly ventilated compartments, the air became stifling, and those who could manage climbed to the deck to escape the reek, even sleeping there if the weather allowed.

Of the hundreds of emigrants aboard, only a very small group were from Nicola and Martha's homeland. Most came from Western Europe, although a handful came from as far east as Russia. At first, Nicola tried to converse with the strangers using hand gestures, but the passengers soon settled into cliques with their fellow countrymen as the initial excitement of their journey gave way to grim endurance.

Every few days, the Yanneys were herded with everyone else onto deck and formed into long lines for further examinations. Those who could not rise from their beds might be given a cursory visit from one of the ship's physicians. After what seemed a far longer trip than their journey from Tripoli to France, Nicola and Martha heard a rumor passing from bunk to bunk. Rising from their beds, they followed after their steerage mates and shuffled onto deck.

The atmosphere quickly changed, with excited voices rising all around them. Everyone was looking over the port side. Peering into the distance, Nicola and Martha saw a dark strip on the horizon and sighed with relief. The last day of their ocean passage had finally come—they had made it to the New World. As they waited and watched, a dim shoreline appeared and passed before their eyes as the steamship skirted south of Long Island. A signal flashed from somewhere on land. A message had been relayed to the quarantine station, and the ship was instructed to proceed and rendezvous with the inspectors.

The passenger liner turned into a large bay and the stewards reappeared, herding those who were not already on deck up for the final shipboard examination. All around Nicola and Martha the passengers talked excitedly in a dozen languages as the stewards began organizing the crowd into long lines for the last time. Some continued to ignore the barked orders and pressed themselves against the railing at the edge of the deck for another glimpse of their new country.

Off the bow, Nicola saw a tugboat speeding toward them from the quarantine station. The steamer came to a stop in the water as the tugboat pulled alongside. Onboard were the inspectors from the port authority. They would give the passengers and crew one final exam before clearing their ship to dock. If the inspection revealed any signs of contagion, the entire ship could be stuck in quarantine for days or even weeks. Having endured several exams already, Nicola and Martha knew what to expect and slipped obediently into line.

The uniformed inspectors climbed onto the ship and walked up and down the lines, scrutinizing each passenger as they searched for any sign of cholera, yellow fever, scarlet fever, smallpox, typhoid, measles, or diphtheria. Martha, who was starting to recover in the fresh air and the calmer waters, felt uncomfortable beneath the gaze of the inspectors. Once every manifest and vaccination record was checked and no signs of contagious disease were found, the ship was cleared to dock.

The tugboat departed as the steamer resumed its course, turning into the Hudson River. No one returned to steerage. Waiting on deck, Nicola's excitement grew. In another hour, he and Martha would be on Ellis Island, where their fate would be decided. They had sacrificed so much, leaving their homes and families behind and enduring the miserable journey; but if all went well, they would set foot in America by the end of the day.

Cheers suddenly swept over the crowd as many of the passengers excitedly pointed over the starboard bow. Nicola and Martha raised their eyes in the direction of the outstretched hands. In the distance, they spied a figure standing atop a tall pedestal. As the shouts of joy continued, tears fell from the young couple's eyes as they gazed at the Statue of Liberty. The long weeks of hardship and misery suddenly fell away and a grin spread across Nicola's face. As they neared Lady Liberty, he caught a glimpse of Ellis Island. The steamer, however, continued its course and docked at a pier across the channel.

Before the Yanneys lay a city greater than either had ever imagined, a sprawl of buildings stretching as far as they could see. Nicola knew that not far from the dock was a large Syrian neighborhood. Several thousand of his countrymen lived there, densely packed into a few city blocks. Its streets were lined with small shops displaying exotic fabrics and other goods imported from their homeland. Arabic was the only language heard issuing from the many street-side cafes and the apartment windows above. "Little Syria," as the neighborhood was known, was the largest Syrian settlement in America and the destination of most newly arriving immigrants coming from the Middle East.

Though Nicola and Martha knew several families who lived there, the young couple was heading in the opposite direction. As they waited aboard the steamer, the first- and second-class passengers disembarked and strolled into the city. Only when they were gone did the stewards escort the steerage passengers off the ship. Instead of going into Manhattan, Nicola and Martha were taken across the pier and separated into a small group with a handful of their fellow Syrians. They were then loaded onto a barge which started back across the channel.

Like the vast majority of immigrants coming to America, Nicola and Martha had chosen to travel to New York and enter through Ellis Island. Half a million people had already passed through the new immigration facility, which had opened only a year earlier. The Yanneys had chosen this way because it was the quickest route, but it was also fraught with risk. Though they had passed all the shipboard exams and those of the inspectors from the quarantine station, there was one final hurdle barring the newlyweds' entrance to America.

Many had made it just as far as Nicola and Martha, only to be turned back during the final and most extensive examination that was administered on Ellis Island. Afraid of being turned away, some immigrants tried for different ports along the Eastern Seaboard, or sailed to Canada or Mexico, hoping to cross into the United States undetected. As the Yanneys headed for the island, the fears that had subsided upon their first glimpse of the Statue of Liberty returned. The final inspection would determine their fate. If they were denied entry, all of Nicola's hopes and plans for the future would be for naught.

When Nicola and Martha walked onto the dock at Ellis Island, their ears were filled with confusing shouts in a dozen languages. Amid the din, a young man approached them and called out in Arabic. The interpreter gave them quick instructions and led Nicola and Martha with their small group through the facility's main door. As they made their way up a long, steep stairway, unbeknownst to the young couple, the final inspection had already begun.

From afar, physicians watched as they climbed the stairs, looking for signs of lameness, heavy breathing, or any behavior that might indicate a serious illness. After they reached the top of the steps, Nicola and Martha met another line of physicians. As they passed before each one, their hands, neck, face, and hair were examined. The last inspector looked intently at their eyes and the inside of their eyelids, checking again for the highly contagious trachoma, the dreaded disease responsible for more denied entries than any other affliction.

In the line ahead of them, Nicola saw physicians holding pieces of chalk. Occasionally, one stepped forward and placed a large X on an immigrant's shoulder. Those with marks were escorted away and disappeared into a different part of the facility. Martha looked to her husband, worried what might happen as they passed in front of the remaining inspectors. Relieved, they both came to the end of the line unmarked, each deemed healthy enough to proceed.

Only one more obstacle remained. Nicola and Martha were directed to a long line, at the end of which sat a man on a tall stool behind a desk. When they reached the head of the line, Nicola stepped forward. The official held their ship's manifest in his hands, and the same interpreter who had met them at the dock now stood at his side. Looking at the manifest, the official quickly interrogated Nicola, asking about the information he had given the stewards back in Koura. The man also inquired how much money Nicola was carrying. Though nervous, he answered the questions. After a few minutes, the official gave a curt nod and the interpreter told Nicola to move aside. Martha stepped forward, and the same round of questioning began. Satisfied, the official gave another nod signaling that the interview was finished.

As Nicola and Martha walked away from the interview, a look of joy and relief spread over their faces as the realization dawned on them—they were being allowed into the United States. Still in disbelief, they followed a guide who showed the couple to the money exchange. Nicola and Martha carefully fished out the money and valuables they had kept hidden in their clothing during the crossing and traded them for the strange American currency. Afterward, Martha waited while Nicola arranged for the little baggage that had been stowed during their long journey to be sent from Ellis Island to their final destination.

Though they had arrived in America, their journey was far from complete. The interpreter pinned a tag to Nicola's coat, on which was written a single word in large English letters illegible to Nicola and Martha: *Omaha*. With the interpreter's help, Nicola purchased two tickets at the railroad ticket office, then returned to Martha and waited at the ferry terminal. When the time of their train's departure drew near, they left the Ellis Island facility, passing beneath a sign that read "Welcome to America."

Another barge took them to the train station on the western shore of the channel. Escorted to the platform and showing their tickets to the conductor, the Yanneys boarded a train bound for Chicago. Neither Nicola nor Martha had ever seen a locomotive, but Nicola remembered John's stories. Now, he and Martha were the ones riding across the country. They settled into their seats and stared out the windows as their train pulled out of the station. As it picked up speed, the young couple watched the city pass before their eyes and give way to a countryside covered in snow.

Nicola and Martha did not realize how far they had yet to travel. Though Nicola had been told that America was vast, he had little idea of what it meant that Omaha was fourteen hundred miles from New York. Already exhausted from the long ocean passage, the couple endured several monotonous days as the train sped westward, making multiple stops along the way. Nicola noticed how different the open country was from the mountains and hills of Koura. Though the locomotive traveled at a great speed, the passing scenery seemed endless. Nicola and Martha used the strange American money to buy food on the train, trusting themselves to the honesty of the conductor. Halfway through their trip, the train pulled into a large station and the conductor motioned for them to get off the car, then directed them to another train.

The second leg of their journey passed much the same. After two more days, the train pulled into another large station. A conductor pointed to the tag still pinned on Nicola's coat and told the newlyweds that they had arrived at their destination. Grabbing their few belongings, they stepped onto the platform. It was midwinter and the air was bitterly cold.

Though thankful that their long journey had finally come to an end, Nicola and Martha stumbled from the train stooped with fatigue. The trip from Koura to Nebraska had taken twenty-six days. The new land, the incomprehensible language, the constant crowds, and the piercing cold were unlike anything they had ever known. In their bewilderment, however, they suddenly heard a most welcome sound. Raising their heads in disbelief, they searched for the source. Again, the greeting in their native tongue rang out from across the platform. A man from the local Syrian community was calling their names. Hurrying to meet him, Nicola embraced the man as they kissed each other's cheeks.

Steeling themselves against the cold, the Yanneys followed their Syrian friend out of the station and looked around. They were in the middle of a large city. Though Omaha was not as immense as New York, over one hundred thousand people lived there. Just to the north of the train station was a bustling downtown. Nicola and Martha could see horse-drawn carriages and electric streetcars speeding down the busy streets that lay between the tall buildings. Martha was grateful to learn that their lodgings were only half a mile south of the train station, but in a quieter neighborhood where their fellow Syrians had settled among other immigrant and American families.

Nicola and Martha were warmly welcomed into the community and treated to a meal in the home of one of the prominent families. Many of the Syrians were away, but those who were still in town gathered to greet the new arrivals. A few of the faces were familiar, themselves having come from Koura years earlier. After the Yanneys' long and lonely trip, the companionship was refreshing. For the first time since France, Nicola and Martha enjoyed good food and drink and, relaxing with their newfound friends, began sharing stories of their travels.

While the good company was a consolation to the tired couple, the lodgings were less than desirable. Though a far cry from the horrors of the steerage, Martha was disappointed when they were shown to their new home. The house itself was divided into tiny single-room apartments, each with a stove, a bed, and a few rudimentary sticks of furniture. The other Syrians lived in similar houses scattered throughout the neighborhood. The majority were men around Nicola's age or older who were either unmarried or who had left their families in Syria. Only a handful of women had accompanied their husbands like Martha. Because almost all were pack peddlers who traveled for months at a time, they needed only the barest necessities for the little time they spent in Omaha. The money they saved by living so frugally was used to buy new stock to sell and pay down their debts, or was sent overseas to support their families still living in Syria.

A few days after arriving in Omaha, Nicola was rested enough to begin working. Two of the most experienced peddlers were cousins, and both had traded in their peddlers' packs to become suppliers. Since their stores provided the merchandise that the rest of the peddlers sold, Nicola approached one of them and asked for work. The store owner agreed to suggest routes and supply him with a first round of goods to sell. Nicola, in turn, would split all of his profits with the supplier.

The supplier also told Nicola about their community. There were almost two hundred Syrians living in the southern part of the city. A number of them were from Damascus. Others, like the Yanneys, were from the regions of Koura and Mount Lebanon. Many were Melkite Catholics, but those from Koura were Orthodox Christians. The peddlers traveled from Omaha into central and western Nebraska, as well as Iowa, Missouri, Minnesota, and even up into the Dakotas. Some were long-range peddlers and returned to the city only a few times a year. Others peddled shorter routes that took them away for only three or four weeks at a time. Martha was welcome to work, as well. The other women in their community often peddled, though only in and around the city.

Giving Nicola an enormous leather pack, the supplier loaded it with sixty pounds of merchandise, including decorative wares imported from their homeland along with more common household items. Nicola would quickly find out what sold best on each of his routes. After coaching him in a few English words and an understanding of American currency, the supplier sent Nicola on a shorter route around the city to practice.

Once Nicola felt comfortable, the store owner suggested a longer route that would take him far from Omaha, but would bring good profits. The supplier assured him that he would get used to the heavy pack, and if he was successful, Nicola might buy his own horse and buggy in a few years. Though it was considered a demeaning occupation in their homeland, in America, peddling could pay well. After five or ten years of hard work, many peddlers—like the supplier himself—were able to stop peddling altogether and open their own supply stores or groceries.

Martha was unhappy when Nicola returned to their apartment and told her that he was leaving to peddle for a month. She already missed home and the quiet countryside. The other women in the peddlers' colony would take care of her while he was away and help her to adjust to her new life in America. Nicola told his wife that peddling was the quickest way to pay off their debts and help their families in Koura. Once they saved enough money, he promised to find different work.

On his supplier's recommendation, Nicola first set out on a route with several men from their neighborhood. Boarding a train at the nearby station, they headed west. Whenever they came to a new town, the men split up and went in different directions, then met again that night or a few days later. Nicola quickly grew accustomed to the work and began to make more sales. When his supplies dwindled, he sent a telegram to his supplier in Omaha, who sent whatever Nicola needed on the next train.

Nicola chose midrange routes so that he could return to Omaha as often as possible. Whenever he came home, he banked the money that he had made with his supplier and returned any unsold items. Hurrying up the hill to their apartment, he greeted Martha warmly and shared his adventures with her as she cooked him dinner. Martha was relieved to see her husband and listened to his stories with interest. Nicola, however, was growing more concerned every time he came home.

While he was away, Martha tried her hand at peddling. Her days were long and tiresome, and she returned home to an empty apartment every evening after tramping many miles across the city. At night, she wove small carpets and knit doilies and other handicrafts for Nicola to sell on his trips. From time to time, she received news from her husband through their supplier or one of the other peddlers' wives. Nonetheless, she was afraid for Nicola when he was away so long. Despite making friends with the other women, Martha was homesick and terribly lonely.

The young couple's lives soon changed forever. Returning from one of his spring trips, Nicola was greeted excitedly as he stepped through the door. Martha had been waiting for weeks to tell him the wonderful news. She was pregnant. Nicola embraced his wife, and they both gave heartfelt thanks to God. He now prayed even more fervently while he was away peddling, and when he returned home every month, he was eager to see how much the baby had grown. Now more than ever, Nicola was torn between the thought of leaving his pregnant wife alone and his need to make money. Already paying off his debts and sending money to his loved ones in Fi'eh, he returned to his work with urgency in order to begin saving for his growing family.

Because each of the peddlers traveled different routes, only a few dozen were ever usually in Omaha at the same time. During the holidays, however, all of the men returned to the city for a week to rest, relax, and visit with their friends and families. The mood in the neighborhood was festive as Nicola joined his friends to celebrate Pascha (Orthodox Easter).

Feasting from house to house, singing folk songs, and sharing both humorous and harrowing tales from their time on the road, the Syrians made the most of their vacation. Everyone in the community had heard the news of Martha's pregnancy and congratulated the couple, praying that she would have a safe delivery and hoping that their firstborn would be a son, considering it a special blessing. After a week of celebration, the men reloaded their packs and buggies and set out again. Nicola joined them reluctantly, knowing that in a handful of months he would be called home as the time for Martha's delivery drew near.

In the midst of autumn, the women in the community began to prepare to help with the upcoming birth, and Nicola stayed closer to Omaha. Though Martha showed no signs yet, the time for the baby's arrival was at hand. The couple celebrated their first anniversary, and Nicola reflected on how much their lives had changed in the past year. Though living in a foreign land on the other side of the world, they had found a community of friends and were working to make a new home for themselves. Most importantly, they were starting their family.

Three days after their anniversary, Martha went into labor. Her friends gathered in the Yanneys' small apartment when the news spread that the delivery was near. Nicola prayed for hours, waiting anxiously nearby. When the midwives opened the apartment door, he bounded into the room. Martha beamed with the infant swaddled at her side. Both she and the baby were healthy. She had given birth to a boy. Nicola was overjoyed as he cradled his newborn son.

Since he was a boy, the child's name had already been decided. As was their custom, their firstborn son would be called Elias, in honor of Nicola's father. Their son's middle name—like that of all of their children—would be Nicola, after their father.

The proud parents rejoiced at the birth of Elias Nicola Yanney and immediately sent letters to their families in Fi'eh and Qilhat. Born in the United States, Elias was an American citizen. He would grow up free, in a land of prosperity, never knowing the want and oppression that his parents had suffered in Koura. Though he dearly missed his loved ones and his homeland, the brand-new father was elated. Dreaming of his newborn son's bright future, Nicola knew that he had made the right choice in coming to the New World.

CHAPTER THREE

Homestead

JANUARY 1894 TO JANUARY 1899

NICOLA WORKED AS A PEDDLER for the next year and a half, visiting towns and villages across the Great Plains. Sometimes, he trekked deep into the countryside, calling on isolated farmhouses. If he came across an especially kind family, he was invited to spend the night in their home. Often, however, he bedded in a barn loft or out in an open field. If the night was cold, he found a haystack in which to sleep.

Though he longed to be home with Martha and Elias, Nicola sometimes enjoyed his travels. In good weather, the journeys were pleasant. He had long grown accustomed to hauling his heavy pack as he wandered across Nebraska and met its people. The landscape was completely different from Koura. There were no mountains on the plains, and very few hills or trees. The endless expanse of prairie was broken only by the waters of the Platte and the railroad that ran parallel to the broad, meandering river. Most of the settlements had sprung up beside the railroad. After spending a day or two peddling a spot along his route, Nicola made his way to the local depot and boarded a train that took him to the next stop.

The Americans that Nicola met were most often friendly. After a few trips, he had learned which items his customers needed most. They, in turn, began to look forward to his visits. Often, he was invited into a family's parlor or kitchen, as much out of curiosity as interest in his wares. Nicola used the opportunities to practice his English, and his customers were delighted by his stories. They were especially keen to hear any tales he could tell about the Holy Land.

Every three or four weeks, Nicola returned to Omaha for a short rest. His pack was nearly empty whenever he came back, and his pockets were filled with money. Though he still had to split the profits with his supplier, his peddling trips were successful enough that Nicola had mostly repaid the debt incurred from their passage, while still managing to support his father and relatives back in Koura. He and Martha had also started saving money for their next move.

Nicola knew that his small family would not remain in Omaha for much longer. Though they had grown close to the members of the local Syrian community, Martha was especially unhappy in the city. Nicola, too, was ready to move. His time traveling the countryside and his visits with the farmers made him yearn for something of his old life in Koura. As soon as he found a place for his family to settle, he could farm again and finally bring George down from Canada. Nicola hoped that family members from even farther away might also join them. Most of all, however, Nicola missed his wife and son while he was away on his long trips and wanted to be closer to home.

Whenever he pulled into the depot in Omaha, he raced back to their apartment. Martha greeted her husband and placed Elias into his arms. Unused to his father, the baby sometimes cried. While Martha prepared their meal, Nicola played with Elias and marveled at how much his son had grown in a month. After praying, the family ate together. Martha listened while Nicola recounted his latest visits with his American customers. Though she was excited to spend a few precious days with her husband, she could not hide her sadness.

In ways, Martha was even lonelier than before Elias's birth. The baby required her constant attention, and most days she was isolated in their cramped apartment. Though she visited the other Syrian women in their neighborhood when she could, they were often busy peddling around the city—something that Martha was no longer able to do. While Elias slept, she might find a spare hour to sew or embroider handiworks for Nicola to sell. She rarely saw her husband, however, and with the other peddlers on the road for months at a time, their house was often empty.

When she did venture out of their neighborhood, Martha was overwhelmed. Used to Koura's quiet villages, she found the hectic city almost unbearable. The rumbling of train cars and the shrill whistles of the locomotives from the nearby stations were constant. The crowded streets were filled with recklessly driven carriages. Not without reason, Martha feared that she and Elias might get struck down while crossing the busy roads near their apartment. She could not communicate with her Italian, Polish, and Czech neighbors, and the language of the Americans caused her the most hardship of all.

While Nicola was slowly learning English out of necessity, Martha was not. The language remained incomprehensible to her and she had little time and opportunity to learn, making even the simplest tasks difficult. When she went to the local groceries, the few English words she had learned were often misunderstood by the clerks. The purchases she did succeed in making were done through pointing and gestures. Even the items themselves were unfamiliar, and the American shopkeepers did not haggle as she was used to doing in the markets of Koura. Sometimes, Martha gave up in frustration and waited until Nicola came home, dictating a grocery list for him in Arabic to go and buy for her.

Martha's greatest sadness, however, was that her family had no church. In Koura, her Orthodox faith had touched every facet of her life. Her family and the entire village celebrated the feasts and fasts together. Living so near the Balamand monastery, Martha had stopped there or in one of the village churches almost every day to light a candle and offer prayers. There were a few other Orthodox families in their community in Omaha, but most of the local Syrians were Maronite or Melkite. Being Catholics, they attended a Bohemian church a short walk from their neighborhood. Martha did not. She knew the differences between Orthodoxy and Catholicism and would not compromise her faith. Even though she longed to pray in church and receive Holy Communion herself, she most especially desired to have Elias baptized. Martha, however, would only do these things in an Orthodox church. Having no other recourse, she prayed at home as the monks and priests in Qilhat had taught her.

When it came time for her husband to leave home again, Martha sometimes cried. Seeing his wife's unhappiness, Nicola redoubled his efforts. On every peddling trip, he looked for a place where he could move his family and find work to support them. Peddling was in its heyday and his fellow Syrians were making good profits. Nonetheless, long before his peers, Nicola decided to give up his travels in order to settle his family in a permanent home. If he could find a piece of land to rent, he wished to return to his farming roots.

Not long after Elias's first birthday, Martha found out that she was pregnant again. Nicola rejoiced at the news, but could not imagine raising his growing family in Omaha. Their tiny room in the peddlers' house was already too cramped without the addition of a second child. Even more so, Nicola did not want his children to grow up in a city filled with so many temptations. Already, he could see how its worldly influence was affecting his friends. The couple decided that the time to move had come. They would wait until after the delivery, and once Martha and the child were strong enough, the family would relocate to a quiet home far from the city, where Nicola would no longer have to leave his family for weeks at a time.

The Yanneys did not have to wait long. Nicola found a place to move during one of his peddling trips. A fellow villager from Fi'eh named Mike Hayek lived in the town of Kearney, two hundred miles west of Omaha. Mike had originally started out in the same peddlers' colony but had struck out on his own several years before Nicola and Martha's arrival. Moving to central Nebraska and finding success there, he began encouraging others to join him. Nicola had visited the Hayeks during his own journeys and liked the area. He had also become acquainted with an American who had a quarter-section homestead for rent where Nicola could start his own farm. He liked the location. It was peaceful and quiet, but there were other farmers nearby and a village several miles to the south. The village of Gibbon lay on the Union Pacific line, and the larger town of Kearney was twenty miles away.

In the months leading up to the birth of their second child, Nicola made the final arrangements to rent the land while he continued to peddle. The extra money would help the Yanneys with their move. Nicola also decided that he could make day trips peddling close to their new home if he needed to supplement his income. Mike Hayek ran a small store and could be his supplier.

Near midsummer, Martha went into labor and gave birth to a little girl. Nicola named his daughter Anna after his older sister. Once Martha and Anna were strong enough, the family packed up their belongings and bid farewell to their friends in Omaha. Arriving at the village near their homestead, Nicola bought a horse, wagon, and other supplies, and drove his wife and children seven miles north through the rolling hills to a place called Buckeye Valley.

As the wagon rose from a hollow, Nicola turned off the dirt road and headed up a gentle slope. Turning again on a path that skirted alongside a ridge, Nicola drove on for a quarter mile and finally pulled their wagon to a stop. Martha and her children laid their eyes on the homestead for the first time. Except for a few scattered trees, the windswept land was empty. The tall prairie grass rippled in the warm breeze. The soil was dry, but there was a source of water nearby and the ridge provided some protection from the wind. Nestled into the hill at the base of the ridge was a two-room sod house that would be the family's home.

Martha inspected the house as they unpacked their supplies. Unlike the limestone homes of Koura, it was made from thick slabs of earth cut from the prairie. With its west side dug deep into the hillside and its almost two-foot-thick walls, the house would stay cool in the summer and warm in the winter. With only a little fuel, Martha's cooking stove could keep the whole soddy warm even on the coldest of days. The inside, however, was dark and damp, and without constant maintenance the vacant house had quickly deteriorated. Rodents, snakes, and bugs had burrowed into the walls, and the earthen roof was beginning to sag. When it rained, drops of mud fell from the ceiling.

The Yanneys went to work immediately, patching the vermin's

holes and smoothing the interior walls with a sharp blade. The roof was patched, and after the dirt floor was leveled and swept, Nicola wetted and tamped it with an old fence post, making it smooth and hard. Martha hung sheets of muslin above their heads to catch the dirt and bugs from falling onto their beds and furniture. Nicola bought plaster and whitewashed the walls. Once the dirty windows were washed and the broken panes replaced, the inside of the soddy looked bright and clean, not so different from the homes of Koura.

While Martha continued to refurbish the house, Nicola turned his attention to the rest of the homestead. He only had a few months to prepare. Both he and Martha had experienced light snowfalls in the foothills of Koura, but nothing had prepared them for winter on the open plains. Even though their years in Omaha had exposed them to the bitter cold, Nicola knew from his travels that winter on the homestead would be far worse than anything Martha had endured in the city. No groves of trees or closely huddled buildings would protect them from the blinding snows and the relentless wind. In the worst weather, the family would be beyond the reach of help for days and sometimes weeks at a time. Stables and pens had to be built for their animals and more supplies had to be brought from town and stored for the winter in case the roads became impassable. Nicola also needed to plant a field with winter wheat.

Preparing the homestead was too much to do alone, and Nicola would not have finished all that he had to do without help. Ever since arriving in America, Nicola had been in touch with his sister. Anna and her family were still living in Pennsylvania, and through her, he had managed to contact his youngest brother in Canada. Nicola and his brother had been close growing up together in Fi'eh, but George had been alone for three years ever

The Yanney family with Nicola's brother George in 1897

since getting separated from their brother John on the way to New York. George was a bright but sometimes melancholic boy, and Nicola imagined what his youngest brother must have suffered during his years of loneliness.

Once Nicola had found the land in Buckeye Valley, he wrote to his brother explaining his plans and asking George to join him. Not long after he and Martha had moved onto the homestead, Nicola received a letter in reply and excitedly shared the news with his wife. George was coming. A few days later, Nicola drove to the train depot. When the train arrived, a young man that he barely recognized stepped forward to greet him. The two brothers embraced and wept to see each other after their years apart.

Looking at his younger brother, Nicola saw that he was no longer the teenaged boy he had last seen leaving for America. Though still rather short, George was becoming a handsome young man. As they collected his baggage at the station, Nicola noticed how well George spoke with the Americans. Nicola was becoming proficient at speaking the language as well, but during his years in Canada, George had become fluent in both English and French.

Though their reunion was joyous, the brothers had little time to spare. Meeting his sister-in-law, nephew, and niece, George joined the family for a meal prepared in his honor. After he settled his belongings in the house, he and Nicola threw themselves into their farm work. The brothers visited their neighbors—many of whom Nicola knew from his years of peddling—to seek advice and inquire about buying and borrowing tools and implements. They also made trips into Gibbon and the larger town of Kearney, and soon had all the equipment they needed. After building a barn for the horses and a chicken coop, they put up pens for the pigs they planned to raise. The hay on their land was cut and bundled for feed, and the brothers began clearing ground to plant in the coming spring.

Just as the weather turned cold, the homestead was finally ready for winter and the soddy's transformation was complete. Beds for Nicola and Martha had been moved in, along with beds for George and Elias and a crib for Anna. Decorative rugs covered the bare floor. Martha's pots and pans were hung from hooks pressed into the sod wall near the small metal stove and the large basin that served as her kitchen. Nicola had bought a dining table and chairs along with a sofa. Martha was pleased with the results. The cramped peddlers' lodging lay far behind them, and, though modest, the soddy had begun to feel like a home. The Yanneys would live there for almost a decade. It would be the site of their greatest joys and deepest sorrows.

With winter fast approaching and the farm prepared as best as they could, the brothers turned to peddling. Nicola stayed close to home, visiting neighboring farmsteads and villages. With his years of experience, he knew what would sell best. Packing up simple items—thread, needles, flatware, linen, and other household goods—Nicola returned to some of his former customers, who welcomed him and were happy to hear that he was living in Buckeye Valley. George decided to work a longer route that took him from far western Nebraska all the way to Omaha. The profits that the brothers made from peddling paid their rent and the expenses they had incurred in fixing up the sod house and readying the farm. Nicola and George were so happy to be reunited and so encouraged by their success that they decided to call their small business "The Yanney Brothers."

When there was less work to do on the farm, Nicola peddled during the daytime. Now, however, he was able to return in the evenings to enjoy a meal with his family. Martha was especially thankful to have her husband home every night. After dinner, the family prayed together, then tucked the children in their beds. In the light of their oil lamps, Nicola tallied the family's expenses and profits in a small notebook, then practiced slowly tracing the English letters. Inspired by George, he had decided to learn to read and write the Americans' language.

When George was home, he, Nicola, and Martha stayed up after the children were asleep, reminiscing and reading letters from their father and other loved ones in Koura. Things had gotten slightly better in Syria since they had left, but many still dreamed of coming to America. Writing back, the Yanneys shared about their life in the New World and encouraged others to join them.

When it became bitterly cold outside, the family heated the sod house with whatever fuel they could find. While Nicola was away, Martha had to tend the stove all day to keep the house warm. In Koura, her family had burned olive pits to heat their home during the winter. With no olives and scant trees on the plains, Martha collected hay and dried sunflower and corn stalks. Cow manure from their neighbors' pastures, however, was the best fuel. At first hesitant to cook over manure, necessity compelled Martha to try. Surprised, she found that it burned with little smell, and gave their food a flavor similar to cooking over hickory wood.

Throughout the winter, when not peddling, Nicola fed and watered the animals, helped collect fuel for Martha, made regular trips back and forth to Gibbon for supplies, and hauled water to their house. As the weather grew warmer, he also began preparing for spring. Once the ground thawed, Nicola tilled large patches for planting onions and other vegetables. Later, he and George plowed their fields and seeded hay for their livestock. Though there were still frosts throughout the spring, Martha rejoiced that the long, dreary winter was over and that she and the children were no longer confined to the house.

By May, the prairie had fully come back to life. The grass was green again, and the first shoots in the fields and the garden were breaking through the soil. Even the outside of the soddy was pretty in the springtime. The grasses and wildflowers bloomed on the eaves, and meadowlarks sang as they nested on the roof. Remembering the orchards of his homeland, Nicola planted several fruit trees around their new home.

With Nicola and George's hard work, the farm was soon able to provide most of the family's food as well as a small income. The chickens that they kept laid enough eggs to sell, and several pigs were fattened for slaughter. Nicola sold to his neighbors the hay that their livestock did not need, and the extra produce from their garden went to their friend Mike to sell at his store in Kearney. George helped when he was home, but he and Nicola continued to divide their responsibilities, with Nicola focusing on the farm work while George spent much of his time peddling on his long route. The brothers soon expanded their business and sold goods like flour, grain, nuts, and cooking oil, along with clothing and hardware, to nearby farming families.

One year after moving to the homestead, Nicola and George took a brief break from their work to travel all the way back to Omaha. Due to the success of their endeavors, they had both made a fateful decision. Finding their way to the courthouse, the brothers stood before the district judge. Under oath, Nicola and George renounced their allegiance to the Turkish sultan who ruled Syria. Though the naturalization process would take several more years to complete, Nicola knew that his family would never return to Koura. The United States was his children's homeland, and he, too, would someday become an American citizen.

Nicola and George returned to the homestead and busied

themselves with their thriving farm and business. Soon, however, the family was occupied with other preparations. Before he and George had left for Omaha, Martha had informed her husband that she was pregnant with their third child. The time for her to give birth came during their second spring on the homestead, and a few neighbor women came to help with the delivery while Nicola and the children waited expectantly. Born on an auspicious day—the feast of the Ascension—the Yanneys' third child was a boy whom Nicola and Martha named John.

Martha had little time to recover. Though their religious custom was to let mothers rest for forty days after giving birth, Martha had no female family members or friends to help her as she would have had back in Koura. Nicola did his best to care for Elias and Anna and did what household chores he could, but he had to return to his farm work. Martha was soon back to her normal busy schedule.

Much of her time was spent preparing meals on her tiny stove top. Caring for the baby, washing and mending clothes, watching Elias and Anna, and keeping varmints out of the house left her with little spare time. Keeping the soddy clean was a never-ending battle. On many mornings, Martha would rise to find the bedsheets and furniture covered in fine dust. Despite the muslin that hung from the ceiling, mud would drip for days after a heavy rain, and insects would occasionally drop onto beds and into simmering pans.

While Martha tended the house and the children, Nicola and George spent their days cultivating the quarter section. They leveled and cleared more ground for growing crops, then cut long furrows back and forth with their plowshare. Carrying the heavy seed sacks they brought from town, they planted the fields by hand. Though there was water nearby, irrigating the dry soil was arduous work. Nicola hauled the water in buckets and dug long irrigation trenches. During the summer and fall, he harvested their produce from the large garden and their budding orchard. When the wheat or hay was ready, the brothers cut it with a scythe and bundled it for feed, and the extra was sold. The chicken coops, pigpens, and the stable needed constant cleaning and maintenance, and the animals had to be fed and watered. When Nicola and George were not busy on the farm itself, one or both were on the road peddling their goods or running errands.

Not long after John's birth, something happened that changed the course of the Yanneys' lives—a small Syrian community began to gather in central Nebraska. A handful at a time, friends from Fi'eh started coming to America. At first, they followed Nicola and Martha's path, living and working in Omaha as peddlers for several years. Even Nicola's best friend, John Shada, and his brothers had come back to America with their wives and young children and were living there in the peddlers' colony. Syrians from other villages were also drawn to the city, hoping to find work at the World's Fair that Omaha would be hosting in 1898. Slowly, however, several families came to the same realization that Nicola and Martha had years earlier, and began moving west.

Nicola, Martha, and George were excited when their old friends from Koura moved to the area. Most were drawn to Kearney because Mike Hayek could provide them with goods to peddle. As more of their countrymen came, the Yanneys began to gather with the small community, driving into town or hosting their friends on the homestead. Nicola became one of the leaders of the group, collecting food and funds from the families to help organize their gatherings.

Even without a church of their own, the Syrians celebrated Saint Simeon's feast day together as they had back in Fi'eh, as well as Christmas, Pascha, and other holy days. Nicola especially desired to help the newcomers, knowing how difficult it was to keep his Orthodox faith in the foreign land, especially without a church or a priest. Though their gatherings were filled with folk songs, dancing, and food, Nicola always remembered to offer prayers and lead his friends in singing hymns, knowing that it was their faith that bound the small community together more than anything else.

Nicola felt blessed with his life in America. He had three beautiful children, and when he found out that Martha was pregnant with their fourth child, he gave thanks to God once again. He had reunited with his youngest brother, and their small farm and business were prospering. The greatest surprise of all was that their local Syrian community was growing. Nonetheless, Nicola felt a growing sorrow in his heart. Though he loved his new home, his mind frequently returned to Koura. Memories of the village churches and the monks chanting in the monastery brought tears to his eyes. Nicola had remained a devout Orthodox Christian, praying often, marking his everyday tasks by the church calendar and keeping the feasts and fasts. It had been years, however, since he had been able to go to confession, attend the Divine Liturgy, or receive Holy Communion.

Nicola's sadness was punctuated by the bittersweet news that he received from his friend John who was still living in Omaha. A Syrian Orthodox priest had recently visited the city, and had stayed for a week. A few families from Kearney had received the news in time and had traveled there to meet him. The priest had blessed their marriages and performed several baptisms. He had also served the Divine Liturgy. By the time the news had reached the Yanneys on their distant homestead, however, the visiting priest had left Omaha. Nicola was happy for his friends, who were overjoyed to have their children baptized, but was disappointed to have the missed opportunity.

Nicola had heard rumors of the priest, and now all his friends spoke very highly of him. He had come to the United States a few years earlier to pastor the only Syrian Orthodox church in the country, located in New York, not far from where Nicola and Martha had first set foot in America. It was said that the priest traveled across the country, searching for Syrian Orthodox Christians. As his friends attested, the rumors were true. Nicola, however, wondered how his family might ever meet the traveling priest. Even if he ever did return to Omaha, word of his visit would never reach the Yanneys in time, living so far from town.

In his disappointment, Nicola prayed for guidance and turned to his faith for consolation. Opening a thick, leather-bound Bible, he remembered God's mercy and care for his family even in their isolation. It was a secondhand Arabic Bible that he had purchased a few days before Christmas. It would become one of Nicola's most precious possessions, preserved and handed down in his family for generations. In the blank pages at the end of the book, Nicola decided to record the momentous events in the life of his family. Most importantly, he would study the Holy Scriptures and read them aloud to Martha and the children.

Seeing Elias, Nicola pulled his eldest son onto his lap. He was five years old and would soon begin attending the country schoolhouse that was only a half mile north of their homestead. Nicola began to read to Elias from the open Bible, showing him the Arabic letters and having him slowly repeat the words. Although the American teacher would help his son learn to read and write English, Nicola would teach Elias his family's language and, more importantly, his family's faith.

After Elias's reading lesson was over and the children were in bed, Nicola opened his Bible to a page near the front and wrote:

> In God's name and with His grace, this record is written by His poor servant who longs for His powerful Lord, Nicola Elias Yanney from the Orthodox village of Fi'eh, resident of Buffalo County, Nebraska, United States of America. Whoever reads this record and finds any mistake in it, please correct it in God's name, and God will correct his life in this world and in the life to come because no one is perfect except God, who has no mistakes.

Nicola laid his pen aside and closed the Bible. In a few days, his family would celebrate Christmas, and in another year a new century would begin. Nicola thanked God for His many blessings, and wondered what gifts divine Providence would bring them.

CHAPTER FOUR

Joys and Sorrows

JULY 1899 TO MARCH 1902

NICOLA PAUSED FROM HIS WORK. Though it was only mid-morning, he was already covered in sweat and knew that it would be another blistering day. He had lived in Nebraska for over six years and was still not accustomed to its extremes. Regardless of the weather, the demands of his farm never ceased.

Winters were especially bitter. Nicola remembered when he and Martha first arrived in Omaha during the coldest part of the year. Then, however, they had been in the big city, far from the merciless plains. In the wintertime, simply feeding the livestock or doing the daily chores could be dangerous. If he got caught outside in a blizzard, he could quickly get frostbite. Nicola had even heard of homesteaders getting lost in a whiteout and freezing to death only a stone's throw from their front door.

After the long winter, spring was often slow in coming. A late freeze or May snowstorm could wipe out the crops. Heavy rains and melting snow made the roads into town impassible for days at a time. A sudden flood or swollen river could sweep away a team of horses and drown an unsuspecting man. A friend of Nicola had been carried away by a raging current when he tried to cross a river on his way to the Yanneys' homestead. His horses had drowned, and he had almost frozen to death, stuck for five hours in the middle of the stream, perched precariously on his wagon seat in the frigid March waters. The man's life had been saved only when a passerby saw him trapped and went to the nearby village for help.

Summers were no less dangerous. Torrential rains often accompanied the summer storms. When the rain refused to fall for weeks on end, however, a single lightning strike could spark a devastating prairie fire. Worst of all was the late summer's relentless, oppressive heat. Koura could be hot, but the heat and humidity in Nebraska were unlike anything Nicola had ever experienced.

Autumns were mostly mild and pleasant, and Nicola looked forward to that time of year. Later in the season, after most of the harvesting was done, his workload lessened and he could enjoy more time with his family. Keeping up with the farm was always difficult, however, especially when George was away peddling. Nicola was always glad to see his brother return home, and not simply for his help on the farm. George's stories and good company eased the monotony of their daily labors.

As Nicola returned to his work, he looked forward to the end of the day. After tending the livestock and watering all the crops, he could retire to the cool soddy, hopefully before the children went to bed. It had been a long season on the homestead. Since early spring, he had been toiling on the farm from morning until dark. Though the fields had been tilled and planted months ago, the farm required his constant attention. He still had to weed and irrigate the crops, make deliveries, and keep up with all of the repairs. In the little spare time he was able to muster, Nicola still peddled locally.

Martha had been just as busy. Though the homestead was preferable to the noisy city, the isolation was difficult for her. She dearly missed her family in Koura, but Elias, Anna, and little John kept her company during the long hours when Nicola was working. Besides caring for her young children, Martha filled her days with housework. For weeks at a time, she saw her husband only in passing, a common fate of homesteaders.

Although his presence made their small sod house even more crowded, George was a great help to the family. Whenever he was home, he worked diligently at his older brother's side. Over the years, the prairie had given way to their labors. Together, they had been able to cultivate more of the quarter section and increase their yields. The brothers were always wary, however, knowing that a drought or a hailstorm—all-too-common occurrences on the plains—could wipe out much of a year's crops. For whatever fruits they coaxed out of the earth, the family was grateful to God.

Near the end of July, Nicola put aside his work briefly. The wheat had been cut and some of the produce from their gardens had already been picked. Although there was still much to do before summer's end, Nicola was needed at home. Martha was expecting their fourth child. The household demands had become difficult for her as the days grew hotter, and she took refuge inside their sod house whenever she could. Nicola and the older children helped with the chores and made ready, excited that the baby would come soon.

On the last day of July, Martha went into labor. Word was sent to a neighbor woman and her Syrian friends in town to come to the farm and help with another delivery. Nicola waited with the children outside. Hours later, when the door of their soddy opened, they rejoiced at the news that Martha had given birth to a boy. Both she and the child were healthy. Welcomed back inside, Elias, Anna, and John gathered around their mother and baby brother. Thanking God, Nicola decided to name him Moses.

Nicola and the children helped as they could while their mother and baby Moses rested. With such a heavy workload needed to keep the farm and household running, Martha was up and working again within a few days. News of Moses' birth quickly spread to the Syrians in Kearney, and several friends made the long journey out to the homestead to bring food and gifts to the family. The men talked with Nicola and helped in the fields, while the women sat with Martha in the house, watching the sleeping baby and exchanging hushed conversation. The visits were a balm to Martha's loneliness.

By early September, Martha's strength had returned. Moses was growing bigger day by day, and the family had settled back into their familiar routine. Now recovered, Martha rose well before sunrise every morning, trying her best not to wake the baby and the other children. She said her prayers, then lit a lamp and kindled the small iron stove to begin her cooking for the day. Nicola was often already awake. After his morning prayers, he was off to check on the livestock and begin his chores. As the adults crept through the house, the children began to stir. Martha nursed Moses, woke the rest of the children, and returned to her cooking.

After watering and feeding their horses, pigs, and chickens, Nicola returned to the soddy with a basketful of eggs. Martha fried the eggs and poured her husband a cup of the strong coffee that she had boiled for him. When the food was ready,

Nicola blessed it, then sat down with his children to enjoy breakfast. While they ate, they often talked about the day's work or a story from the Bible or the life of a saint. After the meal, Martha returned to her housework while Nicola went back to the fields to bundle grass, tend the gardens, and prepare any deliveries he might have scheduled.

With the children awake and fed, Martha's day began in earnest. Elias and Anna helped her with what chores they could. In another year, Elias would be attending the small schoolhouse just north of their homestead. For now, however, he stayed by his mother's side along with his younger sister and brother. One of the day's first duties was washing the clothes, diapers, and linens. Martha pulled down the tub and scrub board and sent Elias to fetch the water. When Moses woke, Martha swaddled and carried him while she continued her work. After hanging the laundry outside to dry, she swept the floor and wiped the dust and grime from their furniture. The older children helped her carry the rugs and bedding outside to beat clean. In between nursing and changing the baby, she continued her cooking.

At midday, Martha rang a small bell hanging from the eaves, signaling Nicola and any wandering children to come in for dinner. After a large meal, Nicola went back to his work until evening. With the hay and the wheat already cut, much of his time was devoted to repairs, deliveries, clearing ground, and preparing the farm for winter. The brothers' many hours of work were paying off. The Yanneys were now more than able to survive from the farm. The pork, eggs, and produce kept them well fed. The surplus that they were able to sell, coupled with the profits they made from peddling, enabled the family to pay their debts and continue to send money to their family in Syria.

After dinner, Martha continued with her cleaning. With Elias and Anna's help, she fetched more water and collected fuel for their stove. Between her preparations for supper, there was produce to preserve and set aside for the winter. While the children played outside, she kept her ears alert for their cries or worse. Though the poisonous snakes were rarely seen, the Yanneys' homestead was on the edge of the prairie rattlers' range. Martha had heard stories and always feared that a rattlesnake might be hiding in the tall grass near the children.

When supper was nearly ready, Martha rang the bell again. The days were growing shorter—a welcome sign that meant the brothers' workload would soon lighten. Martha hoped that in the coming months the family might be able to travel to visit their friends in town before winter came. Nicola made his way in from the fields and joined the rest of the family at the table after washing. Giving thanks for another meal, the family enjoyed the fruits of their labors. Elias especially loved the delicious apples they had begun to collect from their growing fruit trees.

After the supper dishes were cleaned and the last chore was done, the family settled into pleasant conversation. Occasionally, news arrived from Koura. The letters were read with much excitement, telling of their loved ones and other village news of marriages, births, and baptisms. Sometimes the news from home was sad or troubling. Nicola's father was still alive and well, but things were growing worse in Syria again. Family members from both Fi'eh and Qilhat wanted to leave. Nicola got out his pen and ink and sent back greetings, describing the children and their life on the farm. He encouraged his loved ones to come to America, sending them money whenever he could.

Often, Nicola read aloud in the evenings, and continued to use the family Bible to teach Elias to read Arabic. After the older children were put to bed, Martha nursed Moses and began her preparations for the next day. Nicola opened his ledger and recorded his customers' bills, along with the family's income and expenses. After saying their evening prayers, Nicola and Martha blew out the lamp and went to sleep long after dark.

One evening near the end of September, after an uneventful day on the homestead, the family gathered for supper. George had returned home several weeks earlier, bringing money and new stories from his travels. The brothers had worked together all day on the farm. The evening was warm and pleasant, but the previous night had been quite cold. Nicola and George knew that the weather would turn soon, and they were making preparations. After the family atc supper, the children were tucked in. Elias, Anna, and John were especially fond of their uncle, who would sometimes bring them little trinkets, much to their delight. Nicola, George, and Martha finally went to sleep a few hours later.

In the middle of the night, Nicola awoke startled. Outside, and coming closer, he heard the sounds of gunfire and shouting. He sprang from his bed and raced to the window. Beneath the full moon, he saw a crowd of men approaching their soddy. Nicola could not make out their faces, but as he listened, he recognized the voices of his friends. They were calling out to him in Arabic. Quickly pulling on his clothes, Nicola wondered what could have brought them twenty miles from town all the way to their homestead at one o'clock in the morning. George and Martha hurriedly dressed and followed Nicola to the door.

In the bright moonlight, Nicola counted over a dozen people hollering excitedly and shooting their pistols into the air. In their midst stood a dignified, bearded figure. Nicola was overwhelmed, suddenly realizing the reason for the surprise visit. The priest whom his friends had met the previous year in Omaha was standing in front of his house. Ever since hearing of the Syrian missionary, Nicola and Martha had desperately hoped that they might somehow meet him. Knowing this, the Yanneys' friends had brought the man all the way to their homestead.

Overcome with emotion, Nicola and George ran out to the priest and embraced him. With tears streaming from their eyes, the brothers thanked him for traveling so far to meet them. The kindly priest smiled and blessed them. Nicola and George immediately fell to their knees and kissed the ground on which he stood, then kissed his hands and his feet. Still on their knees before the small crowd, the brothers began praising God for bringing them a priest after so many years. Seeing Nicola and George weep, the priest himself was moved to tears.

Martha stood behind Nicola and George, gazing at the priest. Continually crossing herself and raising her hands to heaven, she could not cease thanking God for His unexpected mercy. After seven years, she could confess her sins and receive Holy Communion. Most importantly, she could finally have her four children baptized. Since leaving home, Martha had mourned being so far from an Orthodox church. Now she was unable to believe her eyes or contain herself. Her long years of sorrow suddenly became a torrent of joy, and the ground beneath Martha's feet became wet with tears. God had heard her cries and brought her family a priest from the other side of the world.

Still weeping, Nicola looked to his wife and his brother. With immense gratitude, he then turned to his friends who had convinced the saintly priest to travel so far to meet them. It was one of the greatest gifts that Nicola had ever been given. There, in the middle of the night on their little farm—an ocean away from his beloved Koura and a thousand miles from the nearest Orthodox church—stood Archimandrite Raphael Hawaweeny.[3] Their meeting would change the course of Nicola's life.

Two days earlier, Father Raphael had struck out from Omaha. It had been his second time in the city. During the previous year, he had traveled there to visit a group of Syrians who had come to Omaha to work as merchants and performers at the World's Fair that the city was hosting. During his first visit, Father Raphael had found a lively Orthodox population. Besides the newcomers drawn by the fair, he had met a number of Syrian families who had lived in Nebraska for several years. Most were peddlers who hailed from a small village in the region of Koura, not far from the Balamand monastery. During his week in Omaha, Father Raphael had baptized their children, blessed several marriages, served the Divine Liturgy, and confessed and communed them all. Upon his departure, he had promised to return to visit them again as soon as he could.

The following autumn, the missionary priest fulfilled his word. Coming back to the city, he was surprised to find most of the Orthodox community had moved to a smaller town two hundred miles away. Father Raphael stayed in Omaha for a few days to minister to the small group that remained there, then boarded a westbound train for Kearney. His train ran late, however, and he missed his connection. Stuck forty miles from his destination, Father Raphael had to wait for another train and sent a telegram telling the local Syrians of his delay.

The next train for Kearney arrived eight hours later. When he boarded it, Archimandrite Raphael was wearied from his journeys. He had left his headquarters in New York two months

3 *Archimandrite* is an honorary title for a celibate priest who has been given special responsibilities.

earlier and had been traveling constantly ever since. His trip had been filled with long days and little time to rest. Kearney would be the farthest westward stop on his missionary journey, already his third such trip in the four years since he had come to America. After Kearney, he would head east again, returning home by a different route that would take him another two months to complete. Father Raphael collapsed into his seat exhausted.

His train finally arrived in Kearney after midnight. It was late September, and the temperature was unseasonably cold. He felt the chill wind as he stepped off the train car. His heart was warmed, however, when he saw a crowd of people standing on the platform to welcome him. Almost the entire Syrian community had waited there for hours, so eager were they to meet him. As many ran forward to kiss his hand, Father Raphael gave the little flock his blessing, then exchanged greetings with those he recognized from his previous visit to Omaha. One of the leaders of the community escorted him to a carriage. The horse-drawn buggy was open and the wind was frigid. Already feeling ill, the priest shivered all the way to his host's home.

Warming himself next to the fireplace, Father Raphael sat up for hours talking with the people. Though he was tired from his long trip and was now suffering from a cold, the missionary stayed up until four o'clock in the morning. The entire crowd from the train station had followed him to his host's home. It had been years since many of them had seen an Orthodox priest. Finally, unable to stay awake any longer, Father Raphael dismissed them with the hope that he would serve a liturgy for them in the morning.

After sleeping for only a few hours, Archimandrite Raphael awoke still feeling sick and exhausted. Although everyone had gathered again for the Divine Liturgy, he was too ill to serve it.

Instead, he led them in a short prayer service. By that evening, however, Father Raphael was feeling better. In talking with the gathered Syrians, he learned of one family that lived on a distant farm and had not yet received word that he had come. The husband was highly respected in their community, and both he and his wife were devout. They had been sad to learn of Father Raphael's visit the previous year only after he had already left Omaha.

The kindly priest was moved by the family's plight. He was also interested to hear of Nicola's education at the monastery school. One of the reasons for his cross-country tour was to find pious men who might be ordained to serve the scattered Orthodox Syrians. Hearing this, the Syrians suggested that Father Raphael meet the Yanneys. Feeling recovered from his cold and exhaustion, the zealous missionary surprised them by offering to go to their farm that very night.

The Syrians were overjoyed, and news of the spontaneous trip spread through their community. At nine o'clock in the evening, fifteen of the Yanneys' friends piled into four wagons to accompany Father Raphael on the eighteen-mile trip to the homestead. Unlike the previous night, the evening was warm. Because the recent weather had been good, the dirt roads were smooth and dry. Traveling beneath a full moon, and inspired by the beauty of the night and the presence of their esteemed guest, the Syrians sang church hymns and folk songs during the entire four-hour ride.

As they drew near the farm, their singing and shouting grew louder. Several of the men drew out their pistols and fired shots into the air to wake their unsuspecting friends. The Yanneys came running out of their small home, astonished by what was happening, and fell at Father Raphael's feet. The priest greeted them warmly. The friends smiled and wept as the missionary blessed Nicola, George, and Martha. Still in shock, the Yanneys invited the priest and their friends inside. Martha rushed into the house and set out whatever food and drink she could find. The brothers escorted Father Raphael indoors and made what room they could for all of their guests. The children were wakened briefly to meet the priest. He happily blessed them and kissed their heads. They were soon fast asleep again, despite the great throng of people now packed into their small soddy.

Martha offered her guests hospitality, and everyone talked excitedly as they crowded around the family's table. Though the Yanneys wanted to stay up and visit, their friends—tired from their long journey and the previous night's gathering—soon began to fall asleep. With little room in the home, they dozed in their chairs or curled up on the floor. Nicola and Martha offered Father Raphael their small couch to sleep on, which he graciously accepted. The Yanneys tried to fall asleep as well, still incredulous at what had just happened. After so many years of not seeing an Orthodox priest, one had just shown up on their doorstep to spend the night in their home.

When they rose in the morning, Father Raphael served Matins. The priest had brought a few service books with him, and several of the Syrians helped read and chant, including Nicola and George. All reverently attended the prayers. After Matins, a container of water was brought for a blessing service. Father Raphael offered prayers and petitions, asking God to sanctify the water, then sprinkled it over the family and guests and throughout the soddy. Nicola and George proudly escorted him across the farm as the priest blessed their fields and livestock with the holy water.

The rest of the day was spent visiting and eating. The Syrians reminisced about their homeland and discussed both the good fortune and the struggles of living in the New World. The missionary priest talked about the chapel he had established in New York and his vision for establishing more churches throughout the country. Before leaving, Father Raphael told Nicola and Martha that he would serve the Divine Liturgy in town in a few days. There, he would hear their confessions and baptize their children. In the evening, the Yanneys' guests finally departed for Kearney. Nicola, Martha, and George stood outside their soddy and watched as their friends and their priest disappeared from sight, still astounded and thanking God.

On the following day, the family climbed into their wagon and made the trip into town themselves. There, they stayed with friends for the remainder of Father Raphael's visit. Early on Sunday morning, they gathered with the rest of the community for the Divine Liturgy. Having gone to confession the night before, Martha felt that her heart's desire was fulfilled as she and Nicola stepped forward to receive Holy Communion for the first time since leaving Koura. Then she watched as Father Raphael baptized, chrismated, and communed Elias, Anna, John, and Moses, along with several of their friends' children. Nicola's friend John Shada was there as well. He and his family had recently moved to Kearney from Omaha. Just as John had stood beside Nicola at their wedding in Fi'eh, he now stood beside the baptismal font, fulfilling his promise to be godfather to Nicola's children.

After the baptisms, Nicola watched as Father Raphael married a young Syrian couple. He also chrismated and communed an American woman who had previously married one of the Syrian men from their community, then performed the Orthodox wedding ceremony to bless their marriage. After spending the rest of the day with the little flock, Father Raphael bid them all farewell, intending to leave Kearney on the following morning in order to begin his long journey back to New York. The Syrians all cried. One of their holy days—the feast of the Elevation of the Cross—was only two days away. Together with his friends, Nicola begged the priest to stay with them for a few more days so that he could serve another Divine Liturgy and celebrate the feast with them.

Archimandrite Raphael agreed, knowing that it might be years before he could return. Two days later, they all gathered together with their priest once more. Nicola and George helped with the service again. Father Raphael preached about the Cross and encouraged his flock, admonishing them to keep their Orthodox faith even as they made a new home in America. On the following day, the Syrians accompanied him to the train station and bid him a tearful farewell. As he boarded the train, Father Raphael blessed them. He promised to pray for them and hoped he could return, wondering how such a small, isolated community would be able to preserve their faith. The Syrians stood on the platform and waved, watching until his train disappeared.

After Father Raphael's departure, everyone's lives soon returned to normal. Though they had all been inspired by his presence, the local Syrians were less than fifty in number, too small to form their own congregation or build a church. Nonetheless, they hoped that Father Raphael would visit Kearney frequently. Unfortunately, because of the distance, theirs was the most difficult community for the missionary priest to get to, and he was responsible for all the Syrian Orthodox communities throughout North America. Though he kept a rigorous schedule, it would be another fifteen years before Father Raphael would return to Kearney.

Though they wanted to stay in town visiting with their friends, the Yanneys had to return to their homestead. There was still much work to be done on the farm to prepare for winter. One of the first things Nicola did upon arriving home, however, was to open his Bible. Finding a blank page near the back, he inked his pen and wrote out lines for each of his children. He recorded the dates and places of their births and the names of their godparents. At the end, he wrote: "The baptism of my children was performed by Archimandrite Raphael Hawaweeny at Kearney, Nebraska on the thirteenth day of September, Eastern Calendar,[4] in the year of 1899."

THE NEXT YEAR was a pleasant one on the homestead. Nicola and George's successful farming and peddling ventures continued. Elias began attending the country schoolhouse a half mile north of their farm. Every day, he marched through the pastures across the gently rolling hills. In bad weather, his father or uncle might drive him up the dirt road to the school in the family's wagon. Starting school was difficult for Elias. Unused to being separated from his mother for much of the day, he was also learning to speak, read, and write English, all while his father was still teaching him to read Arabic.

Elias eventually excelled in his subjects and became a favorite of both his teacher and his fellow students. A year later, Nicola and Martha decided to send Anna to school with her brother—an opportunity she would not have had living in Koura. Despite the Protestant missionaries opening several girls' schools in their homeland, few girls attended school in Syria, especially in the

4 Also known as the Julian calendar. Some parts of the Orthodox Church follow the Julian reckoning, which at this time was twelve days behind the American civil calendar. During the twentieth century, the two calendars diverged by thirteen days.

villages, where they were far from the missionaries' compounds.

Nicola wrote to his father and loved ones in Fi'eh about their providential meeting with Father Raphael, the children's baptisms, and Elias starting school. Though the mail service was slow, it was usually reliable. Nicola's letters were sent by steamship. Once it arrived in Tripoli, the mail had to be carried up to the village and hand-delivered to the family. It could take months for Nicola's letters to arrive, and months again to receive a reply.

Another family member that Nicola had kept in contact with was his brother Simon. Almost twenty years older than Nicola, Simon was the oldest of the Yanney siblings. Though he had lived in the city of Beirut for a time, several years after Nicola's departure to America, he had sailed for Brazil to visit their brother John and live in the Syrian immigrant community there. Several months after Father Raphael's visit to the homestead, Nicola and George received a message from Simon. To their delight, he wanted to join them in Nebraska.

The younger brothers had kept their extended family apprised of their farm and the growing community on the plains. More and more families were coming to the area from Fi'eh and other places in Syria. Hearing the news, and desiring to see his younger brothers, Simon asked if he could live and work with Nicola and George on the homestead. His younger brothers responded by sending Simon money for his steamship passage and purchasing him a train ticket. From South America, he had to travel a circuitous route to England before crossing again to Ellis Island. Eventually making it to Kearney, Simon arrived almost a year after Father Raphael's visit.

When Simon stepped off the train, Nicola and George embraced him warmly. It had been many years since they had seen him, and, like Nicola's meeting with George, the reunion was a joyous one. Both were eager to hear news of their brother John, and were glad to hear when Simon reported that he was well, living and working on a coffee plantation. John had married a Portuguese woman and had started a large family. As for Simon, Nicola and George noticed that he had aged much since they had last seen him. He was almost fifty years old and frail from his long journey. Taking him back to the homestead to meet Martha and the children, they made him rest after his many weeks of travel.

Despite his weakened health, Simon's personality remained unchanged. He was highly intelligent, and in his travels he had picked up many languages. A buoyant personality, he was soon regaling his niece and nephews with tales of South America and the other places he had visited throughout the world. Once he had recuperated, Simon became reacquainted with old friends from Fi'eh and made new friends who had come to Kearney from other towns and villages in Syria.

Nicola and George were happy for Simon's help and included him in their business dealings, glad that "The Yanney Brothers" had now grown to three. While the brothers worked on the farm, Simon was entrusted with traveling back and forth to Kearney and the nearby village of Gibbon to pay bills and place orders. Simon enjoyed his dealings in town and meeting new people. Having him on the homestead created a difficulty, however. The two-room house was already cramped. Their small home had been big enough for the family when George had joined them five years earlier. At that time, Nicola and Martha had two children, and George was often traveling. But recently, George had been spending more time on the farm, and there was no longer enough space for the four children and now four adults. The brothers decided to build a second soddy.

The Yanney family in 1901

Nicola borrowed a sod-cutter from one of his neighbors and hitched it to his horse. The brothers took turns, one driving while the other two rode on the cutter, sinking its blades deep into the soil. Plowing back and forth over the pasture, they cut large blocks of sod, keeping them moist by cutting only enough to lay each day. Within a few days, the new house began to take shape. Friends came from town to help, and the men stacked the heavy, six-inch-thick blocks, carefully overlapping the seams of each layer. As the the walls of George and Simon's home rose, spaces for a door and a few windows were framed in with lumber.

Once the walls were finished, work on the roof began. With help from their friends, Nicola and George hoisted a heavy beam and set it lengthwise between the top of the gables. Limbs and boards were run from the beam to the side walls, over which they placed many smaller limbs. Finally, thick slabs of sod were cut and laid like shingles over the small limbs. The men then stripped the grass from the floor, filled the holes with loose dirt, and pounded it flat. Others patched the holes and rough places in the walls and shaved them smooth with a sharp blade.

The brothers were happy with their new house. However, building it had taken precious time away from the farm. After moving in two beds and a few pieces of furniture, Nicola, George, and Simon returned to their work, readying the homestead for the winter. Martha was happy to have more space in her home, but with Simon's arrival and George at home more often, she had more mouths to feed. Not yet six, Anna was already learning to help her mother with the cooking.

Simon's presence invigorated the brothers, and their evenings together around the dinner table were filled with lively conversation. Their business continued to thrive, helped in part by the growing Syrian community, and the three made plans to expand. More joyous news came a month shy of the first anniversary of Simon's arrival in America. Martha informed Nicola that she was pregnant with their fifth child. With Anna now attending school with Elias, Martha only had the two youngest boys at home. John was four years old and able to help his mother with simple chores. Moses was a precocious two-year-old.

As Nicola and his brothers finished their harvesting and began to prepare the farm for yet another winter, Martha began the familiar preparations for another child. Because the baby would come in early spring, the weather might make it difficult for any but a close neighbor to arrive in time to help with the birth. Martha was not worried, however. Though her Syrian friends were half a day away in good weather, the Yanneys' neighbors had helped them before, and they had become especially acquainted with an Irish family who lived only a few miles north of their homestead.

In the two years since Father Raphael's visit, the Syrians had continued to gather together to celebrate holy days, often under Nicola's leadership. They missed attending the Divine Liturgy, however, and because their local community had continued to grow, Martha wondered if the missionary priest might come back soon to baptize the baby as he had her other children. Though a few of the men had stayed in contact with Father Raphael, there had been no news of his returning to Kearney.

Since leaving Kearney, Archimandrite Raphael had been incredibly busy. Besides pastoring his large congregation in New York, he was busy raising money to build a new church and buy a cemetery, all while continuing to travel across the country, ministering to his scattered flock. Father Raphael was still looking for potential candidates for ordination, but had yet to find anyone suitable. With the influx of Syrian immigrants, there was a desperate need for clergy. A handful of priests had come from Syria to visit their families in America, and the archimandrite had convinced a few to stay, but no one was available to send all the way to Nebraska.

As the Yanney family settled in for winter, their excitement grew as the time for Martha's delivery drew closer. By mid-February, however, Nicola became concerned. The baby was not due for a few more months, but Martha had fallen ill. Each day she grew worse. Nicola tended his wife as best as he could, and sought help from their friends and neighbors, but none of their remedies worked. With no priest to anoint Martha, bring her Holy Communion, or hear her confession, Nicola prayed fervently at his wife's side and comforted her as best as he could. In agony, Martha went into labor too soon.

George raced to one of their neighbors for help. Help came, and Martha gave birth to a little girl, but lost consciousness soon after her delivery. She never woke. Nicola squeezed his wife's hand and stroked her face, gently shaking her, looking for any sign of life, but Martha was gone. In shock, Nicola buried his face in his hands until he heard the baby's weak cries. He cradled the tiny infant in his arms, then went to tell his children.

The children had been waiting in their uncles' house. When Nicola told them that their mother had died, the older ones began to cry and begged to see her. Elias was eight years old, and Anna was six. John and Moses were still too young to fully understand what had happened, but began to wail along with Elias and Anna, and their father and uncles.

Arrangements had to be made quickly in order to bury Martha the next day. The Yanneys' Irish neighbors had a small family cemetery nearby and offered to let the family lay Martha to rest there. News was carried to Kearney, and that night friends began to arrive from town. A few of the Syrian women washed Martha's body and dressed her in her nicest clothes. Others cared for the premature baby, trying anything to feed and keep her warm.

When the time for the burial came, Nicola and the children came to see Martha for the last time as she lay on her bed. The grieving husband kissed his wife's forehead, then wrapped her in a blanket and gently carried her to their wagon. Those who had come from town followed the family as they made a slow procession to the cemetery. The weather was unseasonably warm and the day almost springlike as they drove through the rolling hills. The cemetery sat at the top of a gentle slope three miles north of the Yanneys' homestead. Choosing a spot in the corner of the cemetery, Nicola's friends and brothers took turns digging a shallow grave, then placed Martha's body in the ground.

With no priest to perform the funeral service, a few hymns and psalms were sung and recited from memory as all the mourners wept. The huddled group finished by slowly chanting "Memory eternal."

Nicola placed a shovelful of earth on his wife's grave, and everyone followed, coming forward to pay their final respects and to embrace the family and offer their condolences.

A somber meal was served at the homestead. After several hours, most offered their condolences once again and returned to Kearney. A few stayed to help with the children, and especially the infant. The baby was weak, and her condition soon became grave. Family and friends tried to feed and nurse her, but nothing could be done. Just as he had seen Martha grow weaker by the day, Nicola watched helplessly as his infant daughter's life faded away. As her condition grew worse, Nicola prayed over his daughter, naming her Nour. Because no priest was present, he then anointed her with water to baptize her. Nicola had seen the rite done many times, but Nour's was the first baptism he had ever performed.

Over the course of a week, the baby continued to grow weaker. She died nine days after her mother. Saddened for the Yanneys, their neighbors again offered the use of their cemetery. Wrapping his daughter's tiny body and placing it in their wagon, Nicola and his family made another procession to the cemetery and buried Nour beside her mother. A few days later, he returned to mark their graves with a wooden cross.

In a quiet moment in the days that followed his wife's and daughter's burials, Nicola opened the family Bible. His last entry had been one of joy, recording his children's baptisms. Picking up his pen, he wrote: "Our wife Martha passed away on Monday morning at ten o'clock on February 11th, 1902. She was buried on Tuesday in an Irish cemetery in the state of Nebraska." Below this, he added, "Our baby daughter Nour passed away on Wednesday morning, February 20th, 1902."

Nicola closed the Bible and laid his pen aside. Though just a young man, he had tasted his share of suffering. He had lived in want and poverty, endured discrimination, lost his own mother and brother, and had been forced to leave his homeland. Nothing, however, had prepared him for the loss of Martha and Nour. Only twenty-nine years old, Nicola Yanney was now a widower with four young children to raise by himself. His grief overwhelmed him. The dreams that had brought him and Martha to America had ended, empty and bitter.

Over the coming weeks and months, Nicola and his children wept and prayed for their mother and baby sister every night. The younger ones still did not understand why their mother never came when they called. Trying to settle his children in their beds and tucking them in, their father comforted them as best as he could. Eventually, they fell asleep. Nicola blew out the lamps and lay awake, inconsolable, crying to God in the dark.

CHAPTER FIVE

A Church on the Plains

APRIL 1903 TO JANUARY 1904

THE SHOPKEEPER WARMED HIMSELF NEXT to his pot-bellied stove. A four-inch-thick book rested in his hands. He opened it and gently touched the pages. As he read, his lips formed the words he had so often heard in church as a boy. He sometimes paused to reread a passage, then continued. His concentration was broken only by the ringing of the bell over his front door. Carefully laying the book aside, he looked up and greeted his customers. They smiled in return, not surprised to find their friend seated in his favorite spot, poring over his Bible.

Mike Hayek had lived in Nebraska for almost twenty years. At the age of seventeen, he had decided to leave his home in Fi'eh in order to make his fortunes abroad. America had been different than he had imagined. The work was hard, and he had not become rich overnight, but the people were friendly. Mike was especially impressed with how the Americans governed themselves to live in peace and freedom. Realizing that he was never going home, he applied to become a naturalized citizen. A few years later, the process was completed and he himself had become an American.

When Mike first arrived in the New World, he had made his way to a peddlers' colony in Omaha where several of his fellow countrymen lived and worked. Traveling far and wide for four years, Mike sold any items he could carry. He did well as a peddler. A natural salesman, he charmed his customers with his broken English and stories of his homeland. After a few years of working for his supplier, Mike had decided to strike out on his own, with dreams of opening his own store. His travels had taken him all across the Great Plains, and one town had particularly impressed him.

Kearney, Nebraska, was a boomtown that had sprung up at a junction of the Union Pacific and Burlington Northern lines. Money was pouring into the community from out-of-state investors. An artificial canal and a power station had been built to generate electricity for the many factories and businesses that were opening. A huge cotton mill—the largest manufacturing facility in the state—was being erected a few miles west of town. The locals had even strung cables down their main street and installed an electric streetcar and street lamps. In only a few years, the once-tiny settlement on the Platte River had become a modern city of ten thousand people. Best of all, there were no other Syrian peddlers living there with whom Mike had to compete.

Convinced of his plan, Mike moved to Kearney in 1888. Though the economic boom soon collapsed and the town dwindled to half its former size, the community was good to him. He continued peddling and began saving money for his store. Within a few years, he felt established enough to start a family. Arrangements were made with a young Syrian woman whose family had immigrated to Omaha. Mike returned to the city, obtained a marriage license, and was wed. Mike, his new wife, Sadie, and their Syrian friends celebrated the joyous occasion, and then the young couple returned to Kearney. Mike's one regret was that the newlyweds had not been able to marry in an Orthodox church.

Though not yet thirty years old, Mike was finally achieving the success that had called him across the sea a decade earlier. He was happily married. He and Sadie had bought a house, and he was soon to open his store. Best of all, his wife was expecting their first child. Once again, however, Mike felt a pang of sorrow in the midst of his happiness. In the long years since he had left Koura, he had never been able to attend the Divine Liturgy, and he longed to worship in his own tongue and receive Holy Communion again. Even more, he wanted his child to be baptized.

At the time, no Syrian Orthodox churches existed in all of North America. Even the Greeks and Russians—with whom the Syrians shared a common Faith—had only a few churches, all of which were more than a thousand miles from Kearney. Mike was familiar with some of the American Protestant churches from the missionaries he had known in Syria during his youth. Their churches were too different and strange for him to join. With a heavy heart, the Hayeks resigned themselves to their fate. Their only consolation was their growing community of Syrian friends.

Throughout his time in America, Mike had kept in contact with his loved ones in Fi'eh. Writing about his successes and the freedom he had found, he encouraged them to join him. Several eventually made the crossing, moving to the colony in Omaha as Mike once had, and took up the peddling trade. Within a few years of their arrival, Mike's fellow villagers had repaid all their debts and, just as he had, decided to stay in America. Missing his friends and family, Mike began encouraging them to move to central Nebraska. Nicola and Martha Yanney were among the first to join him.

The small group gathered together for feast days and social occasions at the Hayek's house, the Yanney homestead, or, as their community grew, some other family's home. They reminisced and exchanged the latest news from Fi'eh. Soon, the Hayeks had two children and the Yanneys had three, and both families lamented the fact that they could not have their children baptized into the Orthodox Christian faith. Word had reached them, however, that a priest from Syria had arrived in New York and was making visits to communities all across the country. Mike, Nicola, and their friends hoped that the traveling missionary might somehow hear of them and come to Kearney. Because they were so small in number, however, they had little hope.

In the summer of 1898, Mike received surprising news. The Syrian priest was on his way to Omaha. The city was hosting a World's Fair, and the local Syrian community swelled as artisans and performers came from their homeland and around the United States to work there. The missionary had planned his visit to coincide with the fair. Mike and his wife immediately boarded the train for Omaha with their two young children.

Meeting Father Raphael Hawaweeny was a turning point in Mike's life. He had not seen an Orthodox priest since leaving Koura, and now, one of great distinction stood before him. During his week-long stay in Omaha, Father Raphael was a guest of honor at dinners in the Syrians' homes and at banquets on the fairgrounds. He visited the faithful, prayed in their living rooms, encouraged and exhorted them in their faith, and heard their confessions. When the Hayek family arrived from Kearney, he received them warmly.

Father Raphael performed the wedding service for Mike and his wife, solemnizing their marriage with the sacramental rite. The missionary priest also baptized their daughter and son, along with several children of the Shada brothers who had recently returned to Nebraska. Mike met privately with Father Raphael and made his confession for the first time in fifteen years. Later, at the Divine Liturgy, he and his family received Holy Communion together. When he boarded the train back to Kearney, Mike was renewed in his faith. Deeply moved, he hoped to see Father Raphael again, as the priest had promised.

When Father Raphael returned to Omaha in the fall of 1899, he found that most of the Orthodox Syrians had moved in the intervening year. The Shada brothers and most of the others from Koura had followed the Hayeks and the Yanneys to the Kearney area. When the missionary priest arrived at the Kearney train station in the middle of the night, Mike Hayek stood at the head of the excited crowd that had gathered to meet him. Considered a leader of their local community, and the only one with a house fitting to host such a dignified guest, Mike proudly escorted Father Raphael home in his carriage.

While staying at the Hayeks, Archimandrite Raphael served two liturgies, confessed and communed the faithful, performed two marriages, and baptized several children. Just as the saintly priest had inspired Mike in Omaha the previous year, so his visit to Kearney had a profound impact upon the entire Syrian community. Like Mike, they had all been raised in an atmosphere of religious piety and devotion. Yet for many years, they, too, had been separated from the liturgical and sacramental life of the Church.

When Father Raphael departed after his week-long stay in Kearney, Mike and his friends hoped to see the priest again soon.

To their disappointment, however, it had already been three years since his last visit. Father Raphael's many responsibilities prevented his return. Although he had tried to bring more clergy from Syria to help minister to the scattered communities, only a few had stayed. Those few priests were on the East Coast, where the vast majority of the Syrian immigrants were living. Because of the continued immigration, they were overwhelmed organizing their own parishes and helping the new arrivals flooding their congregations. Despite Mike's and his friends' requests, there was little that Father Raphael or the handful of Syrian clergy could do for the small, isolated community at the farthest edge of his missionary territory.

Mike and his friends had discussed their situation over the years and had recently come up with a plan. The immigration from Syria had affected their small community as well. Since Archimandrite Raphael's visit, the original settlers had been joined by more loved ones from Fi'eh, as well as families from the towns and villages of Tripoli, Deirmimas, Fourzol, and Marjeyoun. In only a few years, their local community had nearly doubled in size. Twenty Orthodox families now lived in the area. Even a few of the local Melkites—who usually joined the Roman Catholic Church when they came to the New World—wanted to pray with their Orthodox friends, finding the American Catholic services unfamiliar and in a foreign language.

With the community's growth, Mike realized that they now had more resources at their disposal. Their need had also become more pressing. There were numerous baptisms and weddings that needed to be performed. It was Martha Yanney's unexpected death, however, that had been the starkest reminder of their need for a priest. In discussing their plight, Nicola, George, and Simon Yanney, John Shada and his brothers, and the recently arrived

Abood family all agreed with Mike. They could no longer wait for years between visits from a priest. Instead, they would contact Father Raphael, plead for his help, and make their proposal. If they promised to provide enough money to support their own priest, perhaps he would send them one.

Though not wealthy by American standards, Mike was the most successful man in the Syrian community, and he was willing to put his money behind their plan. He could not do it alone, however, and knew that he would have to convince others to help. As he and his friends visited the other families and talked about their idea, they knew it would require sacrifice and dedication. Even though their community had grown, most of the families were relatively poor. John Shada was doing well as an established peddler. Only Nicola and his brothers were farming, though their income was modest. The rest were of humbler means, peddling or working as laborers. Accomplishing the plan would nonetheless require everyone's support.

Despite the difficult commitment being asked of them, most of the Syrians were convinced of their need for a church and a priest, and they agreed to help. Bolstered by the support, Mike and his friends composed a message and sent it to New York, then waited for a reply. Their plan was good, but Father Raphael would have to give his blessing. Mike and his friends hoped and prayed that he would.

ARCHIMANDRITE RAPHAEL read the telegram. It was quite bold. One of his smallest congregations—and the most distant—was pressing him for help. According to their message, they were, in fact, demanding that he act. The Kearney community stated emphatically that they needed a resident priest and promised to provide a salary to whatever priest he could send.

Father Raphael recalled the crowd that was waiting for him when he stepped off the train in the middle of the night. The people were certainly devout. Their community had reportedly grown since his visit, but they were still very small. In almost eight years of ministering to the Syrian communities across North America, Father Raphael had only officially established four parishes. Those churches were all in large cities—New York, Boston, Montreal, and Worcester—and each had hundreds of Orthodox families. Though their intentions were commendable, he wondered how the Syrians in Kearney would be able to support a priest.

After considering the fervent request, Father Raphael made a decision. He would make their community his fifth official church, but only on certain conditions. Firstly, as promised, they must provide a salary for a priest. This would take great effort on their part, and would prove the seriousness of their commitment. Secondly, they would have to buy or construct a building to use as their church—an even more difficult task, given the congregation's size.

Father Raphael decided on this requirement for practical reasons. Though small, the group in Kearney had become too large to meet in any one member's home. Some of his other communities were meeting in borrowed facilities. The archimandrite had friendly relations with the Episcopalians, and several of his informal congregations regularly met in their churches. Father Raphael, however, wanted the Kearney congregation to have their own building. The Syrians there lived on the far southern edge of town. They would need a place nearby to worship that was always available to them. Father Raphael was unsure whether this obligation was beyond the small group's ability, but if they would commit to fulfilling these two conditions, he was willing to grant their request.

Father Raphael had one more requirement, however. It was the most difficult one of all. The very reason that Kearney had been so long without a pastoral visit was the fact that Father Raphael had so few priests to serve his scattered flock. For five years, he had been searching for pious laymen whom he might ordain. Thus far, he had found no candidates. While a handful of priests had come from Syria, a few had already returned home. Including Father Raphael, there were only four Syrian Orthodox priests to serve the entire continent of North America. Because he had no spare clergy to send them, he would tell the Kearney community to choose a man from among themselves who was worthy of ordination.

Father Raphael remembered that most of the Syrians in Nebraska were from a village near the Balamand monastery. A few of the men had even attended the Orthodox school run by the monks. Perhaps they would have some good candidates from which to choose. The missionary priest thought especially of the midnight wagon ride and his meeting with the pious farmer and his wife. Father Raphael had received word of the wife's untimely death, and prayed for the repose of her soul and peace for the grieving widow and his children. Sending his response to Kearney, he wondered what the small community would do.

When Mike and his friends received Father Raphael's telegram, they were elated. Pascha was coming, and they would share the news with the entire community when everyone was gathered to celebrate the feast. Meanwhile, Mike already had an idea about a church temple. They had no funds to construct a new building. There was, however, an abandoned building several miles outside of town that might suit their needs.

When the local economy had collapsed a decade earlier and Kearney shrank to half its size, many of the new factories began to close. The massive cotton mill west of town had been shut down two years earlier. Next to the cotton mill, a wood frame schoolhouse had been built to educate the millworkers' children. It had lain vacant ever since the mill's closing. If the Syrians could purchase the school, it might be remodeled into a church. Mike and his friends made inquiries and found out that the school was for sale at a reasonable price. Three miles northwest of Kearney, it would eventually have to be moved into town, but the men knew that buying the abandoned schoolhouse was their best option if they were to have a church of their own.

On Pascha, the entire Syrian community gathered at the home of John Shada. It was the holiest day of their year. The long Lenten fast was over, and gathering together to celebrate had become an annual tradition. The occasion was festive, and the house was filled with food, wine, and singing. In the midst of the revelries, Mike and John called everyone to attention to inform them of Father Raphael's response. If they were committed, Father Raphael would bless them to found a church under the patronage of Saint George. Everyone was ecstatic at the news. In order to move forward, however, two crucial decisions had to be made.

The first one required immediate action; they needed a place to worship. The Syrians listened intently as Mike and John told them about the cotton-mill schoolhouse. They had made inquiries, and the price was affordable if everyone would contribute. Concerns were raised about the school's location since it was over six miles from most of their homes. Mike and one of the Abood brothers already had thoughts about where they might relocate the building. Besides purchasing and moving the schoolhouse into Kearney, they would also need more money in the future to remodel it into a proper church. Everyone enthusiastically supported the idea and decided to take a collection that very evening.

Altogether, they raised one hundred twenty-five dollars, enough to buy the school.

The second decision required greater consideration. In order to have a proper church, they needed much more than just a building. They needed a priest. In his telegram, Archimandrite Raphael wrote that he had none to send. However, if the local Syrians still wanted their own church, Father Raphael would bless them to pick a worthy man from their own community who would be trained and ordained to the priesthood.

There was much commotion as the Syrians fell into discussion and continued their festivities. They were overjoyed at the news that they would soon have their own church, and had already raised enough money to purchase the schoolhouse. As for a candidate for the priesthood, the choice was obvious as their eyes fell on the young widower.

For a year, Nicola and his family had deeply mourned the deaths of Martha and baby Nour. The children had been especially close to their mother. Even as he tried to console them, Nicola found it difficult adjusting to the loss. Martha had been the children's constant companion and caretaker while he had been busy in the fields or away making deliveries. She had worked ceaselessly to keep their house clean and the entire family fed. When the children were hurt or sad, she had always known what to say to console and encourage them.

Nicola struggled in his new role. He stayed closer to home, dividing his time between farming and the housework. He could no longer go on errands that took him away for long, and he relied on his brothers to do more of the peddling and deliveries. Many of the chores fell to Elias and Anna, though Anna's constitution was frail. Even when his oldest children were able to attend school, Nicola still had to tend the two youngest boys. Though he had always been an affectionate father, he and the children grew even closer in their sorrow. Nonetheless, he knew that his efforts fell short. Little seemed to ease their sadness. Nicola was especially thankful for the presence of George, with whom the children shared a close bond.

After Martha's death, Nicola questioned the direction of his own life. He and Martha had left their families and homeland in hopes of finding a better life in America. Nicola now wondered whether their sacrifices had been worth it. Though their years of toil had made them small gains on the farm, they were isolated from their friends and their church. Laying Martha to rest without the ministrations of a priest had especially troubled him.

Though she would have preferred to stay in Koura, his wife had followed him to the other side of the world, only to die far away from her loved ones. Martha and Nour had not even been able to receive Holy Communion before they died, nor did they have a proper funeral. The promises that had enticed the young couple to America now seemed empty. Always a deeply religious man, Nicola realized that his pursuits in the New World had been fleeting and vain. A deep sadness gripped him as he struggled to keep his farm and his family afloat.

In the midst of his children's grief and his own loneliness, Nicola considered remarrying. He knew of a widow who had recently come from Syria to live with her two brothers west of Kearney. The young woman already had two teenaged sons, one of whom had accompanied her to America and another who had stayed in Syria. Nicola approached her about a possible marriage, hoping to find a mother to raise his young children and companionship for himself. The widow, however, declined his proposal. Facing the prospect of spending the rest of his life alone and raising his children by himself, Nicola had nowhere to turn but to his faith.

Nicola's friends had also noticed his struggles. When they paid their respects at the homestead or visited when the family traveled to town, they saw how he wrestled with his grief. Yet, they also saw his unfailing devotion in the midst of his suffering. Nicola was popular among the local Syrians. Many had grown up with him in Fi'eh and knew his upright character. He was pious in his conversation and his conduct. Tutored by the monks, he knew more about Orthodoxy than anyone else in the community, and everyone sought his advice on matters of faith.

In the aftermath of Martha's death, their esteem for him grew even more. They felt sorry for the young widower, knowing that his loneliness was great. If he accepted ordination, he would never be able to remarry, and it would be a heavy cross that he would bear for the rest of his life. Moving into town to pastor their church would save Nicola and his children from their isolation on the homestead and perhaps help ease their grief. However, it was not for pity that the Syrians began to talk about Nicola as their priest. He had been tested, and they had seen in him a steadfast faith and peace even in the throes of his suffering.

Though no official decision was made at their Pascha gathering, a consensus was quickly reached. If any among them was worthy to bear the blessing and the burden of the priesthood, it was Nicola Yanney. He would be the candidate.

After praying for a time and considering his friends' request, Nicola accepted. It was a difficult decision. He would have to give up the farm. Moving into town and being closer to their community might be better for the children. Heaviest on Nicola's mind, however, was the fact that he could never remarry. Though willing to accept the call to the priesthood and remain celibate for the rest of his life, he grieved that Elias, Anna, John, and Moses would never again know the love and tenderness of a mother.

The Syrians in Kearney told Father Raphael of their plans to buy the schoolhouse and that they had a candidate to recommend for the priesthood. The archimandrite was delighted by their enthusiasm. In order to be ordained, the young man would have to be thoroughly examined to make sure that he was worthy and had no impediments to ordination. Though Father Raphael was too busy to come to Kearney to do this himself, he made arrangements for another priest to visit Nebraska near the end of the summer.

By midsummer, the purchase of the schoolhouse was complete. Mike Hayek began to look for a place to move the building. Though the majority of the Syrians lived in the southeast corner of Kearney, he had found a property farther west, next to his own home. Mike provided most of the funds to buy the empty lot. His friends raised the rest. In the meantime, Nicola prepared himself for the priest's upcoming visit.

One of the handful of Syrian priests serving in America, Archimandrite Meletios Karroum had come from Syria a few years earlier, and was pastoring a congregation in Ohio. Sent by Father Raphael, he first stopped to minister to the few Orthodox Christians still living in Omaha, then made his way to Kearney. Gathering the little flock in their newly purchased schoolhouse for the first time, the priest baptized several children and celebrated a service for the beginning of the Dormition Fast. On Sunday morning a few days later, he served the Divine Liturgy.

On Sunday afternoon, the congregation gathered again for another service, followed by their first official church meeting. The kindly priest with his shaggy, uncut beard delighted the Syrians and reminded those from Fi'eh of the old monks at the monastery. Father Meletios presided over their discussions and reminded them that the man chosen to become their priest would be examined. If all went well, the candidate would leave soon for New York in order to be trained and ordained. Nicola was quickly elected as the congregation's candidate, with the agreement that he would leave the homestead and move into town.

After the conclusion of the meeting, Father Meletios pulled Nicola aside and made plans to meet with him privately. On the following day, the two met in the church. Kneeling beside the elderly priest, Nicola made a confession of all the sins that he had committed throughout his life. Archimandrite Meletios examined him to see if the young man had fallen into any moral failings that would prevent him from being ordained. Once they were finished with the confession, he raised up Nicola, knowing him to be a most worthy candidate.

As Nicola kissed the priest's hand and received his blessing, Father Meletios embraced him, commending him to God and telling Nicola that he would soon receive word from New York. The priest then sent a message to Father Raphael, telling him of the congregation's choice, as well as his own recommendation that the young widower be ordained. A few days later, Father Meletios performed a wedding, served one final liturgy in the schoolhouse for the Feast of the Transfiguration, and then returned to Ohio.

Several months after Father Meletios' departure, the congregation began work on their church building. A local mover was contracted and brought a team of horses and a large wagon to move the former schoolhouse six miles to its new home on the southern end of Kearney, next to the Hayeks' house. Over the next few months, the Syrians met together in their new building every Sunday morning for prayers, fellowship, and teaching.

Little by little, they also began to transform the schoolhouse into an Orthodox church. Nicola participated when he could. Remodeling the school reminded him of his youth and rebuilding their village church of Saint Simeon. He still had the children to care for, however, and his work on the farm kept him from coming to town as much as he would have liked.

On the day after Christmas, the new congregation once again gathered in the home of John Shada to celebrate. They also held a meeting to elect their church officers. Mike Hayek was chosen to be the treasurer, and Nicola's younger brother George was picked as secretary. A second collection was then taken to help fund the remodeling of their church. Though the community had not yet heard from Father Raphael, John was also concerned about collecting money to send Nicola to New York. He knew that his friend would never be able to afford the journey himself.

With the end of another long fast, the food and wine flowed plentifully after the meeting as the Syrians danced and sang. Nicola watched as his future parishioners joined in the festivities. In their exuberance, a few of the young men began ringing a bell and leaping over each other's heads. One was suddenly lifted up by his friends and thrown into the air. Landing on his feet, he began to lead the revelers in another folk dance. The celebration lasted long into the night.

Days later, after the end of the Christmas festivities, Nicola and his family made the long, cold journey back to their homestead. He and his brothers still had to begin preparations for their eventual move. Eager for the coming year, Nicola waited for the message from Father Raphael.

CHAPTER SIX

Holy Priesthood

FEBRUARY TO JULY 1904

NICOLA STOOD BEFORE THE JUDGE, with his younger brother and a friend by his side. Raising his hand, he repeated the words of the oath, swearing to support the Constitution of the United States and, once more, renouncing all allegiance to the Sultan of Turkey and any other foreign powers. When he finished, the judge congratulated him, while George and the other witness shook his hand. Nicola Yanney was an American citizen.

George had been naturalized for a year and a half, but Nicola had been too busy after Martha's death to complete what he and his younger brother had begun together years earlier. With his impending ordination, Nicola had finally decided to travel with George to the courthouse in Kearney to fulfill his dream. As the brothers and their friend left the courthouse, Nicola thought of the date. Martha had been gone for almost two years. In two weeks, they would mark the day with special prayers for her repose.

Becoming citizens had been the couple's desire since arriving in America. Though they had missed their life in Koura, the freedom to worship and live without fear of persecution had convinced both Nicola and Martha to stay in the United States. Over a decade after arriving in the New World, Nicola had now realized their old dream. Yet he was alone. Though he loved his new country and was proud to be an American, Martha's death had changed his dream.

Nicola had felt a deep stirring long ago in his childhood, serving in church and praying in the monastery. The tragic circumstances of his recent life and the congregation's need had renewed that calling. Through his ordination and Father Raphael's training, Nicola would serve his people, who had come to America with great hope and yet felt lost so far from their church. Nicola would minister to those who had gone years without making their confession or receiving Holy Communion, who had been unable to have their marriages sanctified or their children baptized. He would bring consolation to families who had suffered like his own. In their last hours, he would be at the bedsides of the dying to anoint and encourage them, and he would bury the departed with the prayers and final blessing of the Church.

Throughout the autumn and early winter, no word had come from New York as Nicola and his family and friends continued to wait. Their community still met in the little schoolhouse every Sunday, which they were continuing to remodel into a church. With the approach of spring, however, some were growing impatient, wondering what was taking Father Raphael so long to respond.

Unbeknownst to the Syrians in Kearney, Archimandrite Raphael was waiting himself. Though a native of Damascus, even before coming to America, he had been serving as a priest of the Russian Orthodox Church. When he arrived in New York to minister to the Syrian immigrants, he had done so under the authority of the Russian hierarchy. Over the years, they had watched the young priest travel across the country, selflessly ministering to his scattered flock. Toiling ceaselessly, he had raised funds to purchase and remodel a large church in Brooklyn and had established an Orthodox cemetery for his congregation.

His superiors were impressed with Father Raphael, especially the head of the Russian's diocese in America. Archbishop Tikhon had arrived in the United States three years after the Syrian archimandrite. Father Raphael had warmly welcomed the Russian prelate to his new post. The two became close friends, and Archbishop Tikhon soon came to rely on the missionary priest to minister not only to the Syrians but also to the Russian Orthodox faithful. When he himself was busy elsewhere, he often sent Father Raphael to preside at services and church meetings in his stead.

Inspired in part by his friend, the Russian archbishop conceived a visionary plan to serve the different immigrant Orthodox communities in North America. He desired to have a vicar bishop consecrated for each individual ethnic group. Though they would work under the auspices of the Russian diocese, these assistant bishops would have a large degree of autonomy in serving their own flocks. Archbishop Tikhon wanted to begin with Father Raphael. Returning to Russia on church business, he presented his vision to his fellow hierarchs and asked their permission to consecrate Archimandrite Raphael as his vicar bishop for the Syrians.

Many of the Russian bishops remembered Father Raphael fondly from his time in Kiev, Moscow, and Kazan, where he had studied, served, and taught at one of their academies. Hearing

Archbishop Tikhon's plan, they cast a unanimous vote to elevate the Syrian priest. Because of Father Raphael's close ties to his home church, the bishops also contacted the newly elected Patriarch of Antioch, informing him of their decision. The patriarch gave his whole-hearted blessing.

Archbishop Tikhon excitedly told Father Raphael of his election to the episcopacy. Though he had turned down similar offers from the Patriarchate of Antioch because they would have taken him away from his flock in America, the archimandrite gladly accepted. His scattered congregations would be formed into a diocese under his administration. As a bishop, he could better serve them, especially by finding and ordaining young men like Nicola Yanney to the priesthood.

When Archbishop Tikhon returned to the United States, the exciting news of Father Raphael's consecration spread quickly. As spring approached, the prelate received an official proclamation from Russia directing that Archimandrite Raphael be elevated as soon as possible. Days later, a message was sent to Kearney. Nicola was to travel to Brooklyn, where he was to be ordained near the end of Lent, not long after Father Raphael's consecration to the episcopacy. The local congregation rejoiced at the news, and the even greater tidings that accompanied it—Nicola was going to be ordained by Father Raphael himself. Not only were they going to have a priest; the Syrians were going to have their own bishop as well.

With his impending departure, Nicola had to make arrangements quickly. The renovations to the schoolhouse were underway, and the building would be fully transformed into a church by the time he returned. Nicola could not afford the trip to Brooklyn, but his friend John Shada had already raised money to cover his travel expenses. His ordination and priestly training

Fr. Nicola's house in Kearney

required him to be gone for well over a month, but George and Simon would care for Elias, Anna, John, and Moses while he was gone. They would also tend to the homestead for the time being.

Because of his agreement with Archimandrite Raphael and the congregation, Nicola would have to leave the farm and move into Kearney to be closer to the church and his parishioners. While waiting for word from New York, Nicola had begun looking for a home in the southeast corner of town. Though some distance from the relocated schoolhouse, it was the neighborhood where most of the Syrians lived. He had hoped to find a house with land to buy, but with the date of his trip so near, he settled on finding a place to rent. The move itself would have to wait until after his return.

The children were both excited and sad at the prospect of moving. They had visited Kearney with their father many times. They would be near their Syrian friends and could wander downtown among the shops and stores. Nicola knew, however, that the move would be hard on his oldest children. Elias was already ten years old and had made many friends at his school. Though shy at first, he was now popular and excelling in his studies, and was one of his teacher's favorite students. Anna had also been attending the school and making friends. The homestead was the only home that the children could remember and was tied to memories of their mother. While the two youngest boys would find the transition from country to town easier, leaving the homestead would be difficult for Elias and Anna.

Though their oldest brother, Simon, was happy to relocate, George and Nicola himself had mixed feelings about the move. Simon had already been spending much of his time in Kearney, where he enjoyed socializing with his friends and taking care of the brothers' in-town business dealings. Nicola and George, however, had worked for years to cultivate a farm and a business that they now had to abandon. George had been elected as the congregation's secretary. He also sang as a chanter and would need to be closer to the church to help his brother with the services. Though he planned to move in with Nicola and the children at first, George wanted to continue farming, albeit closer to Kearney. He also wanted to start a family.

During his time living and working with his older brother, George had grown into a man. Still a teenager when he first arrived, the Syrian community now looked to him as one of their leaders, and not merely because he was the brother of their future priest. George was a bright, kind-hearted, and generous man. He had just turned twenty-seven, and it was time for him to get married. Before leaving for New York, Nicola approached the eldest Shada brother. One of his daughters had captured George's attention. Her name was Rebecca. She was sixteen years old, and all agreed that she would be a good match for George. Finalizing the arrangements, however, would have to wait until Nicola returned from New York. If all went well,

Nicola himself would be able to perform George and Rebecca's wedding.

As the day of Father Raphael's consecration drew near, Nicola embraced his children, explaining that he would be gone for several weeks and that their uncles would care for them. He also told them that when he returned, he would be a priest. The children were sad, never having been parted from their father for so long. Boarding the train, Nicola waved goodbye to his family as he retraced the route that had brought him and Martha to Nebraska eleven years earlier.

During the fifteen-hundred-mile trip, Nicola marveled again at the size of America. After a few days, he arrived in New York. When he and Martha had first come to the United States, they had been immediately shuttled to Ellis Island, only glimpsing the city from the dock. Now traveling through the sprawling metropolis, he was lost in the maze of buildings and the chaotic bustle. Making his way to Brooklyn, he found the Syrian neighborhood, still the largest Syrian community in the country. Nicola had arranged to lodge with acquaintances from Koura during his long stay in the city.

When the time for Father Raphael's elevation services came, Nicola and his hosts traveled into Manhattan to the newly built, magnificent Russian cathedral. At the end of the evening service, Archbishop Tikhon and another Russian bishop examined the Syrian archimandrite in front of the large crowd. Father Raphael made an official proclamation, promising to strictly adhere to the doctrines of the Orthodox faith in his new role as bishop. He then formally accepted his nomination to the episcopacy.

Father Raphael's consecration took place on the following day, this time at his own church in Brooklyn. That morning, Nicola walked from his hosts' home to the nearby temple that the archimandrite had worked so hard to purchase for his congregation. Named for Saint Nicholas—Nicola's own patron saint—the church would become the cathedral for all of the Orthodox Syrians in North America once Father Raphael was made a bishop. Like the night before, the crowd was so large that Nicola had a difficult time entering the church. Over two thousand Syrians had gathered, many, like himself, traveling from afar to witness the great event. Father Raphael was the first man to be consecrated as an Orthodox bishop in the New World.

As Nicola waited outside trying to make his way into the church, several Russian dignitaries arrived for the service and tried to find their way through the thick crowds. Later, a procession of priests and altar servers carrying lighted candles and banners pushed their way out of the front doors and crossed the street to Father Raphael's residence. Informing him that the hierarchs were waiting for him in the altar, they formed two lines and led the bishop-elect back across the street. As the escort chanted hymns, the entire neighborhood peered out of their windows to listen and gaze at the extraordinary sight.

After Father Raphael arrived in the church, the service began. Nicola could see that the interior had been beautifully decorated. When the time for the consecration came, Archbishop Tikhon and the assisting bishop escorted Father Raphael from the midst of the church, where he had been standing, and led him around the altar table three times. He then knelt at the altar as the bishops covered his head with their hands, invoking the Holy Spirit to endow Father Raphael with the grace of the episcopacy.

As the new bishop rose, Archbishop Tikhon clothed him in episcopal vestments sent as a gift from the Russian tsar. The choir and the crowd repeatedly sang "He is worthy" in several languages, and Nicola joined in the thunderous response. After the consecration, Bishop Raphael led the rest of the service. At the end of the Divine Liturgy, Archbishop Tikhon exhorted his friend about his new responsibilities, and Bishop Raphael promised to serve his people with zeal. The bishops and the rest of the clergy, along with the dignitaries and several hundred specially invited guests, retired to a banquet held in the new hierarch's honor, while Nicola and the rest of the faithful returned to their homes.

Bishop Raphael's consecration had taken place on the Sunday of the Adoration of the Cross. Because it was the middle of Lent, there were many services for Nicola to attend at the cathedral. Nicola saw Archimandrite Meletios, who had come from Ohio for the consecration, and the two exchanged warm greetings. Over the next few days, when things had quieted down and the honored guests had departed, Bishop Raphael met with Nicola. Asking about his family and the parishioners in Kearney, the bishop expressed his condolences, having heard news of Martha's death two years earlier.

Because there were several ranks to pass through before Nicola could be made a priest, Bishop Raphael told him that the various ordinations would take place over the next two weeks. Four days after his own elevation, the bishop called Nicola forward near the end of a church service. The young widower kneeled before him and bowed his head as Bishop Raphael prayed, making him a reader. He then sent Nicola into the middle of the church where he read a passage of scripture before the congregation.

Over the next few days, Nicola helped the other chanters read the Psalms and sing during the services. On the following Sunday, Bishop Raphael ordained Nicola as a subdeacon. For a week he helped serve in the altar, remembering how he had served as an acolyte during his youth in Fi'eh. Carefully watching the priests, he tried to memorize their every move and gesture.

One week after making Nicola a subdeacon, Bishop Raphael had him escorted from the midst of the nave into the altar and had him kneel beside the altar table. Nicola felt the bishop's hands press against his head as he ordained him to the diaconate. Bishop Raphael then presented Nicola to the congregation and dressed him in deacon's vestments. As they had at the bishop's consecration, the choir sang "He is worthy" in response to Nicola's ordination. Nicola served several services as a deacon, leading the congregation in the petitions and assisting the bishop and the priests at the altar during the liturgies.

On Palm Sunday, the cathedral was overflowing. It had been three weeks since Bishop Raphael's elevation, and it was on this great feast day a week before Pascha that the bishop had decided to perform his first priestly ordination. During the middle of the Divine Liturgy, Nicola was once again escorted into the altar, this time by two priests. Circling around the altar, he kissed each corner of the table, then a made a prostration before Bishop Raphael. After the third circuit, the bishop rose from his chair and once again laid his hands on Nicola's head as he knelt beside the altar.

The choir sang responses to Bishop Raphael's petitions as he invoked the Holy Spirit to send down the grace of the priesthood upon the young farmer from Nebraska. Raising Father Nicola up, the bishop presented the new priest to the congregation and dressed him in a new set of priestly vestments. After the eucharistic prayers, Bishop Raphael placed the consecrated Lamb in his hands and told Father Nicola to hold it until the time came to commune the clergy and the congregation. As the priest reverently held the Body of Christ, the bishop instructed him to care for it, for at the end of his life, Father Nicola would have to give an account to God for every particle of the Eucharist and every person who would partake of it from his hand.

Father Nicola prayed fervently during the rest of the service, remembering all of his family and friends in Koura and the parishioners in Kearney. Most especially, he remembered his children and Martha. When the time came, Bishop Raphael called the young priest to his side. Receiving Holy Communion from the bishop's hands, he was then sent into the nave to commune the congregation. Nervously but carefully, he held the chalice and placed the Holy Communion in the mouths of the faithful with a golden spoon.

At the end of the Liturgy, Father Nicola followed Bishop Raphael as the clergy led the congregation in a procession around the neighborhood. When they returned to the church, the bishop congratulated the new priest in front of the congregation. Later, he gave Father Nicola a pocket watch engraved with his name and the date of his ordination. Both the vestments and the watch were gifts from the tsar and Bishop Raphael on behalf of the Russian Church.

Father Nicola examined the gold pocket watch. It was very fine, far more expensive than he himself could ever have afforded. A small golden cross hung from the watch's chain and was inscribed with "Father Nicola" in Arabic. The young priest was deeply touched and thanked the bishop with tears in his eyes. Father Nicola would carry the watch with him for the rest of his life.

Later that afternoon, he sent a telegram to his family and friends in Kearney, telling them of his ordination and that he would be arriving home when his training was complete. Father Nicola then joined Bishop Raphael and the other clergy for the rigorous services of Holy Week. After celebrating Pascha, he spent a few more weeks with Bishop Raphael, meeting with him privately to discuss his priestly ministry and celebrating the Divine Liturgy every day so that the bishop and the other clergy could instruct him.

When the time came for him to return home, Bishop Raphael gave Father Nicola a large crate. Inside were more gifts from the tsar and the Russian Church for his congregation—icons, hanging lamps, service books, and holy vessels for the liturgy. Bishop Raphael also gave the new priest a vessel of Holy Chrism for the many baptisms and chrismations he would perform. Receiving the bishop's blessing and saying goodbye to the clergy who had trained him, Father Nicola boarded the westbound train having experienced a marked transformation since his arrival in the city a month earlier.

His shirt, coat, and trousers had been traded in for the black hat and cassock of an Orthodox priest. A thick beard was filling in around the mustache that he had worn for years. Like Archimandrite Meletios and the priests he had known in Koura, Father Nicola would not cut his hair or trim his beard for the next decade. Many people on the streets and in the train stared at him, but a large silver cross hung around his neck, and even those who had never seen an Orthodox clergyman knew that he was a Christian and guessed that he was a priest.

Father Nicola stared out the train window as the city gave way to small towns and wooded countryside. A day into his trip, the landscape changed. As he gazed on the passing farms and fields, Father Nicola realized the immensity of the task that Bishop Raphael had given him. Though he would still pastor the congregation in Kearney, the bishop had also appointed him as a missionary. Father Nicola was only halfway home from New York when he crossed the invisible line that would mark the eastern edge of his missionary territory for years to come.

When Bishop Raphael had come to America, he, too, had pastored more than just his congregation in Brooklyn. In his agreement with the Russian Church, he had been charged with serving the Syrian communities scattered across North America for two months each summer and two months each winter. Bishop Raphael's missionary labors had eventually given rise to the congregation in Kearney and the entire diocese, and now he had laid a similar burden on his new priest.

Bishop Raphael had only five churches in his diocese and a handful of clergy. Yet there were many Syrian immigrants in America who lived far from either a priest or an established church, and more were arriving each year. In order to serve them all, Bishop Raphael had made a stipulation that any community with three or more Orthodox families could request a visit from a priest once a year. Though a few clergy occasionally traveled from the East Coast to minister to the Syrians who had settled in the Midwest and on the Great Plains, Bishop Raphael now had a priest living in Nebraska. Because the need was great, Father Nicola had obediently accepted the appointment, remembering the many years that he and his family and friends had been without a priest. Yet he also knew the sacrifice it would require. Father Nicola's travels would take him away from his home and his young children for months at a time.

When Father Nicola finally pulled into the train depot in Kearney, his family and parishioners were waiting. The small crowd cheered and greeted him enthusiastically—the congregation of Saint George Syrian Orthodox Church finally had their priest. Elias, Anna, John, and Moses ran to their father as he stooped to embrace them. The rest approached their new priest and bent to kiss his hand, asking for his blessing. After exchanging greetings, they went to the small church where Father Nicola led them in prayers.

When he arrived at the church, Father Nicola saw that the remodeling was nearly finished. An altar table and an iconostasis had been installed. The only things lacking were the very items that Bishop Raphael had sent with him from New York. The parishioners excitedly unpacked the crate and hung the icons and lamps throughout the church. Once Father Nicola placed the holy vessels in the altar, the transformation was complete. The abandoned schoolhouse was now an Orthodox temple.

The Syrian community hosted a festive meal to welcome their newly ordained priest home. Staying up late into the night, they listened intently as Father Nicola described the grandeur of Bishop Raphael's consecration and the crowds that had packed into the churches for the great event. He also told them about his own ordination and celebrating Holy Week and Pascha with the bishop. When he finished, Father Nicola explained that Bishop Raphael had asked him to tend Orthodox Christians living in other communities, and that he would have to spend a significant amount of time away from Kearney. Though some were concerned at the news, they nodded their heads in agreement.

Later, as Father Nicola unpacked his bags, he gave his children the small gifts that he had brought for them. Their eyes grew wide when he let them carefully handle his gold pocket watch. Overjoyed that he was finally home, John and Moses clung to their father. With a heavy heart, Father Nicola explained to the children that he would have to be away from home more often—sometimes for weeks or even months at at time—because the bishop had asked him to visit other towns and cities where the Syrians had no priest or church of their own.

Adjusting to their new life in Kearney and their father's travels were not the only changes that the children had to face. Because their father was now the Syrian community's *khoury*,[5] they were looked upon differently. As Father Nicola gently reminded them, their behavior—good or bad—reflected upon him, their family, and the entire parish. Even the children's names were changed. At birth, they had each received "Nicola" as their middle name. Now, however, their middle names were all changed to "Khoury," so great was the honor of being the child of a priest.

Father Nicola immediately began conducting weekly church services, hearing his parishioners' confessions, and visiting the sick and infirm in their homes. George helped lead the chanters, and Father Nicola trained Elias and several other boys to help him as altar servers. Having gone so many years without the Divine Liturgy, the Syrians eagerly attended the services, filling their small church whenever the doors were open, worshiping in their native tongue, and receiving the Sacraments. Most had to walk a mile or two to the church, but happily did so even in poor weather. Those who lived out of town made the trip into Kearney as often as they could. After the liturgy, Father Nicola invited visitors and any parishioners who desired to join him for Sunday dinner.

Not long after his return from New York, Father Nicola visited the eldest Shada brother again. As his father had arranged for his marriage to Martha, so he made arrangements for the betrothal of his younger brother to Rebecca. His good friend John Shada, an uncle of the bride-to-be, was especially happy with the upcoming union, and the families began planning for the festivities that would take place in a few months. Meanwhile, Father Nicola received his first missionary call. A telegram came from Michigan, where several friends and relatives from Fi'eh had

5 The Arabic word for priest.

settled in the state's upper peninsula in the town of Ironwood.

Though Father Nicola had been home for less than two months, he was already saying goodbye to his family again. Telling his children that he would only be away for a few weeks, he left for Michigan. The trip to Ironwood took him as long as his journey to New York had. When he arrived, he was greeted by familiar faces who welcomed him and congratulated him on his ordination. Father Nicola stayed in the home of one of the leaders of the local community and performed the two baptisms for which he had been called. He also heard confessions and served a liturgy for the small group. Like those in Kearney, it had been years since they had seen a priest. Though they were still a small group, Father Nicola encouraged them to start a church as they had in Kearney. Promising to visit regularly, he returned home.

When he arrived in Kearney, Father Nicola found another couple waiting to be married. A widower and cousin to the Abood brothers wanted to wed a young woman who had come to America from his home village. It was Father Nicola's first wedding. Two weeks later, the day of George and Rebecca's wedding arrived. The Yanney and Shada families celebrated for three days leading up to the ceremony. The entire neighborhood joined in the festivities, with dancing, feasting, and loud singing filling the usually quiet street. Though a few of their American neighbors complained, the Syrians' celebrations proceeded uninhibited. The groom filled a tub with ice-cold beers for his guests to enjoy, and John Shada handed them out in the midst of the revelry.

When the time for the wedding came, the couple and the whole community gathered in the beautifully decorated church. Father Nicola handed two large candles to George and Rebecca and began the service. As he prayed for them, the priest remembered his own wedding in Fi'eh. It seemed to Father Nicola to have happened very long ago. Yet, next to George stood his friend John. The rest of the Shada brothers and many others who had attended his own wedding lined the walls of their small church, just as they had when he and Martha had been crowned in Koura. Like himself, each now had children of their own who had never walked the streets of their parents' village or known the place that their ancestors had called home.

The ceremony neared its end as Father Nicola led his brother and Rebecca around a small table in the middle of congregation. Removing the crowns from their heads, he blessed them once again, then spoke briefly about marriage. The crowd listened intently to the widowed priest's words. After Father Nicola congratulated his brother and sister-in-law, the couple left the church to the Syrians' joyful cries. As George and Rebecca and the rest of the community continued their wedding festivities, Father Nicola hurried home. Finishing his packing, he bid farewell to his children and the newlyweds, then headed to the train depot, leaving on another missionary journey.

Father Nicola had arranged for the children to stay with George and Rebecca while he was gone—an arrangement that would be repeated many times in the years to come. Their uncle was already like a second father to Elias and Anna and the younger boys, and they would all soon grow close to their new aunt. She, in turn, would help her brother-in-law carry his priestly burden by caring for his children when he had to be away from home. Little did any of them know how much Father Nicola's missionary journeys would someday cost him.

CHAPTER SEVEN

Syrian Orthodox Missionary

JULY 1904 TO APRIL 1906

TROUBLING NEWS WAS WAITING FOR Father Nicola when he arrived in Saint Louis. He had been invited to the city to perform several baptisms and to serve the Divine Liturgy for a special occasion. A startling telegram, however, was waiting for him when he arrived. Back in Kearney, his newly married brother and his best friend had been arrested.

The festivities leading up to George and Rebecca's wedding had apparently been too raucous for their American neighbors. Immediately after Father Nicola's departure, George had been charged with disturbing the peace and disorderly conduct. John Shada had been accused of distributing alcohol on a Sunday to three underaged boys. While Father Nicola was traveling through Missouri on his eastbound train, George and John had already made their first appearance in court. A large crowd of friends and family accompanied them, and with two separate cases and many witnesses, the proceedings spilled over into the next day.

Unable to return to Kearney, Father Nicola waited for more

news as he began attending to the Syrians in the city. A large contingent of Orthodox Syrians had recently moved to Saint Louis, and the busy priest had many pastoral visits to make, as well as five baptisms to perform and two liturgies to serve. He planned to stay for two weeks, then continue east.

Father Nicola performed the first baptism not long after his arrival. Finding his way to the family's home, he greeted them as they kissed his hand and asked for his blessing, then began to set up for the service. Unpacking the items he had been given at his ordination, he had almost everything he needed—vestments, a chalice and paten for the liturgies, a Gospel book, service books, and his container of Holy Chrism. Since Father Nicola was not able to carry a bulky baptismal font with him, the parents of the child brought out their own large tub and filled it with water. After the godparents and the guests arrived, the candles were lit and the prayers began. It was only the third baptism that Father Nicola had performed as a priest, yet he already knew much of the service by heart, so many times had he seen it in his youth.

Anointing the infant with oil, he gripped the squirming child firmly and plunged him into the water three times. The little boy cried, but his parents and godparents beamed. After Father Nicola finished the baptism, he sat down with the family and their guests to enjoy a special meal prepared in honor of the occasion. Two of the families were from Fi'eh and were old friends of Father Nicola. They excitedly exchanged the latest news from Koura, then asked their friend about his ordination and Bishop Raphael's consecration. Father Nicola also shared with them about John and George's predicament.

More news soon came from Kearney. The trouble was quickly subsiding. Over a dozen witnesses had come forward to testify that the three teenaged boys had, in fact, not been invited to the party. Although repeatedly shooed away by the wedding guests, the boys had returned and helped themselves to the beer. John was found not guilty. George's case was still pending, but he had hired an attorney who was moving to have his charges dismissed as well.

Father Nicola was glad to hear the good news, but was soon dealing with trouble of his own. Though several of the families living in Saint Louis were from Koura, most of the Syrians had come there recently to work at the World's Fair. Like the exposition held in Omaha six years earlier, Syrian actors, craftsmen, shop owners, restaurateurs, and tour guides had been hired from around the country to work in one of the special exhibits. Others had been brought over directly from the Holy Land.

With twelve hundred acres of fairgrounds and several million visitors attending each month, Saint Louis was hosting the largest World's Fair ever. One of the highlights of the fair was the ten acres of grounds that had been set aside for the special Jerusalem Exhibit. Full-scale replicas of the Jaffa Gate, the Dome of the Rock, the Church of the Holy Sepulcher, as well as other buildings, shops, and streets from Jerusalem, had been meticulously recreated for the attendees. Seven hundred people were employed to live and work in the Jerusalem Exhibit, many of whom were Orthodox Christians.

Not only had Father Nicola come to minister to the fair's Syrian workers, he had also been sent there by Bishop Raphael to offer the Divine Liturgy at the World's Fair itself. On Sunday morning, Father Nicola was to serve in the chapel of the Church of the Holy Sepulcher at the invitation of the fair's organizers. It had been widely advertised and was to be a spectacular event. Most had never seen an Orthodox service, and many fair officials, dignitaries, and visitors from around the world were excited to attend.

Father Nicola arrived early in the morning to prepare for the nine o'clock service, along with four men who would assist him with chanting and serving. When Father Nicola and his companions showed their tickets, they were stopped at the front gate and refused entrance. They had signed their fair passes in pencil. A week earlier, the officials had changed rules, requiring the ticket holders to sign their names in ink. While Father Nicola waited at the gate, others began to pass through, heading for the church and hoping to see the Orthodox liturgy. Despite his protests, the gatekeepers refused to let him or his companions in for another two hours.

Inside the Church of the Holy Sepulcher, a large crowd had gathered for the service. As people ran back and forth from the gate to the church to inform the attendees of Father Nicola's predicament, a Roman Catholic priest who had been invited to observe the liturgy decided to serve a Latin Mass while they waited. Hearing of the misunderstanding at the gate, one of the fair officials finally telephoned the gatekeepers, instructing them to allow the priest and his companions to enter.

When he arrived at the church, Father Nicola was surprised to find over one thousand people waiting for him. By that time, however, the Roman Catholic service was well underway. Father Nicola had to wait for another hour. After the Mass and a special music program, he stood up and addressed the crowd, explaining what had happened and apologizing for being late. Though the crowd had already been waiting for him for two and a half hours, Father Nicola did not dismiss them.

Asking the attendees to reverse their seats, he explained that Orthodox Christians worship toward the east, in the direction of the rising sun. Father Nicola then had several men take down the altar that had been temporarily erected and reassemble it in the correct place on the opposite end of the church. Meticulously setting out the chalice and paten and preparing the holy bread, he finally started the Divine Liturgy for which the crowd had gathered almost three hours earlier.

Over the next week, Father Nicola continued to visit the Syrians in Saint Louis. In the middle of the week, he returned to the Holy Sepulcher replica to baptize a child whose parents had come from Damascus to work in the Jerusalem Exhibit. Having waited four months for an Orthodox priest, they were elated that Father Nicola had come to the World's Fair and asked him to perform their son's baptism. A few days later, the missionary priest baptized several more children, including the daughter of one of his friends from Fi'eh. Before leaving the city, he also served another liturgy.

After his time in Saint Louis, Father Nicola was briefly called back to Nebraska. George and John's trouble had ended peacefully, so he did not have to return to Kearney. Instead, he traveled to Omaha. Several relatives of his parishioners still lived and worked there, and he stopped in the city briefly to baptize three children and perform a wedding. From Omaha, Father Nicola finally headed east, destined for the Syrian Orthodox communities in Upper Peninsula Michigan. Though he had visited them two months earlier, there were more baptisms to perform in the towns of Ironwood and Iron Mountain. Along the way, he visited other communities and ministered to the Orthodox Christians he found there.

Though Ironwood and Iron Mountain were several hours apart, both Syrian communities had been settled by villagers from Fi'eh. Jobs on the railroad, as well as the local mining and lumber industries, had first drawn them there. Most, however, had ended up as peddlers and merchants like their friends and relatives in Nebraska. After a few days in Ironwood, Father Nicola traveled to Iron Mountain to baptize two more children and to visit his childhood friend Abraham Khoury. Abraham and Father Nicola had grown up together in Fi'eh, but his friend had left the village a year before the Yanneys, finding work in America as a fruit merchant.

Abraham had been successful over the years and was a generous man. Very happy for his newly ordained friend, he invited the priest to stay with his family. Over six feet tall, Abraham towered over Father Nicola. Yet when they met, Abraham bowed to his friend and kissed his hand. The two embraced, and Abraham congratulated him on his ordination. Father Nicola enjoyed their time together, reminiscing with his old friend about their youth and sharing stories about their time in America. After visiting with the local Syrians for a week, Father Nicola departed Michigan, but not before insisting that Abraham visit him in Kearney.

On his return trip, the missionary priest stopped in Saint Paul, Minnesota, for a week, baptizing a child and visiting members of the local Syrian community. A particularly successful supplier invited Father Nicola to stay with his family and conduct services in a second-floor hall above his store. Bishop Raphael had visited the community three times during his own missionary journeys but had not been able to return for several years. Though there was a Russian church in the nearby city of Minneapolis, the Syrians desired to form their own congregation so that they could worship in their own language. Many came from the same village in Syria and had settled in both Saint Paul and Cedar Rapids, Iowa. Others from their village had ventured farther west to

Sioux City, and even into North Dakota. Hearing from the local Syrians that a number of their friends and loved ones had relocated to the northern plains, Father Nicola planned to visit them. Promising to return to Minnesota when he could, he departed for Wisconsin.

A small but fervent group of Syrians lived in the city of La Crosse. Bishop Raphael had visited them twice, and the group had grown since his last visit. Father Nicola spent a week in the city and performed several baptisms. Because of their fervent faith and dedication, he encouraged them to form a church society in hopes that they might someday build a church.

From La Crosse, Father Nicola traveled to eastern Wisconsin to the town of New London where a larger community of Syrian families had found work in local factories and on the railroad. During his week there, he baptized three children and blessed a young couple's marriage. Father Nicola stayed with them to celebrate the Elevation of the Cross, just as Bishop Raphael had served the feast for the Kearney congregation five years earlier.

From Wisconsin, Father Nicola returned to Kearney. He had been gone for two and a half months, twice as long as his trip to New York had taken. His family met him again at the train station, and the children ran to meet their father. Though happy to see him, he could see that they were sad that he had been gone so long. While home, he spent as much time with the children as he could, but his pastoral duties afforded him little time to rest.

Besides his normal activities of hearing confessions, holding church services, and visiting parishioners, Father Nicola had to arrange a few baptisms. Father Nicola baptized two boys and congratulated their loved ones who had come to the church from near and far for the services. More young men were settling down and starting families or sending for their wives and children in

Syria. Together with the continuing immigration, their community was growing quickly.

George and Rebecca, too, were settling nicely into married life. While he was home, Father Nicola and the children stayed with the couple in their rental house. The newlyweds would soon be starting their own family, however, and Father Nicola realized that he and the children needed a home of their own. He began looking for property near the Syrian neighborhood, hoping to find land to purchase as well as a house. Keeping a large garden would help supplement his meager income. Though torn between his priestly obligations and the needs of his young children, Father Nicola knew that he had to continue his missionary duties. Not only were the scattered Orthodox communities depending on his visits, he himself relied on the money that he made during his missionary journeys. Without the small monetary gifts that he often received during his travels, he and the children would not be able to survive.

Father Nicola worried about his children. In a few short years, they had lost their mother, moved away from the homestead, and, since his ordination, had to endure their father's frequent absence. Because they had been through so much, he was especially lenient and affectionate with them. All of the children except the youngest were now attending a nearby school with their Syrian friends. John and Moses seemed to be adjusting to their new life in town. Father Nicola, however, was concerned about his two eldest.

Anna was still sickly and easily tired at times. Surprisingly, Elias was struggling at school. A very bright boy, he had been popular and had excelled at his studies at the country schoolhouse near their homestead. The school in town, however, was much larger, with a different teacher and classroom for each grade. Father Nicola encouraged his son, trusting that he would make friends and adjust to his new environment in time.

After two weeks at home, Father Nicola was called to visit the Syrians in the southeastern corner of his missionary territory. A number of Orthodox families had settled in several towns in southern Missouri, as well as across the Mississippi River in Illinois, Kentucky, and Tennessee. They had once been served by a Syrian priest living in the area. Coming to see his children in America, the clergyman had been convinced by Bishop Raphael to stay and start a congregation. Eventually, however, he had returned to his homeland. Bishop Raphael had subsequently visited the region on his missionary journeys, but it had been years since the local Syrians had seen a priest.

After a seven-hundred-mile train trip, Father Nicola arrived in the first town. His new charges greeted him enthusiastically. Hailing from the Syrian city of Marjeyoun, they told him of their relatives living in Kansas. Father Nicola had heard of a growing Syrian community in Wichita and planned to visit them. He blessed the marriages of two couples and was asked to perform two baptisms as well. The families of the children lived out of town, however, and would not be able to arrive for several days. Telling them that he would return in a week's time, Father Nicola departed for a city 350 miles away in Illinois.

After spending a few days in Illinois, Father Nicola traveled south again, this time to a town on the far side of the Mississippi River in Kentucky. While there, he baptized more children whose families had come from Marjeyoun. Crossing the river again one hundred miles back into Missouri, the priest returned to perform the baptisms, as he had promised a week earlier. Later that day, one of the Syrians drove him thirteen miles by wagon to a nearby village to baptize a few more children.

For the next three weeks, Father Nicola traveled back and forth across the great river, confessing, communing, and serving liturgies for Orthodox families throughout the region. A few of the communities were almost as large as the congregation in Kearney but had not yet founded a church. After spending an entire month in the area, the missionary priest performed one last baptism before heading north.

Traveling twelve hundred miles from the far southeastern corner of his missionary territory, Father Nicola arrived at its northernmost edge, not far from the Canadian border. Hundreds of Syrians were moving to the state of North Dakota, and numerous families had settled near the town of Rugby. The local Syrians came from different religious faiths, with many Melkite and Maronite Catholics living alongside the Orthodox. Though the Melkites were visited by a circuit-riding Catholic priest and had built a small church for themselves, the Orthodox families had not yet been visited by one of their own clergy. Hearing of their plight, Father Nicola decided to spend two weeks with them before returning to Kearney.

When he stepped off the train in North Dakota, he found the weather dramatically different from that in southern Missouri. The temperature had dropped thirty degrees. Most of the Syrians lived ten miles out of town, and the strong wind blowing across the open plains made Father Nicola's long wagon ride bitterly cold. Because none of them had seen a priest since moving to North Dakota, he had ten baptisms to perform over the course of a week as he traveled from house to house. He also blessed a marriage and served a liturgy, confessing and communing all the faithful. Several of them told Father Nicola of a few smaller Orthodox settlements eighty miles south of Rugby, and also of one in the far northwestern corner of the state. The missionary priest promised to travel there on a return visit, but had an appointment to keep at home.

Father Nicola arrived in Kearney a few days after the start of the Nativity fast. He had been gone for almost seven weeks. Originally, he had planned on heading east for a few more weeks before returning to Nebraska, but a young man from his congregation wanted to be married before Christmas. Father Nicola confessed, chrismated, and communed the man's fiancée and performed the couple's wedding. He then departed for a brief trip to Ironwood, where he heard confessions and served a liturgy. On his way home, he stopped at a few more communities to offer services before the Nativity feast.

By the time Father Nicola returned, Christmas was only two weeks away. Elias, Anna, John, and Moses were happy to have their father home again and were excited for the upcoming holiday. Father Nicola was glad to learn that his eldest was adjusting to his new school and making friends. As the congregation prepared for the feast, the priest chrismated an American woman who was engaged to one of his parishioners, then performed the young couple's marriage.

In between church services and visiting his parishioners, Father Nicola caught up on his correspondence. When he arrived home, he had found a pile of unanswered letters waiting. Most were from family and friends in Fi'eh congratulating him on his ordination. Letters from his closest relatives, however, expressed concern. Having written Father Nicola several times since the summer, they had received no reply, not knowing that the young priest had been away on the first of many missionary journeys.

Besides the holiday season, the Yanney family was excited for another reason. Father Nicola had found a house. A small one-story home, it was located in the neighborhood where most of the Syrians lived. Although Father Nicola did not have enough money to buy the house, one of the Abood brothers who was a successful peddler offered a mortgage loan to the family. Father Nicola also purchased some of the surrounding land and kept his eye on a few more vacant lots nearby.

One week before Christmas, the family moved into their new home with a few belongings and the furniture they had brought from the homestead. After the church services for the feast, Father Nicola and the children gathered together with Simon, George and Rebecca, and other friends and loved ones to celebrate the end of the long fast. Having made two extensive missionary journeys since his ordination, Father Nicola decided to stay home for the next six months to spend time with his children and tend to his congregation.

As spring approached, the Syrians were excited as they made preparations for Lent and Pascha for the first time as a congregation. Father Nicola held services almost daily. In the middle of the fast, however, trouble arose that embroiled the whole neighborhood. Two Syrian men came to blows over a disagreement and ended up in court. The entire community poured into the courtroom, and many stood as witnesses for each of the warring parties.

Father Nicola himself offered to attend the proceedings to help bring peace and act as an interpreter if necessary, though neither man belonged to his parish. Over the years, as more Syrians continued to move to Kearney, several of the newer arrivals were members of the Melkite and Maronite faiths. Some attended the Orthodox church in order to worship in their native Arabic. Religious tensions, however, often surfaced. Compounded by family and village rivalries and sour business dealings, bad tempers frequently led to violent confrontations.

When he was in town, Father Nicola was often asked to help settle disputes between neighbors and spouses, and offer guidance to immigrants as they tried to adjust to their new life. A few of the men in the neighborhood received a great shock when their wives threatened something unheard of in Syria—divorce. Others complained that the Americans' loose morals were eroding their culture and customs. Surrounded by foreign social pressures and competing faiths, Father Nicola tried to be a counselor, pastor, and peacemaker among his people.

As the tensions subsided, Father Nicola and his parishioners looked forward to Pascha. Many Syrians from the surrounding area traveled to Kearney during Holy Week. Father Nicola performed a baptism on the morning of Holy Saturday. Later, at midnight, the congregation gathered for their very first Paschal liturgy in their new church. For the next week, the community feasted together with their out-of-town guests, and two more baptisms were celebrated. With Lent and Pascha over, Father Nicola thought of making another missionary journey, but another troubling situation arose that kept him in Kearney—many of his parishioners were becoming gravely ill.

The sickness started at the home of one of the Aboods. Several family members and a friend came down with symptoms after sharing a meal together. Rumors spread that they had taken ill from food poisoning. The real culprit, however, was soon discovered to be typhoid fever. As the sickness spread throughout their community, Father Nicola visited the bedsides of the sick, anointing and confessing them, and bringing Holy Communion to the most seriously afflicted. The neighborhood panicked when the elderly aunt of the Abood brothers died.

The fever continued to spread and lingered for weeks. Going from house to house, the priest tried to calm his parishioners' fears as he ministered to the suffering. By the time the sickness had run its course over a month later, four members of their community had died. Father Nicola had prayed with and communed each one. The man who had given Father Nicola his mortgage was among the dead, and the loan passed to his younger brother.

Father Nicola stayed in town for a few more weeks, comforting the grieving families and ministering to those who were still recovering from typhoid fever. His responsibilities to his wider flock beckoned, however, and he left for Michigan in the middle of the summer. Over the next five months, he visited the communities in the northern region of his missionary territory. Father Nicola was spending more time away from Kearney than either he or the bishop had originally intended. Bishop Raphael, however, had hoped to establish churches throughout his diocese that could be missionary centers in each region. In founding the parish in Nebraska, his plan was a success—since ordaining Father Nicola, thousands of Syrians in a hundred different towns and cities were being served by a priest.

While in Michigan, the missionary stayed with family and friends from Fi'eh. Besides serving the liturgy, hearing confessions, and teaching, he baptized a few children during his two-week stay in Ironwood, then left for Iron Mountain. After baptizing a child there, he received an urgent message to return to Ironwood. A newborn was near death. Racing back, Father Nicola arrived in time to perform an emergency baptism. Traveling back to Iron Mountain, he baptized more children before heading south to New London, Wisconsin. He then crossed Lake Michigan to the city of Grand Rapids. The local Syrians had not seen a priest for some time. Father Nicola stayed with them for a week, baptizing two children and blessing five marriages, then journeyed to Lansing for a brief visit.

Having spent a month and a half in the Michigan area, Father Nicola took a train five hundred miles west to the city of Cedar Rapids, Iowa. The Orthodox community in Cedar Rapids was small but thriving. The first Syrians had come to the city as peddlers a decade earlier. Before Father Nicola's ordination, they had received yearly visits from a clergyman living in Worcester, Massachusetts. With a priest now stationed much closer, they came to rely on Father Nicola, inviting him to visit several times a year. Many of the Syrian families were from the village of Ain Arab and had relatives living in Worcester and Saint Paul. Others had moved to the northwest corner of Iowa, or had settled on the Dakota plains in the communities that the missionary priest had already visited. One of Father Nicola's brothers-in-law was from a village near Ain Arab, and he had moved to Cedar Rapids as well.

Though they were still a small community, the local Orthodox Syrians were devoted and dreamed of founding their own parish. For the time being, however, most of the peddlers' earnings were being sent to help their loved ones still living in Syria. It would be a decade before they would gather enough funds to build their own church. Before leaving Cedar Rapids, Father Nicola married a young couple and baptized six children.

Making his way back to Wisconsin, the missionary priest first stopped at a community on the eastern edge of Iowa to perform a baptism. When he returned to La Crosse, the congregation welcomed him warmly, and Father Nicola stayed there for two weeks, as would become his custom. Ministering to the little flock, he once again encouraged them in their dream to someday found a church. Though small in numbers, the local Syrians were especially dedicated. Father Nicola then returned to New London, where four more children were waiting to be baptized.

Over the next month, Father Nicola traveled to other communities in his territory, eventually arriving in North Dakota. Though it was almost winter and often bitterly cold on the northern plains, it was a convenient time for him to make an extended visit there. Peddling had first brought Syrians to the state, but many had stayed in order to homestead. By living and working their staked land, the immigrants could own it within five years. Knowing from experience the best time to visit the farmers, Father Nicola waited until near the end of the year when the harvest was finished and most of the farm work was done.

While spending a few weeks near the town of Rugby, Father Nicola performed a few baptisms along with a wedding. Heading south, he stopped in Sioux City, Iowa. Like their kin in North Dakota and Cedar Rapids, many of the Syrians came from the village of Ain Arab. Some had found work as peddlers, while others labored in the city's large stockyards. During his week-long stay, Father Nicola baptized a child and encouraged the local Orthodox community. He then traveled across Iowa to visit a small village in the northeast corner of the state.

In early December, Father Nicola finally returned to Nebraska. Before going home, he stopped in Omaha to visit his friends in the peddlers' colony. One infant was deathly ill, and Father Nicola performed the baptism before the child died. Having suffered the same loss himself, he tried to console the grieving parents. After baptizing a few more children, he boarded the train for Kearney.

When Father Nicola arrived back home, he was met by his family. Embracing them, he gave Elias, Anna, John, and Moses the little gifts that he had collected for them during his travels. Over the next few days, he told his family about his long trip and brought them greetings and news from the other Syrian settlements. They, in turn, related all that had happened in Kearney and their neighborhood since he had been away.

Father Nicola placed an advertisement in the local newspaper to let his parishioners and the wider community know that the services in their church had resumed. A couple approached the priest and requested that he marry them, and another family asked him to baptize a child that had been born during his absence. As Christmas approached, Father Nicola was called back to northern Iowa to perform a wedding. He left town again for a few days, but returned home quickly to spend the final weeks before the feast with his family and the congregation of Saint George.

After the winter holy days, Father Nicola and his children began to settle into a daily routine together. Early in the new year, he was called to the nearby town of Lexington to baptize one of his parishioners' children. With more immigrants coming to Nebraska each year, many Syrian families were beginning to seek business opportunities in towns and cities besides Kearney. When Father Nicola returned home from his short trip, he received a request from a young couple living in Kansas. Wanting to be married before the start of Lent, they traveled to Kearney so that their priest could perform the wedding.

As Father Nicola made preparations for the long fast, he received exciting news. Despite his travels and busy schedule, he had stayed in regular contact with his loved ones in Fi'eh. He, George, and Simon had continued to send letters and money to their father and other family members, so Father Nicola was not surprised when he received a letter from his orphaned nephew. He had last seen Michael as he and Martha were leaving Koura. His nephew had been a young boy of seven years at the time. Thirteen years had passed since then, and Michael Yanney was now a grown man and newly married himself. Seeing no future in Syria, he had contacted his uncle in Nebraska about helping him come to America. Father Nicola and his brothers gladly sent funds for the young couple's passage, along with instructions on how to get to Kearney.

A few months later, when Michael and his wife arrived at the train depot, Father Nicola barely recognized him. As thin as he himself had been at twenty, and several inches taller, his nephew wore a thin, youthful mustache. The priest noted Michael's resemblance to his father, who had died four months before he had been born. Father Nicola had been eleven years old at the time. The uncles embraced their nephew and his wife, and listened intently as he related news from Fi'eh and messages from their elderly father. Elias Yanney had now reached the age of eighty-nine, nearly as long as any elder in their village had ever lived.

Father Nicola and his brothers assured Michael that he could find good work in Kearney. Once he and his wife were rested from their long journey, the priest promised to introduce his nephew to Mike Hayek and some of the other Syrians in their community. He also told Michael that the young couple could stay with the family until they wanted to find a home of their own. Michael was grateful for the help. His uncle had always been respected in their village, and since becoming a priest, his esteem had risen even higher. Father Nicola was grateful, too. His nephew had been reared and educated at the Balamand monastery, and he hoped that Michael would someday become a leader in their congregation.

Besides their reunion with Michael, the Yanneys were also excited for another reason. Ten months earlier, Rebecca had given birth to her first child, whom Father Nicola was soon to baptize. George had named his son John Elias George Yanney. A few days after celebrating Pascha, the Yanney family and their fellow Syrians returned to the church for the baptism of one of the Shada brother's children. On the next day, they gathered again to baptize George's firstborn son. Father Nicola was delighted for his younger brother, who had been a faithful companion through the years and was helping him to raise his own children. The family threw a party for their friends and neighbors to celebrate the happy event. On the following day, Father Nicola baptized another child, then immediately left town on his spring missionary journey.

The missionary priest's first stop was Kansas. A growing community of merchants had settled in the large city of Wichita and the nearby vicinity. Most of the families hailed from Marjeyoun and peddled across the southern plains. Father Nicola heard their confessions and served the Divine Liturgy in the home of one of their prominent members. Staying in Wichita for a few more days, he baptized several children, then departed for Fort Dodge, Iowa.

While in Fort Dodge, Father Nicola baptized a child born to one of the local Syrians since his last visit to the town several months earlier. Intending to continue east to Cedar Rapids, his trip was interrupted by alarming news. George and Rebecca's son was terribly ill. When Father Nicola arrived back in Kearney, he sped home. His brother and sister-in-law were sick with worry, and his own children were quiet and anxious. Father Nicola anointed and prayed over his infant nephew. Sadly, the little boy died a few days later in the early hours on Sunday morning.

George and Rebecca were devastated. Father Nicola consoled them and the children, but had to leave to prepare the church for that morning's liturgy. There, he made the announcement to the congregation and prayed for his nephew at the end of the service. The funeral was planned for the following afternoon.

On the next morning, while the family grieved and began to prepare the child for the funeral, they made a startling discovery. The little boy's body was still soft and supple. No signs of rigor mortis had set in. Little creases had even appeared on his skin where his garters had been fastened, and when his parents stroked his hands, they appeared as if they might clasp onto something.

Father Nicola postponed the funeral as excited rumors spread throughout the neighborhood that George and Rebecca's son might not be dead after all. Neighbors called a doctor to the Yanneys' house, and the family waited anxiously, hoping that their son might somehow still be alive. When the physician arrived, he examined the body and confirmed the worst. The little boy was indeed dead.

George and Rebecca were distraught. The hope caused by the delay made their grief even greater. After Father Nicola helped them finish dressing their son, a few of the neighborhood men carried his body to the church. There, Father Nicola performed the most difficult of his priestly duties—the funeral of a child. In the late afternoon, after the service and amid tearful prayers and loud cries, the entire congregation escorted George and Rebecca to the local cemetery.

A year earlier, the church had purchased a number of cemetery plots to be set aside for parishioners. Four graves had already been used by those who had died in the typhoid outbreak. A fifth had been opened for George and Rebecca's son. As the Syrians lowered the small coffin into the earth, Father Nicola said a final prayer and cast the first handful of dirt into the open grave. The Syrians wailed inconsolably. Not long after the funeral, the Yanneys erected a stone over the little boy's grave. In a few years, two more members of their family would be buried nearby.

CHAPTER EIGHT

Travels and Trials

MAY 1906 TO MAY 1908

After his nephew's death, Father Nicola stayed in Kearney as long as he could. After a few weeks, however, his missionary duties called him away. With his brother gone, George and Rebecca once again became the children's caretakers, and they poured their attention into Elias, Anna, John, and Moses while they continued to mourn for their son.

Resuming his spring missionary journey, Father Nicola traveled to Cedar Rapids, where he baptized two children. One was the son of his brother-in-law, and Father Nicola stayed with his relatives and told them about the death of George's son. Before leaving Iowa, he married a young couple, then departed for Kansas, where a large group of immigrants from Marjeyoun were holding their semiannual reunion.

Coming from as far away as Florida, Ohio, and New Mexico, two hundred Syrians had gathered in Wichita. Considering Father Nicola their pastor since his first visit to their community, they had called him to the city to hold church services in conjunction with their jubilee. Packed into a few homes in the Syrian neighborhood, the long-sundered friends and family spent a week feasting and enjoying one another's company. The locals were especially excited. Several days before the priest's arrival, the leader of their community had been betrothed to a young woman whom he had courted in Syria. Now reunited in America, grand plans were being made for their wedding celebration.

As the festivities in Wichita concluded, Father Nicola congratulated the couple and promised to return for their wedding. Due to marry another couple in Omaha, he boarded a train bound for Kansas City, then caught his connection to Nebraska. After the wedding in Omaha, he returned to his family. George and Rebecca were still grieving. In the midst of their sorrow, however, George shared happy news—Rebecca was pregnant with their second child. He also told his brother that they were considering moving out of Kearney. George still wanted to return to farming.

Father Nicola wondered about his children. John was now attending school with Elias and Anna. Elias had made many friends, and spent much of his spare time playing marbles with them. Anna, however, was not faring as well. Her health was often poor and was a growing concern for Father Nicola. The doctors could give little help, and he prayed fervently. His youngest son, Moses, would soon be joining his older siblings at school. Father Nicola began thinking about how the children might remain at home while he was away. Though George was not moving out of town yet, the children would need to stay in Kearney so that they could continue their education.

While he paused from his travels, Father Nicola had the opportunity to buy more property surrounding the family home. Earlier in the year, he had acquired the two lots adjacent to the house, and a third at the north end of the block. Because the properties had gone unclaimed, Father Nicola was able to buy them by paying the back taxes and fees. Once he bought the last lots from two of his neighbors, the family owned four acres of land around their house. Father Nicola still owed a mortgage to the surviving Abood brother, but hoped to cultivate his new property. He and the children could raise produce and plant fruit trees on the land, and George could farm there until he and Rebecca moved.

Father Nicola was traveling again by the middle of the summer. Returning to Cedar Rapids, he performed three marriages in a single day. He then headed south to Wichita to marry the young couple as he had promised. By the time Father Nicola arrived, over a hundred out-of-town guests had joined with the local Syrians for the wedding festivities. For days, they danced and feasted, some trading in their American work clothes for their traditional Syrian finery.

Gathering in the groom's home, Father Nicola performed the ceremony. After the priest congratulated the happy couple, the bride was spirited away and hidden by her husband's friends. Father Nicola remembered his own wedding and smiled at their custom. The new bride was soon returned after the groom threw a lavish wedding feast for his guests.

After visiting for a few days in the city, Father Nicola traveled to Omaha to baptize the son of a couple he knew from Fi'eh, then turned east toward Michigan, visiting other communities along the way. Arriving in Ironwood over two weeks later, he baptized another child whose parents hailed from Koura. Over the next month, he traveled throughout the region to families living close to Ironwood and Iron Mountain, serving the liturgy and confessing the faithful, and baptizing more children. Before leaving

Michigan, Father Nicola performed the wedding of a bride and groom who had each come from his and Martha's home villages of Fi'eh and Qilhat.

From Upper Michigan, Father Nicola headed south. Stopping briefly in Iowa, he performed a wedding before visiting the Syrian families living along either side of the Mississippi River. For two weeks, the missionary priest once again traveled hundreds of miles back and forth across the great river to the scattered communities, confessing and communing the Orthodox faithful under his charge and baptizing nine of their children.

Traveling north toward Saint Louis, Father Nicola stopped to visit two families from Koura who were living near the town of Jackson, Missouri. Baptizing their children, he became reacquainted with a young man who had been raised in a village neighboring Fi'eh. Though Father Nicola was several years older, he remembered the young man and his older brother. The Hamaty brothers had studied at the same monastery school that he had attended. Promising the man and his family that he would return regularly, the missionary priest continued to Saint Louis for a brief visit.

From Missouri, Father Nicola returned to Cedar Rapids before heading into Minnesota. Visiting a few communities on his way north, he stopped in a town on the western edge of the state to perform a few baptisms. With autumn already drawing to a close, it was time for Father Nicola's annual visit to the homesteaders in North Dakota.

First going to Rugby, Father Nicola performed a handful of baptisms over the course of a week as he made his rounds to the Orthodox families in and around the town. He encouraged the local community to remain faithful. Many of the Syrians living in the area were Melkite Catholics. Though the two local Syrian communities sometimes cooperated and there were occasional intermarriages, religious disputes between the local Orthodox and Melkites were common.

From Rugby, Father Nicola traveled eighty miles south to the two small villages that he had learned of during a previous visit. Twenty-five Orthodox families had settled there. Coming from the same village, many had relatives living in Sioux City. Like most of the Syrians who had come to North Dakota, the families had largely given up peddling to become homesteaders.

Roaming the northern plains at the approach of winter was often difficult. Trains only took the priest so far into rural North Dakota, and Father Nicola had to do much of his traveling by open wagon. The wind was often bitter, and rain and driving snow were common. Arriving at the first family's home, he spent the next few days traveling the ten miles back and forth between the two communities, visiting with the isolated Orthodox farmers, baptizing six children, and blessing two marriages.

With Christmas only a month away, Father Nicola left North Dakota. Receiving several telegrams, he traveled to western Minnesota for a baptism and Ironwood for a wedding before returning home. When he arrived in Kearney, the missionary priest had been away for over five months. A few days later, he married a young couple in Kearney, but within a week, he was called away again.

Making a quick trip to eastern Iowa, Father Nicola baptized several children. From there, he returned to visit the Syrians living in Sioux City. Staying with them for a few days, he performed two more baptisms, then boarded a train for Omaha. Reuniting with friends in his old neighborhood, Father Nicola baptized three children early one morning, then raced to the depot. He was due to perform a wedding in Kearney later that same day, and was glad there were no delays as his train sped westward.

After the wedding, Father Nicola traveled to Wichita for the third time that year to preside over an even larger reunion hosted by the local Syrians. Returning home, he rested from his missionary labors for the next two months, celebrating the feasts of Christmas and Theophany with his family and tending to his congregation. Not long after Father Nicola's return, Abraham Khoury arrived from Michigan to visit the Yanneys. The two reminisced together with George and Simon and other friends from Fi'eh, and Father Nicola brought all of them news and greetings from their acquaintances across the Great Plains.

Early one Sunday morning, Abraham accompanied Father Nicola to help prepare the church for the services. The stove had to be lit to warm the building before the rest of the parishioners arrived. Though the church was little more than a mile from the Yanneys' home, the weather was bitterly cold. By the time Father Nicola and his friend had the fire started in the stove, they were half frozen.

As they huddled together warming themselves, Abraham asked the priest why the church was located so far from their neighborhood. Only two families lived close to the church, while the rest of the congregation had to walk a mile and a half to get there. The two agreed that the church should be closer to the families' homes so that the women and children would not have to walk so far, especially in bad weather. After the Sunday morning liturgy, Abraham spoke to the congregation about their problem. His business in Iron Mountain had been successful and he wanted to help his friends. If the congregation desired to relocate and would purchase one lot in the middle of their neighborhood, he would buy a second adjacent lot, and the church could be moved.

The parishioners were stirred by the offer and discussed it excitedly over the next several weeks. Many wanted to move their church, but a vocal minority opposed it. When a vote was eventually taken, the majority decided to proceed with the move and soon found two properties for sale directly north of Father Nicola's land. The congregation purchased one of the lots, and Abraham fulfilled his promise, buying the second lot and deeding it to the parish. Meanwhile, the priest tried to keep the peace between opposing factions.

Several weeks before the start of Lent, Father Nicola received a request from a family in Saint Paul to baptize their child. From Minnesota, he continued east into Michigan, where he performed a wedding. Two weeks later, he was called away from home again to serve the funeral of a young Syrian man living in southeastern Iowa. Father Nicola returned to Kearney in time for the beginning of the fast.

Seven weeks later, he celebrated Pascha with his family and the congregation. Elias and several other boys from their community served in the altar to help the priest with the midnight service. The rest of Father Nicola's children settled beside their aunt, who held a four-month-old infant daughter in her arms. Their uncle George and cousin Michael led several men in chanting the festal hymns. At the end of the long services, Anna, John, and Moses were roused with the rest of the Syrian children and directed to step forward to receive Holy Communion from their father.

After resting for a few days, Father Nicola left on his spring missionary tour. He first headed east to Saint Louis. Most of the Syrians living there were of the Maronite faith, but several Orthodox families had remained in the city after the closing of the World's Fair. After baptizing a boy whose parents had come from Fi'eh, Father Nicola married a young couple, then left for

Kansas. Staying in Wichita for two weeks, he then traveled to several isolated farmsteads in the southern part of the state.

From Kansas, the missionary priest proceeded to southern Colorado. It was Father Nicola's first time visiting the state. Several Syrian families had moved to the area, following a local coal-mining boom. Not miners themselves, they had opened dry goods stores in the towns that had sprung up near the mines. Originally hailing from a region south of Koura, the families had been in America for several years but had not yet been visited by an Orthodox priest.

Over the next two days, Father Nicola baptized seven of the families' children. He intended to stay with them longer, but on the third day of his visit, he received an urgent telegram from George—Anna was gravely ill and Father Nicola needed to return home immediately. The family had discovered that Anna's ailments were caused by heart problems, and her health had begun deteriorating in the weeks after Pascha. Bedridden by the time that Father Nicola received the telegram, Anna was so weak that her uncle and aunt feared for her life.

Father Nicola raced home, anxious at every delay on his long route back to Kearney. By the time he arrived, Anna was unconscious. Kneeling beside her bed, Father Nicola desperately prayed over his daughter and anointed her. She was barely alive and quickly slipping away. He had come too late to speak with her one last time. Anna died early the next morning, six weeks shy of her twelfth birthday. Father Nicola embraced his sons as they all wept.

News spread quickly through the neighborhood and the town that the Syrian priest had been called back home from his missionary work and that his daughter had passed away. Parishioners began arriving at the house, offering their condolences to Father

Nicola and his sons and wailing with the family in their grief. Together with several women, Rebecca washed her niece's body and dressed her in her nicest clothes. Father Nicola began making arrangements to serve the funeral early the next afternoon. The local newspapers were notified of his daughter's death, and a coffin was delivered to the house. Anna's small body was gently placed in the coffin, loaded onto a wagon, and escorted to the church. There, the community gathered with Father Nicola and his family to pay their respects and offer their prayers.

With no other Syrian Orthodox priest living within a thousand miles of Kearney, Father Nicola had to serve his daughter's funeral. As he prayed before the coffin, the entire congregation wept, both for Anna and for her father. At the conclusion of the funeral, Father Nicola placed his priestly stole on Anna's head and said the prayer of absolution. He had arrived too late to hear her confession or to give her Holy Communion.

As the chanters began a slow dirge, everyone in the packed church stepped forward to kiss the little girl. The crowd wailed. George, Rebecca, and the boys came up to Anna's coffin to say goodbye. Finally, Father Nicola stooped and kissed his daughter for the last time. He then poured oil and ashes over her in the sign of the cross as a final blessing. When the coffin's lid was closed, the wailing drowned out the chanters' song, and the procession to the graveside began.

In the two years since the church had purchased their cemetery plots, the congregation had already used five graves. Anna's would be the sixth. All had been unexpected and untimely deaths. As the crowd stopped at the newly dug grave, Father Nicola led them in the final prayers and hymns, then stood with his family as the coffin was lowered into the ground. The grieving father cast the first handful of earth into his daughter's grave. The rest of the crowd followed, then embraced their priest and his sons and the rest of the family.

The crowd slowly departed, but Father Nicola stayed at the grave for some time. Half of his family—Martha, Nour, and now, Anna—were gone. Only Father Nicola and the boys remained. In the weeks after Anna's death, a constant stream of parishioners came to the Yanney home, bringing food and offering their condolences. They had all known hardship and experienced tragedies over the years, but none more than their priest.

Father Nicola stayed in Kearney for several weeks after the funeral, mourning with his sons. Although he needed to resume his seasonal missionary journey, he could not leave the boys alone so soon after Anna's death. Losing their beloved sister and playmate deeply affected Elias, John, and Moses. In the years following their mother's death, Anna had helped care for her brothers, especially the younger two. As her own health rapidly declined, Anna's brothers did their best to comfort her as she had always cared for them. In her last days, the boys grew angry and frustrated, helpless as they watched their sister fade away.

Every night, Father Nicola prayed with his sons, including Anna's name together with their mother and the baby among the departed. He also remembered his daughter in the petitions during the church services and prayed the memorial services for her. Father Nicola grieved for himself and especially for his sons, knowing how hard losing their mother and now their sister had been for them. He himself had been close to Elias's age when he had lost his own mother and older brother.

With his missionary duties mounting, Father Nicola prepared to leave home three weeks after Anna's funeral. Years earlier, he had imagined the sacrifices that he would have to

The Reverend Nicola Yanney, 1909

make in accepting the priesthood. When he had been appointed as a missionary, he had embraced the calling in obedience to Bishop Raphael and out of love for his fellow Syrians. Like many of them, he, too, had lived for years without a priest or a church. Though his pastoral duties and constant travels wearied him, Father Nicola did not complain. Nor did his parishioners' grumbling at his frequent absence greatly trouble him. However, he was deeply grieved at the thought that his children bore the brunt of his priestly burden.

Before leaving town, Father Nicola baptized George and Rebecca's daughter. A few days later, he boarded the train with a heavy heart, thinking of his boys. Traveling first to Omaha and then to Iowa, he baptized more children, then continued his tour of the communities in the northeastern portion of his missionary territory, confessing, communing, and serving the liturgy for the hundreds who were awaiting his visits.

Only a week after Father Nicola had left town, trouble arose. When he was away from home, altercations often occurred between members of the Syrian community. Without Father Nicola there as a peacemaker, many of the disputes ended up in the local court. The latest conflict, however, involved more than a few individuals or families. This time, the entire congregation was embroiled.

Though they had voted to relocate the church and had already purchased the property, the former schoolhouse had not yet been moved. The opposing faction was still resistant. One third of the congregation had voted against the plan, among whom were a few of the most successful families in the parish. The rest of the congregation, however, wanted to move the church into their neighborhood immediately and had grown tired of waiting.

With Lent and Pascha finally over, and with their priest out of town, the supporters pressed forward. Though they had waited for several weeks after Anna's death out of respect for Father Nicola and his family, they now made arrangements to move the church. Fearing that the opposition might call the police or contact city officials to delay their plan, several of the supporters hired a team to move the building on the Fourth of July. Over the holiday, the city offices would be closed and the sheriff would be occupied elsewhere.

The movers arrived with a team of horses and began their work. Within a few hours, the church had been placed in its new location in the midst of the Syrian neighborhood. Father Nicola was informed of what had happened. With the deed done, he would have to set about bringing peace when he returned home in a few months. In the meantime, he hoped that tempers would cool and that those who had opposed it would finally accept the move.

Father Nicola continued his eastward journey through Illinois, Wisconsin, Iowa, Michigan, and Minnesota over the next two and a half months, visiting cities like Chicago and Saint Paul, spending several weeks in smaller towns and villages in the Upper Peninsula, and staying with families on their isolated farmsteads. During the trip, he performed a dozen baptisms and three marriages.

After making his last stop in Grand Rapids, Father Nicola returned to Kearney. Looking out his window, he could now see the church just a block north of his house. Calling the Syrians for services, the congregation came together for the first time since the divisive move. The ill will was just beginning to subside, and Father Nicola made rounds, visiting those who were still upset and encouraging them to make peace. With time, he knew that the community would reconcile, even if begrudgingly at first.

Since the church had been moved to its permanent location, Father Nicola began discussing further improvements that the congregation might make to the building. Throughout much of Syria, the Ottoman Turks had made it illegal for Christian churches to ring bells. Now that they were in America, the priest wanted to add a bell tower to their church, with a large bell that could be rung to announce the church services. The townsfolk of Kearney had begun taking a greater interest in the Syrian missionary priest and his extensive journeys, and Father Nicola hoped to approach the wider community for help in raising funds for the expensive bell.

Father Nicola performed a baptism and a wedding in Kearney and celebrated the Exaltation of the Cross—a feast especially beloved by the congregation of Saint George since Bishop Raphael's visit. Though he had only been home for less than a month, Father Nicola received several calls to North Dakota. It was earlier than usual for his annual visit to the state, but more Syrians were settling there. Spending over a month in North Dakota, Father Nicola returned to all of the settlements that he had previously visited, serving the liturgy and baptizing numerous children. He then traveled to a town in the far northwestern corner of the state where there was a new and growing Syrian community.

A settlement of one hundred Syrians was living seven miles northwest of the town of Williston. Homesteading farmers, several of the families were Melkite Catholics, but most were Orthodox. Father Nicola knew many who had come there from Cedar Rapids, Sioux City, and Saint Paul. Although the Melkites were visited by their own missionary priest and the local Syrians maintained their separate religions, the entire community socialized and worked together more closely than those in Rugby. They even had plans to build two simple halls—one in town and another near their farms—to use for social gatherings and religious services.

Leaving North Dakota, Father Nicola spent another month traveling through Minnesota and Michigan, where he baptized several children. Though Christmas was approaching, it had been over a year since he had seen the Syrian communities living near the Mississippi River, so the missionary priest turned south before heading home. For two weeks, he traveled between Illinois, Tennessee, Missouri, and Kentucky, visiting families living on both sides of the river and baptizing a dozen children. One day near the end of his stay, he performed baptisms in two different towns, one hundred miles apart and on opposite sides of the river.

With Christmas only a week and a half away, the missionary priest traveled west from Kentucky for a brief stop in Wichita. While there, he baptized a few children and served a liturgy for the community before returning to Kearney. The boys were very happy to see their father. The holidays were subdued, however. Everyone was still mourning Anna, and Father Nicola was especially sorrowful.

News of Anna's death had reached Elias Yanney in Fi'eh months earlier. Worried for his son, he dictated a letter, encouraging the priest in his grief:

> You never part from my thoughts, day or night, not even a single instance as I keep you all in my thoughts. With a heart full of sadness, I send you my condolences for your loss and ask God that He grant you safety and well-being. My heart is filled with sadness for the loss of Anna. My heart is grieving but that is God's will. God said in the holy book to not grieve like those without hope. God also said in a different verse that we were created from dust, and to dust we shall return. The Prophet David said, Be patient as I am patient for God. I reiterate—do not be sad and depressed as that has bad consequences to the body. This is all God's plan and what He decides cannot be changed.

Elias told Father Nicola that he was being cared for by their oldest sister's family, who helped him often and invited him to their home for meals. The elder was, however, concerned for his grandson Michael and asked his sons to help their nephew pay off his debts. With inflation rising in Syria, food and many other items had become very expensive, and he requested that Father Nicola send his regular support money as soon as possible.

After replying to his father's letter, the priest spent the next month resting at home and serving his congregation. Since the Syrians had made plans for the new bell tower, Father Nicola began raising money for the bell. After performing several baptisms in Kearney and a nearby town where some of his parishioners had settled, he made another six-week missionary journey, with plans to be home by the beginning of Lent. Spending several days in both Omaha and Cedar Rapids, he performed half a dozen baptisms and two weddings between the two communities.

Heading south from Cedar Rapids, Father Nicola stopped in southeast Iowa for a brief visit, then returned to two towns along the Mississippi River in southern Illinois and western Kentucky to baptize several of the local Syrians' children. From there, the missionary priest was planning to head north to Chicago, but got called back to Omaha instead. A large community of Greek Orthodox immigrants had settled there, initially drawn by work in the city's stockyards. Two of their members had died, and left without the ministrations of their own priest, they called on Father Nicola to perform the funerals.

With the beginning of Lent only a week away, the missionary priest hurried east to perform a baptism in Chicago, then took a train back west to spend several days with the community in Sioux City. After baptizing three boys and three girls there, he returned to Kearney just in time for the first day of the fast.

During Lent, the men of the parish worked to erect the bell tower over the front entryway of the church, topping it with a steeple-shaped roof and decorative shutters. With the help of the Kearney townsfolk, the Syrians had raised enough money to purchase an eight-hundred-pound bell. Two weeks before Pascha, the new bell was delivered and mounted in the tower. As the feast approached, Father Nicola placed two announcements in the local newspapers, explaining that the upcoming services would start at two o'clock in the morning and continue until daybreak, according to Orthodox custom. Proud of their new bell, the Syrians warned the entire town not to be alarmed when it was rung in the early morning hours of Pascha.

As their festal celebrations began and the bell rang out, Father Nicola and his parishioners were grateful for all that they had accomplished with God's help, and that of their American friends and neighbors. The services were joyous, and the neighborhood feasted together from house to house after they were dismissed from church. On the following day, Father Nicola wrote a letter to one of the local newspapers, thanking the people of Kearney who had contributed toward the Syrians' purchase of the bell and had helped the congregation make such a fine improvement to their beloved Saint George church.

A week after Pascha, Father Nicola traveled to Minnesota to perform a wedding, but returned home a short time later. Over the next two months, he spent time with his family and his parishioners. He was called away only once to northern Iowa to perform a baptism. As the summer drew near, however, the needs of his wider flock beckoned yet again. Packing his bags, Father Nicola said his goodbyes and embraced Elias, John, and Moses. Hauling his travel-worn luggage to the depot, he boarded the train for another missionary journey, not knowing when he would see his boys again.

The Yanney family in 1908

CHAPTER NINE

Home and Abroad

DECEMBER 1908 TO MARCH 1911

ELIAS, JOHN, AND MOSES GREETED their father as he stepped off the train. The weary priest embraced his sons. As usual, he had returned to Kearney just in time to celebrate the Christmas services with his parishioners. Father Nicola looked at his boys with a twinge of regret. He had been away during their birthdays. Elias had turned fifteen two months earlier. John and Moses had turned eleven and nine during the summer. Father Nicola noticed how much they had all grown since he had last seen them.

The rest of the family had accompanied the boys to meet their father. Father Nicola embraced his brothers and offered his congratulations to George and Rebecca. Rebecca had given birth to a boy during the summer. They had named him Nicholas after Father Nicola, for which the priest felt deeply honored. With two small children to care for, and Rebecca pregnant again with a third child, George was ready to move. He had found a farm to rent five miles northwest of town and was planning to relocate his family there soon. No longer able to work, Simon had decided that he would stay in Kearney rather than move to the farm with George.

Father Nicola's nephew Michael had also come to the depot to greet him. The priest congratulated Michael on the birth of his second child. He and his wife now had two daughters—a two-year-old toddler and a two-month-old infant that his wife was caring for at home. Michael worked for the railroad, and he and his family were renting a house together with another family who had recently emigrated from Fi'eh. They lived only a few blocks from the church, and Father Nicola promised to visit them soon to bless Michael's wife and the baby.

As he headed toward home to drop off his bags, Father Nicola worried about his sons' situation. Once George moved, he and Rebecca would no longer be able to stay with the boys whenever Father Nicola was away. Elias, John, and Moses might go to stay with them on their new farm, but the boys' schooling and other obligations in Kearney would make living so far out of town very difficult. Father Nicola pondered over the problem, hoping that a better solution could be found.

Making his way to the church, the priest began his preparations for the Christmas services. For the first time in six months, the church bell rang out to announce the priest's return and to call the congregation to the feast. Though it was only three o'clock in the morning, Father Nicola's parishioners soon filed into the small church. Once again, George led the chanters in singing the festal hymns while Elias helped his father in the altar. For four hours, the Syrians stood and prayed during the long services, with the men on one side of the church and the women on the other side. Afterward, the parishioners warmly greeted their pastor who had been gone for so long, and Father Nicola announced that he would hold festal services on the following two mornings as well.

The parishioners returned to their homes. Although they celebrated the holiday two weeks later than the Americans and did not have the custom in their homeland of exchanging gifts at Christmastime, most had adopted the practice of giving Christmas presents. Finally resting with his family after the feast, Father Nicola unpacked his bags and took out the gifts he had brought his sons. As they shared a meal to break the long fast together, the boys asked Father Nicola about his latest trip. While the family ate, the priest recounted his stories from the road and shared news from the many Syrian communities that he had visited over the past half year.

When he had left Kearney in the early summer, Father Nicola had taken a different route than usual. At first, he had headed to Kansas for two weeks. There were baptisms to perform in Wichita and a nearby village. It was another grand wedding, however, that had called him south at the start of his latest missionary trip. Father Nicola described the lavish, weeklong celebration to his family. Like the members of their own community, the Syrians in Kansas had all started as peddlers, but many had become merchants and farmers. The bride and groom were both from well-to-do families, and five hundred of their Syrian family and friends from across the country had attended the wedding, together with the groom's American neighbors.

Father Nicola stayed at the large gathering for a few days after the wedding in order to perform two baptisms, then left to visit his flock in Wichita. From Kansas, the missionary priest had headed south into Oklahoma. It was his first time in the state. During the wedding festivities, he had met several Syrians who were living in two different cities in Oklahoma. One community of families had immigrated from Koura. The other hailed from Marjeyoun and were relatives of the Syrians in Wichita. Between the two communities, a half dozen children had yet to be baptized, so Father Nicola spent over a week ministering to them.

From Oklahoma, he turned east toward the settlements near the Mississippi River. As always, Father Nicola journeyed by train. Aboard the passenger cars, he spent many hours reading and praying as the ever-changing scenery passed outside his window. Sometimes, he struck up conversations with his fellow passengers. Most had never seen an Orthodox priest before. It had been over four years since his ordination, and Father Nicola's beard was now long and bushy. His uncut hair was pulled back into a ponytail. Dressed in his priestly garb, his unusual appearance often stirred the curiosity of onlookers. Seeing the cross around his neck, they knew that he was a Christian of some persuasion.

Though many simply stared, others were bold enough to ask him about his religion. Father Nicola explained his background and told them about Orthodox Christianity. Many were fascinated to meet a man who had grown up in the very lands that they themselves had only read about in their Bibles. Wondering why he was traveling so far from Nebraska, his fellow passengers listened as Father Nicola explained his missionary duties and told of the many places that he visited each year. The priest's newfound acquaintances were often dumbfounded.

Crossing the Mississippi River, Father Nicola spent the next few weeks traveling between Tennessee and Kentucky, then came back to Missouri and went down into Arkansas. In each place, he stayed for a day to two with the scattered Syrian families. Though some lived in town not far from the local depot, many lived on outlying farms. Often, stepping off the train after a day's journey, he still had hours to go before arriving at his destination. Meeting their honored guest at the station, his hosts drove with Father Nicola in their horse-drawn carriages far into the night.

After touring the southeast region of his missionary territory, the priest had then traveled north to Michigan to visit several communities, including a brief stop in Ironwood. From there, Father Nicola had gone to spend time with the little flock in La Crosse and then proceeded into Iowa. During the first days of autumn, he had returned to Ironwood for a two-week stay with the congregation before being invited to Saint Louis to perform a wedding. Over the next month, he had continued his journeys, visiting many communities, including Abraham Khoury and his family in Iron Mountain. While there, Father Nicola was called back to Ironwood for a long-expected reunion.

The Abraham family—Habeeb, Mineshi, and their children—had just arrived from Syria. Father Nicola's family grew excited as he recounted the news. The Abrahams were close kin from Fi'eh. Habeeb's family had been especially helpful in caring for the elderly Elias Yanney, and Mineshi was Father Nicola's niece, the daughter of his sister who had remained in Syria. The priest had looked forward to meeting Mineshi and her husband again, and was eager to hear news of his father and loved ones. Father Nicola's niece had been a young child when he and Martha had left Koura. Though Mineshi had only distant memories of her uncle, she had long heard of him while growing up in their village. It was a great honor to have a priest in the family, and she was delighted to be meeting him only weeks after she and her family had arrived in America.

After meeting the Abrahams and helping them settle into their new home, Father Nicola had continued his travels into

Minnesota and North Dakota. For three weeks he had crisscrossed the northern plains, visiting numerous communities. With the feast of the Nativity drawing near, he headed south once more to Wichita. There were several children in the community who needed to be baptized, and many out-of-state relatives had returned to the city for the holiday. Knowing that their priest could not stay until the actual date of the feast, the local Syrians asked him to serve a liturgy on Western Christmas.[6]

Father Nicola had stayed in Wichita for another week to perform the baptisms, then, at last, had headed for Kearney. Exhausted, he was happy to finally be home with his family, and especially to see his sons. By his own count, he had visited fourteen states, performed eight weddings, and conducted seventy-five baptisms during his six-month journey.

Although Father Nicola tried to stay close to home for the next few months, he had little time to rest. Several calls took him to Iowa and Michigan briefly, as well as across the state of Nebraska. The priest also had to attend to pastoral issues closer to home. To help lead the congregation while he was away, Father Nicola sent a telegram to Bishop Raphael, asking him to confirm John Shada as the chairman of the parish society and his brother George as the secretary. Father Nicola's other tasks were more troubling.

While he had been gone on his latest trip, several parishioners had ended up in the local police court. The disputes ranged from use of indecent language and disturbing the peace to public drunkenness and harassment, and had caused dissension in their community. During one arraignment, so many Syrians had attended the proceedings that the court had to reconvene in a

---

6 Father Nicola and his parishioners celebrated Christmas on January 7 according to the Julian calendar.

larger room. The judge warned the spectators that the defendants' behavior reflected poorly on all of them, and he implored them to keep peace in their neighborhood. Back from his long missionary journey, Father Nicola tried to instill a spirit of forgiveness and foster reconciliation among his contentious parishioners.

With the approach of Lent came a season for Father Nicola to fast, pray, and spend many hours in the penitential church services. It was a welcome respite from his normally hectic routine. As Pascha drew near, however, he began to make preparations for another trip. George and Rebecca had moved. Having no other recourse, Father Nicola arranged for Elias, John, and Moses to stay on the farm with their uncle and aunt. Though Elias might be old enough in a year or two to care for his brothers, the boys were still too young to live by themselves. With their house vacant for several months, Father Nicola tried to rent it out together with the land. The extra income would help to supplement his meager salary.

A month after Pascha, the missionary priest was once again traveling, this time heading for two communities in southeastern Colorado. Though only a handful of Syrian families lived in the area, there were nine children to baptize since his last visit. After staying with them for two weeks, Father Nicola returned to Nebraska to the city of Lincoln. The priest regularly ministered to several families living there, serving the liturgy for them in a nearby Episcopal church. This time, however, he came to marry a young couple. The local Syrians were especially excited—it was the first wedding in their small community.

After the wedding, Father Nicola returned to Kearney to serve a liturgy at his parish and to perform a special baptism. The priest's nephew and namesake—now almost eleven months old—was to be baptized after the Sunday morning service. George had asked John Shada to be the child's godfather.

Sadly, however, the joyous occasion was marred by more trouble in the parish. On Sunday morning, an altercation occurred between a married couple and John's brothers. The husband claimed that as he entered the church for the morning service, he saw one of the Shadas beating his wife, and that three more of the brothers—including John—quickly became involved in the row. The couple charged the four brothers with assault and battery. On the following morning, the Shada brothers appeared in court and pleaded not guilty. Following their court appearance, Father Nicola worked with both parties and managed to bring enough peace that the plaintiffs dropped the charges. The brothers, in turn, agreed to pay the court expenses.

On the following day, Father Nicola was called away from home. A young Syrian man had fallen ill in Iowa, and the priest boarded a train for the five-hundred-mile journey. By the time he arrived, however, the young man had died. After performing his funeral, Father Nicola decided to spend the next month visiting his communities in Iowa and eastern Nebraska.

Though the missionary's ministry was primarily to his fellow Syrians, Orthodox Christians of other ethnicities lived within his vast missionary territory and often looked upon him as their pastor, including several Greek families in La Crosse, southeastern Colorado, and other communities across the plains. Two weeks after burying the young Syrian man, Father Nicola was called to the other end of the state to serve a funeral for a Greek man in Sioux City. Remaining there for a few more days, he baptized five Syrian children, including the daughter of the local community's most wealthy and prominent member, Rizk Beshara.

Father Nicola not only had to deal with bickering in his own congregation but also encountered troubles during his missionary visits. After his time in Sioux City, the priest spent a few days with his friends in Omaha, baptizing several of their children, then returned to the city of Fort Dodge in central Iowa to perform another baptism. A large number of Syrians from the area had gathered at the home of the child's family. Father Nicola greeted the crowd and began the baptism. Several confused rabble-rousers, however, thought the service too long and wanted to begin their party immediately. They rushed to the font and blew out all the candles. When they disrupted the prayers, Father Nicola tried to bring calm and continue the baptism. A brawl started, and the godfather of the child was badly beaten while trying to protect the infant. The local police were called, and once the troublemakers were removed, the astonished priest completed the baptism.

Father Nicola returned home via Omaha. A few days later, he baptized another child, this time his best friend's youngest daughter. No altercations had happened in the parish during the month and a half that he had unexpectedly been away. Since it was already the middle of the summer, the tired priest planned to stay in Kearney. One week later, however, he was called to Minnesota. From there, he decided to make his two-week, semiannual visit to the community in La Crosse, Wisconsin.

During his stay, Father Nicola arranged to use the local Episcopal church to serve four liturgies for the Syrian and Greek families under his charge. After performing a marriage and several baptisms, he recorded the services in the sacramental diary that he carried on his journeys. Examining the pages, he realized that he had baptized three hundred people in the five years of his priesthood. Unbeknownst to Father Nicola, he would perform over six hundred more baptisms in the decade to come.

While in the area, he visited other nearby Syrian communities until he received a call to Ironwood a few weeks later. A ten-month-old girl who had yet to be baptized was sick. Father Nicola hurried there to perform her baptism. With her health continuing to decline, the priest stayed in town. A week later, he served the child's funeral.

Another funeral soon called Father Nicola back to Kearney. The fifteen-year-old son of one of the Shada brothers had unexpectedly fallen ill. When Father Nicola received word that the boy was being taken to the hospital, he raced home. The boy died early the next morning before the priest could get there in time to commune him. Like his daughter Anna, he had died of heart trouble. Father Nicola stayed at home for a week, consoling his friends on the loss of their son. He then continued his interrupted journey, returning to Michigan by way of Sioux City.

From there, he toured North Dakota for a month, traveling to even more settlements than the previous year, baptizing fifteen children, hearing a myriad of confessions, and serving liturgies in the farmers' homes. Returning to Michigan for a fourth time that year, Father Nicola spent two weeks visiting communities in both the lower and upper portions of the state. With Christmas only a month away, he then traveled west to Chicago before turning south to his missionary flock living near the Mississippi River. By the time the Americans were observing their own Christmas and New Year, Father Nicola was again among the Syrians in Wichita, serving the feasts for them before returning to Kearney.

Once home, Father Nicola celebrated Christmas with his family and parishioners. He took no missionary calls for a time and brought the boys back from George and Rebecca's farm. For the next four months, the priest and his sons readjusted to life together. Father Nicola noted that Elias, John, and Moses were progressing at school and becoming more involved in extracurricular activities, and he knew that it would be difficult to uproot them again when the time came for his next missionary trip.

Father Nicola continued to instruct his sons in the teachings of their Faith and in the Scriptures. Elias was especially keen, and his father noticed how much his eldest son enjoyed church. As an altar server, he watched every move and memorized every gesture and prayer that his father performed, and was learning the meaning behind each part of the church services. Father Nicola wondered if Elias might one day become a priest himself.

During the winter, Father Nicola baptized a half dozen children in Kearney and buried three parishioners. It was now 1910, and he had been in America for seventeen years. In the weeks before Lent, Father Nicola, George, and Simon received the sad but long-expected news from Fi'eh—their father Elias had died. He had lived to be ninety-three years old. The brothers marked their father's passing with memorial services in the church and remembrance in their private prayers. As they reminisced about him and their days in Koura, Father Nicola was sad that his own children had never met their grandfather nor seen their family's ancestral home. He marveled that his boys were now sixteen, twelve, and ten years old.

With the passing of another Lent and the approach of Pascha, the priest began preparations for his spring missionary trip. After much deliberation, Father Nicola decided that his sons would stay in town. Elias was old enough to take care of his brothers while their father was away, and they had family and friends close at hand. Their uncle Simon had stayed in town when George and Rebecca had moved to the farm. Because he was in declining health and unable to work, Simon lodged with his nephew Michael and his family down the street from Father Nicola's house. Together with George and Rebecca and many friends throughout the neighborhood, they would help look after the boys while their father was away.

One week after Pascha, Father Nicola left on his spring missionary journey. He spent his first month in Iowa, visiting various communities around the state, especially Sioux City and Cedar Rapids. He then returned to Kearney for a few weeks to check on his boys. The new arrangement was working, though Father Nicola worried about the responsibility that his eldest son now bore.

After baptizing two children whose parents hailed from Koura, Father Nicola traveled east to Ironwood for a week. From there, he paid his two-week visit to the community in La Crosse, then journeyed back to Michigan to stay with his friends in Iron Mountain. Called to rural Kansas for a week, Father Nicola returned to Michigan to spend the rest of the month in Ironwood. On his way back to Nebraska, he took two weeks to revisit the Syrians living in Sioux City and Cedar Rapids.

Wanting to stay closer to home with the boys living on their own, Father Nicola spent the next month in Kearney. Though he was hoping for a few peaceful weeks at home, his respite was soon interrupted. Not long after he returned, a disturbance broke out in the neighborhood involving several of his parishioners. In all, six men had been accused and arrested for attacking another lone Syrian, who had called the sheriff and pressed for charges of assault and battery.

When the court convened a few days later, fifty Syrians descended on the courtroom. Witnesses were called, but they gave conflicting testimonies. Due to the plaintiff's injuries, the defendants were found guilty and fined. The supposed assailants, however, decided to appeal the decision in the district court. Though Father Nicola would have to leave town before the second court convened, he sought to make peace as best as he could. Two months later, after the missionary priest had resumed his missionary visits, the district court would throw out the case altogether when it was found that the plaintiff had sustained his injuries while the defendants were preventing him from committing suicide.

In between counseling the warring parties and tending to the rest of his parishioners, Father Nicola had personal business that required his attention. Two years earlier, he had paid off his debt to the surviving Abood brother, but was being forced to take out a mortgage on the house again. Whenever he was in Kearney, the priest hosted parishioners and out-of-town visitors at his home for Sunday lunch. Though he and the boys grew much of their own food on the four acres surrounding their house, Father Nicola's travels, coupled with his low pay and the family's offering their weekly hospitality to the community, put a financial strain on the family. After procuring the loan, he returned to his missionary duties.

Father Nicola spent the next month in North Dakota, visiting the scattered Syrian settlements and baptizing a dozen children. During the following month, he traveled between the various communities in Minnesota and Wisconsin, returning to Kearney a few weeks before Christmas. After the holidays, Father Nicola made a few short missionary trips, but tried to stay close to Kearney. While home, he baptized several children, including the two-year-old daughter and infant son of his nephew Michael. Elias stood near his father as he performed the baptisms. Michael had asked his cousin Elias, now seventeen, to be godfather to his little boy, and the young man had proudly accepted.

As Father Nicola and his family made their preparations for another Lent, they found themselves hosting a number of out-of-town visitors. Parishioners from several nearby towns, as well as friends from Ironwood, had come to Kearney for the upcoming church services that marked the first week of Lent. While they were enjoying the last few days before the fast, a tragedy occurred.

As usual, Father Nicola and George's older brother Simon had regaled their guests with his extensive knowledge and tales from his world travels. Though his health had been declining, Simon was still an energetic and entertaining personality. One evening while strolling through the neighborhood, he suddenly collapsed. Paralyzed by a stroke, Simon was rushed back by his friends to the house. Father Nicola raced to the church, then hurried back to his brother's side. Simon was still conscious, though unable to move, and Father Nicola prayed for his older brother and anointed him, then gave him Holy Communion. The family kept watch and prayed at Simon's bedside, but he died a few hours later.

The funeral was held on the following day. News of Simon's death had spread quickly, and more parishioners arrived from out of town to pay their respects. After the services, the congregation and the visitors made a procession to the cemetery. A new grave had been opened a stone's throw from Anna's headstone. There, with prayers and tears, Father Nicola laid yet another member of his family to rest.

CHAPTER TEN

Circuit Riders

MARCH 1911 TO JULY 1914

A WEEK AFTER SIMON'S DEATH, Father Nicola was called to serve another funeral, this time for a prominent Syrian in Indiana. The man had been a leader in his local Syrian community and was known to Bishop Raphael. Though Father Nicola lived over seven hundred miles away, he was still the closest Orthodox priest available for the burial. Leaving for Indiana during the second week of Lent, he returned a few days later to spend the remainder of the fast at home.

A week after Pascha, Father Nicola undertook a missionary journey that would take him away for the rest of the spring and summer. For three months, he made a tour of Iowa, Minnesota, Michigan, and Wisconsin. While visiting Sioux City, Father Nicola baptized a newborn son of the wealthy merchant Rizk Beshara. Because Bishop Raphael had been encouraging warm relations between Orthodox Christians and Episcopalians, Father Nicola made arrangements to perform the service in a local Episcopal church. The Americans who attended the service marveled not only at the ancient baptismal rite but also at the priest's ornate vestments, along with his uncut beard and long hair.

The Syrians in Indiana also began calling on Father Nicola. After a tour of his northern states, the missionary priest returned to Indiana to visit two different communities. Over the course of a week, he performed several baptisms, then departed for southern Illinois and Missouri. From there, Father Nicola traveled to Kansas to spend a week in Wichita and another week in Oklahoma. By the end of summer, he was almost ready to conclude his trip, and he traveled west to Colorado for a weeklong visit during which he baptized ten children.

Father Nicola returned to Kearney in time to celebrate the Elevation of the Cross with his parishioners. He had not seen his sons in four months, and he pulled out several presents from his bags. As Father Nicola handed Elias the books that he had purchased for him, he thought of the sacrifice that his eldest son was making. John and Moses were still in school. Though Elias should have been in his final year of high school, he was no longer able to attend. He had continued caring for his younger brothers while their father was on his missionary trips. The arrangement allowed the boys to stay in town, but the daily demands of running the household left Elias no time for school. He would never receive his high school diploma.

Father Nicola recognized that his son was exceptionally bright and wanted to encourage him to continue his education despite the difficult circumstance. Elias spent his precious spare time reading, so Father Nicola often searched for interesting books to bring him, especially encyclopedias and history books. Because the boys had lost their mother at such a young age, and because he himself was so often absent, he tried to be a lenient and loving father. However, Father Nicola also wanted his sons to be civic-minded and law-abiding citizens. Above all, he desired them to be devout Christians. Elias and his brothers continued to read the Bible daily as their father had taught them, and while John and Moses were at school, their older brother educated himself through his voracious reading and by taking correspondence courses.

Though he had been away for several months, Father Nicola had little time to rest. Called out of town twice for baptisms, he also performed the funeral service for a Greek teenager whose family lived in Kearney. Only a few weeks after returning from Colorado, he had to say goodbye to Elias, John, and Moses and return to his missionary duties. He spent the next month and a half crisscrossing North Dakota, baptizing twenty children in total. He then traveled east for three weeks into Minnesota and Wisconsin, before his weeklong visit to Wichita in time for Western Christmas.

Father Nicola returned to Nebraska, hoping to celebrate the holidays with his congregation and take some much-needed rest. When he arrived home, however, the entire neighborhood was in an uproar. On the evening of Western Christmas, while Father Nicola had been in Wichita, a fight had broken out among the Syrians that would take five months to resolve in the Kearney courts. Several men had been arrested on assault charges. One of them had been severely kicked and beaten while another had suffered a gunshot wound. Over the next month, the Syrians took sides and followed the case closely, showing up at the courthouse for the arraignments. The conflict would bring heavy fines and deepened grudges for those on both sides of the fight.

Once again, Father Nicola tried to calm tempers and bring peace to his parishioners, dividing his time between Kearney and other communities in eastern and western Nebraska. Three weeks after returning from Wichita, however, he was called back to Kansas again, this time to two small rural communities near the southern edge of the state. From there, he made for Sioux City for a brief stop to baptize several children before continuing to Minnesota.

Father Nicola had been called to Saint Paul for an especially lavish wedding. The son of a wealthy merchant was to be married, and the family had requested that their priest from Kearney perform the ceremony. It was to take place at the merchant's residence, where Father Nicola also held services during his regular visits to the city. Set to be the grandest Syrian wedding in twenty years, the large room was lit with hundreds of candles. In front of six hundred guests who had come from around the country, Father Nicola united the bride and groom. As the wedding festivities continued for a week, Father Nicola stayed in Saint Paul to baptize several children, and he also served the funeral of an aged matriarch who died during his visit.

With Lent beginning soon, Father Nicola traveled to Ironwood where he made a brief stop to serve a liturgy for Cheesefare Sunday and baptize two children before returning to Kearney. Home again and happy to see that his boys were doing well, the priest was especially delighted that Elias had been able to enroll in the local college. Almost fifteen, John was now able to assume more of the household duties and care for Moses, freeing his older brother to continue his studies. Though busy with his courses, Elias was also working part time to help support the family.

Father Nicola stayed at home with his sons until the beginning of summer, then left on a seven-month tour. He spent his first month in La Crosse. From Wisconsin, the priest visited Minnesota, then spent another month traveling back and forth between Wisconsin and Michigan. Called home to Kearney for a funeral in the midst of his journey, he was back in Ironwood two days later to assist with a baptism and to help welcome the congregation's new pastor.

A month earlier, Bishop Raphael had assigned a priest to the community. Father Elia Hamati had recently emigrated from Palestine. He was well educated, and Father Nicola was glad for the congregation. Though the Syrian communities in Ironwood and throughout Upper Michigan had relied on his regular visits for eight years, they had long desired to have a resident pastor. Greeting his fellow priest, Father Nicola commended the congregation to Father Elia and hoped for a fruitful relationship. Heading west, he stopped in Saint Paul and other cities and towns for three more weeks, then traveled to North Dakota, where he stayed for a month and a half.

Halfway through his tour of the state, Father Nicola received a startling telegram that had been relayed all the way from New York. It concerned Bishop Raphael. Father Nicola had not seen the bishop since his ordination but had kept in regular contact with him, updating him about his missionary activities. Many of the baptisms, weddings, and funerals performed by the Syrian clergy were printed in the bishop's monthly diocesan journal. Of all of Bishop Raphael's priests, Father Nicola's reports covered the largest territory. The bishop, too, had continued making his own pastoral tours, all while managing the affairs of his diocese, and Father Nicola had enjoyed reading about the hierarch's latest travels.

The alarming news from New York, however, was that the tireless missionary bishop was terribly ill. A few weeks earlier, Bishop Raphael had been working in his office in Brooklyn when he had suddenly felt a sharp pain in his stomach. The pain increased and became so intense that the bishop could no longer work or even sit upright. Within an hour, he was bedridden. A physician was called but could provide no relief or diagnosis. Over the next few days, Bishop Raphael's condition grew steadily worse. Specialists were called in, and he was finally diagnosed with a serious inflammation of the heart. The man who had traveled across the country ministering to thousands was now confined to a bed, mortally ill and unable to move.

The prognosis became dire as Bishop Raphael continued to deteriorate over the next week and a half. Desperately concerned for their beloved bishop, the cathedral clergy sent an urgent message to all of the Syrian priests, asking that every parish offer special prayers on the hierarch's behalf after the upcoming Sunday liturgy. Father Nicola had been traveling back and forth across North Dakota, called to serve numerous baptisms and a funeral. When the time came to pray for Bishop Raphael, he found himself among a small community of farmers in the center of the state. With the group gathered for the liturgy in a small farmhouse, the missionary priest spoke lovingly of the bishop and led the small congregation in their supplications for his health. After the services, Father Nicola was called away by an anxious family to baptize their sickly child.

On the following day, the nurse tending Bishop Raphael at his residence in Brooklyn announced that he was beginning to recover. The bishop was soon receiving visitors, and a few days later, the man who had been bedridden for weeks and who many had feared would die was well enough to attend services for the Feast of the Archangels. Only a week after the special prayers had been offered, Bishop Raphael was once again celebrating the Divine Liturgy at his cathedral. During the service, he thanked his many parishioners for their prayers.

When news of the bishop's miraculous recovery reached

Father Nicola, he joyfully shared it with the communities he visited. After spending another week in North Dakota, he returned to Wisconsin for two weeks, then traveled through Iowa. Before returning home, the priest stopped in Cedar Rapids for a week. Everywhere he went, the Syrians asked Father Nicola for news of Bishop Raphael and marveled at the manner of his healing. Despite his recovery, however, the bishop would continue to suffer health problems for the rest of his life due to his unrelenting schedule.

Father Nicola spent a few weeks in Kearney to celebrate Christmas and Theophany with his congregation. While home, he negotiated another mortgage for his house and land, then left town again for a short, three-week circuit to communities in Iowa, Minnesota, and rural Nebraska. After another week at home, he headed south into Kansas and Oklahoma. Over the next two weeks, he visited six communities in four states and performed twenty baptisms. Intending to return to Kearney for the first day of Lent, he was unexpectedly called to Sioux City. There, Father Nicola baptized and communed a dying child, then served the funeral before returning to Kearney.

Home for two months, the priest spent the remainder of Lent with his parishioners. Several young men from the congregation, including his eldest son, approached Father Nicola with the idea of founding a new organization for their parish. Though the ladies had their own church society, there was no special club for the men. With the priest's blessing, Elias and his friends formed the Syrian Young Men Christian Society to promote the teaching of their Orthodox faith, do charitable works, and lend aid to the parish. Even though he was busy working and attending college, Elias was elected as the society's president.

As Pascha approached, Father Nicola called the new society

and the rest of the parish to do some much-needed work around the church. The church grounds were cleaned and the entire building was given a fresh coat of paint. When Pascha finally arrived, the Syrian community celebrated for three days with long church services and much feasting in the neighborhood.

Two weeks after Pascha, Father Nicola began his spring missionary journey. Several Syrian families had moved to South Dakota, so he headed north for a brief stay to baptize half a dozen children. From there, he traveled into northern Iowa. Staying for several days in Sioux City, he baptized three Romanian children, then proceeded into Wisconsin. Father Nicola then visited Ironwood, where he had been invited to help with a funeral. With Father Elia now serving the area, however, the missionary priest was freed from making his usual tour of Upper Michigan, and he returned home.

Not since the first years of his priesthood had Father Nicola been able to rest in the middle of his extended spring and summer journeys. Because more clergy were being ordained by Bishop Raphael, however, the weary missionary realized that he might someday have less territory to cover and more time to spend at home. A few weeks later, his unexpected respite was interrupted by a telegram from Iowa. The news was terrible, and Father Nicola rushed to the train station. Sioux City's most prominent Syrian, Rizk Beshara, had been murdered by an American.

When he arrived in the city, the local Syrians were outraged. Beshara—the wealthy merchant in whose home Father Nicola had often stayed and whose children he had baptized—had been killed during a heated argument. While away from home on a business trip, the harried Syrian businessman had dashed through the town he was visiting, looking for a place to stable his horses. When a livery worker chastised Beshara for driving too hard, an argument ensued and turned violent. The American stablehand shoved the Syrian, who fell and struck his head against a wagon wheel. Though he rose dazed and wandered onto the street, he fell over dead only minutes later.

Beshara's widow was distraught. She had several small children. Father Nicola had baptized the couple's youngest daughter only five months earlier. The funeral was held in the same Episcopal church where the baptisms of the Beshara children had taken place. The church was packed for the funeral, with many townsfolk joining Syrians from across the region. Because of the large crowd, the services were partly done in English.

Father Nicola was concerned for the Beshara family. Not only was the dead man's widow left to raise her children alone; settling her husband's estate would be overwhelming. Beshara had business ventures in three different states. With his untimely and violent death, greedy investors were already talking about insolvency, making his widow's future and that of her children unsure. The rest of the Syrian community was up in arms, doubtful whether the murderer would be held accountable for his crime since he was American and his victim had been a foreigner. After the burial, Father Nicola wanted to stay in Sioux City to console the grieving family and ease the Syrians' fears. A few days later, however, he was called away. Leaving the grieving widow and her children in the care of their family and friends, the missionary priest traveled two hundred miles across the state to perform a wedding in another town.

From northern Iowa, Father Nicola traveled to Omaha, where he was expected by several families still living in the neighborhood of the old peddlers' colony. As always, he was warmly welcomed. The priest was scheduled to perform a wedding and several baptisms during his brief stay. Most of the children's parents hailed from Fi'eh and had known Father Nicola for many years. The priest was always happy to visit his friends in Omaha, and most especially to see John Shada's nephew, Sam. Sam and his wife, Selma, had previously lived in Kearney but had moved back to Omaha a few years earlier. Father Nicola was closely related to the young couple through Martha. Selma's mother and Martha had been sisters. The priest and Sam were personally close as well.

Father Nicola often stayed in the couple's home while he was in the city. This particular visit, however, was special. He had been called to baptize their third child. Father Nicola had baptized Sam and Selma's first two boys and, sadly, had buried their firstborn. Wanting to solemnize their close relations, Sam and Selma had asked the priest not only to baptize their son, but also to be his godfather. Father Nicola had gladly accepted. Though he had several children to baptize during his visit, on his first day in Omaha, he performed only one baptism—his godson's. After celebrating with Sam and Selma and their friends, the missionary priest baptized six more children over the next few days, then headed back through Iowa.

Father Nicola spent a week visiting two communities in Iowa and one in Minnesota. His destination, however, was La Crosse, Wisconsin. Well into summer, it was time for his two-week stay in the city. The priest had five baptisms to do, followed by a noteworthy wedding. A young Syrian woman—a spiritual daughter to Father Nicola—was to be married to a man that she had met two years earlier while he was peddling in La Crosse. Considered the belle of the local community, she was beautiful and popular, and both Father Nicola and the families had blessed the courtship.

Over the course of several days, many guests arrived from far and wide. In typical fashion, the wedding festivities went on for days both before and after the ceremony. On a Sunday morning after the liturgy, near the end of Father Nicola's stay in La Crosse, he performed the marriage service in a church packed with four hundred guests.

After leaving La Crosse, the missionary priest headed south. It had been two years since he had performed any baptisms in the Syrian settlements near the Mississippi River. Spending a few weeks in the area, he returned to Kearney in time to celebrate the Feast of the Dormition. After the festal liturgy, Father Nicola baptized an infant girl born to a local Greek couple. The child's godfather was also a Greek man who had immigrated to Nebraska from Athens. With no church of their own, the local Greeks sometimes attended the Syrian church and looked to Father Nicola as their priest.

Immediately following the baptism, Father Nicola left by train for Colorado. Over the next two weeks, he visited the Syrian colonies in the state and baptized ten children, then returned

Fr. Nicola with Sam Shada at St. George Church in Kearney

to Kearney. Aside from traveling into rural Nebraska to perform several baptisms, Father Nicola spent much of the next four months at home. Elias was about to turn twenty years old. He had been working as a court reporter and was soon to finish his degree from the local college. Though he was earning his teaching certificate, Elias had begun to doubt if he wanted to be a teacher. John was halfway through high school, and Moses was in the middle of his freshman year. Father Nicola enjoyed the rare uninterrupted time with his boys.

Months earlier, while Father Nicola had been traveling to Sioux City for Rizk Beshara's funeral in the early summer, Bishop Raphael had started out on his own journey. Exhausted by his relentless schedule and still suffering in the aftermath of his previous illness, the bishop had been compelled by his personal physician to take a vacation. Bishop Raphael decided to leave his residence in Brooklyn, but instead of spending his time resting, he took the opportunity to visit his congregations in upstate New York.

Everywhere he went, large crowds of Syrians gathered to listen to him speak. Over the next month, Bishop Raphael preached, confessed, and communed hundreds of parishioners. He eventually returned home, never having rested and still exhausted. Soon, the saintly bishop was on the road again for another month-long trip, this time touring his parishes in Pennsylvania.

Back in Kearney, Father Nicola was preparing to celebrate Christmas with his family and parishioners. Having spent several months at home, he decided to make a two-month trip before the beginning of Lent. A few days after Christmas, he boarded a train for Kansas City, then caught a connection to Wichita. He spent the next week in the city, celebrating the Theophany services for the local Syrians and baptizing five of their children.

From Kansas, Father Nicola made a tour of Oklahoma. More Syrians from Marjeyoun were settling there, and the missionary priest made an extensive visit to the ranchers and merchants living throughout the state. For the next month, he traveled to villages, towns, and cities across Oklahoma, serving many liturgies and baptizing twenty-five children. At each stop, family and friends gathered for the baptismal celebrations. The homesteaders were especially grateful that a priest had traveled so far to see them on their isolated farms.

Father Nicola returned to Wichita for a week, then headed north to visit his communities in Iowa. He ended his trip with a stay in Sioux City, where he married a young couple, baptized five children, and chrismated a teenager. Though still recovering from the murder of Rizk Beshara, the local community was flourishing. During his week in Sioux City, Father Nicola expressed his hopes that the Syrians might be able to build their own church. He celebrated Clean Monday with them, then returned to Kearney for the remainder of Lent. Anticipating another extensive missionary trip after Pascha, he tried to rent out his four acres of land to supplement his income.

When Father Nicola arrived home, Elias told his father that he no longer wanted to be a teacher. Instead, he wanted to study accounting. The college he needed to attend was located in Omaha, however, and he would have to move away from home. With John now old enough to care for Moses while he was gone, Father Nicola gave his blessing for Elias to enroll in school and helped him move. Though he would only be away from home for a year, the parting was particularly hard on the priest. After leaving Elias in Omaha, Father Nicola wrote his son, encouraging him to maintain his upright character and to focus on his studies:

> The apple of my eye and the vision of my heart, Elias, my support and my dear son in the Lord: I ask God not to deprive me of you. I send you blessings and prayers, and thousands of kisses on the cheeks, as many as the sands of the sea. As I write these lines, tears are flowing down my cheeks, especially when I read your letter in which you said that life has tempted you. . . . My dear Elias, may you be pleasing to God. Be the best version of yourself. Avoid crude and offensive talk. Do not joke coarsely or easily give your heart to others. Be conscientious of your health before anything else. Oh, Elias, the apple of my eye, every time I come home, I see how gloomy it is without you. Oh, my dear, had I known that it would be so hard to let you go, I swear to God that I would not have let you go. Nonetheless, I know well that you left to study, not to frolic. I ask God's special blessings on you, that you take care of your brothers and your fellow countrymen. Make me proud. Keep me posted about yourself and write me often so that I always know you are fine. I kiss your cheeks thousands and millions of times. . . . Take care of your studies and your health before anything else. . . . Lastly, I kiss your cheeks and ask God to grant you safety and well-being. Your father who thinks of you always.

Whenever Elias wrote home, Father Nicola wept from missing his son.

While the missionary priest had been busy visiting Kansas, Oklahoma, and Iowa, Bishop Raphael had decided to undertake a tour of his southern parishes. For two months the bishop made pastoral visits in Mississippi, Louisiana, Alabama, and Texas, encouraging and exhorting his people everywhere he went. The Syrian diocese had grown greatly in the decade since his elevation to the episcopacy, boasting thirty congregations and several other thriving communities. Bishop Raphael had continued to train and ordain young men to the priesthood to serve his scattered flock, and during his tour was now seeing firsthand the fruits of his labors.

The bishop returned home during the middle of Lent. He served in his cathedral for the remainder of the fast, celebrating Pascha and spending the Paschal season in New York. Bishop Raphael's recent travels, however, had made him desire to visit the rest of his parishes. In early summer, he decided to embark on what would be the last of his missionary journeys, this time visiting congregations in the northern and western portions of his diocese.

Three weeks after Pascha, Father Nicola was called back to Sioux City to perform the most difficult of duties. The missionary priest had returned to the city two months earlier in the middle of Lent to bury a young woman. Now he was being called to serve the funeral of a child. While there, he baptized another child a few days later, then decided to begin his spring missionary journey by first visiting his communities in rural Nebraska and South Dakota. From there, he turned east to Minnesota and Wisconsin.

As he continued his summer travels, Father Nicola received word that Bishop Raphael was also beginning a cross-country journey. At the furthest point of his circuit, the bishop intended to visit his priest and parishioners in Kearney. Delighted, Father Nicola sent a telegram informing his congregation. As he thought of the upcoming visit, he looked forward to returning home—he had not seen Bishop Raphael in ten years. Their reunion would have to wait, however. Both missionaries still had months of travel ahead of them.

Bishop Raphael Hawaweeny

CHAPTER ELEVEN

The Death of a Saint

SEPTEMBER 1914 TO MARCH 1915

THE EXCITING NEWS SPREAD QUICKLY—BISHOP Raphael was on his way to Kearney. Father Nicola had received the telegram from Omaha only that morning. The bishop had left New York two months earlier on a tour of his churches, planning to visit Nebraska as the westernmost stop on his journey. Father Nicola had been expecting to hear from him for weeks. It was now mid-September, and word had finally come.

With the bishop due to arrive in a matter of hours, Father Nicola immediately sent word throughout the Syrian neighborhood. It had been fifteen years since Bishop Raphael had visited Kearney. At that time, he had been a young missionary priest, traversing the country in search of his scattered flock. Now, he was a venerable hierarch making an inspection of his diocese. The Syrians cleaned their homes and began cooking food for the festivities that would take place during the bishop's stay. Those who remembered his first visit shared their memories of the saintly man.

The congregation of Saint George had more than quadrupled in size since Bishop Raphael's last trip to Nebraska. Several of the founding families remained, and they remembered the former missionary priest with love and admiration. He had been a kind and warm pastor. Even from afar and after becoming a bishop, he had been attentive to their needs, blessing them to form a church even with such limited resources and ordaining Father Nicola to serve them. Over the years, they had eagerly read the monthly magazine that Bishop Raphael sent them—reports of new congregations, diocesan business, and especially the articles he wrote teaching about their Orthodox faith. They marveled at his continued travels across North America as he founded thirty Syrian churches.

Although his many responsibilities had kept Bishop Raphael from visiting them sooner, he was finally coming back. Those who had waited for him at the train station years ago excitedly shared their memories of the meeting—how the sick young priest had stayed up for hours talking with them, the baptisms and liturgies that he had served in their crowded living rooms, and especially his late-night trip to the Yanneys. Now, they would proudly meet him again, no longer a handful of families, but a congregation of two hundred people.

As his parishioners busied themselves and reminisced, Father Nicola had his own preparations to make. He sent telegrams to the Orthodox families living outside of Kearney, telling them that the bishop was coming that very evening and would be staying until Sunday. Father Nicola contacted a local band to play at the train station when the bishop arrived and arranged for a car and driver to chauffeur him to the church. He also spoke with the local newspapers, giving the details of Bishop Raphael's visit and the times for the Sunday morning church services at which the bishop would preside. Father Nicola then returned to the church and his house, making sure that everything was clean and ready for their guest. The priest and his sons would be hosting the bishop in their home.

Like his parishioners, Father Nicola was eager for the visit. He had not seen Bishop Raphael since his ordination. Just as the bishop had crisscrossed the country, so he, too, had traveled back and forth across the Great Plains many times. He was weary from his constant journeys and from struggling to pastor so many people. He confessed and counseled many isolated Syrians who saw a priest only once or twice a year, and tried to preserve them in their faith. It was a difficult task. Some were being tempted to join nearby Episcopalian or Protestant congregations out of convenience. Others were losing their faith and piety in the pursuit of wealth. After ten years as a circuit-riding priest, Father Nicola understood a small part of Bishop Raphael's burden, and revered him all the more.

Father Nicola owed the bishop much. Bishop Raphael had brought hope to his family in the midst of their loneliness. His visit had been the answer to Martha's prayers, coming to their homestead and baptizing their children. After her death, the bishop had given the young widower a new purpose in ordaining him to the priesthood. Bishop Raphael's ministry had become his own model as a missionary priest. Yet it was for more than personal reasons that he yearned to see his bishop. As difficult as it was tending such a scattered flock, there were also rising tensions at home. Resentments were beginning to divide his congregation, and Father Nicola needed Bishop Raphael's help.

That night, hundreds gathered at the depot to welcome their bishop to Kearney. Bishop Raphael's train arrived at half past nine, and as he stepped from the passenger car, cheers erupted from the crowd and the band began to play. He had traveled thirty-six hours from his last stop in Ironwood, Michigan, and was exhausted from his journey. Nonetheless, he greeted the crowd warmly, remembering the midnight welcome that he had received on the same platform long ago. A young man in his early twenties stood next to Bishop Raphael and helped him with his luggage. Emmanuel Abo-Hatab had immigrated to America a few years earlier. Recently elevated to archdeacon, he was now serving as the bishop's secretary.

As Bishop Raphael drew near to greet the crowd, Father Nicola noticed how much he had aged. Though they were in regular contact, it had been ten years since he had seen him in person. Bishop Raphael's once-thick black hair and beard were now almost entirely white. His lined face looked careworn. His eyes were still bright, however, and the same kindly smile spread over his face as Father Nicola stepped forward to receive his blessing.

Welcoming the bishop and his deacon, Father Nicola noticed that both wore their hair short and that their beards were closely trimmed. Their travel clothes were also those of American gentlemen rather than the robes traditionally worn by Orthodox clergy. Father Nicola had heard that Bishop Raphael preferred that his priests dress like the pastors of other denominations so that they were easily recognizable as Christian clergymen. The bishop, however, had never forced Father Nicola or any of his fellow priests to adopt the modern American style.

After they had exchanged warm greetings, Father Nicola escorted the esteemed guests to the waiting car. A long procession followed them as they drove slowly from the train station to the church. Bishop Raphael had never seen the converted schoolhouse. It was a humble building. Inside, the parishioners had built an iconostasis and an altar table, over which a wooden canopy had been erected. Small icons were hung around the interior of the church. Some were hand painted and mounted in carved frames; others were simply paper prints covered in glass. The ornate brass lamps that Father Nicola had brought home with him from New York still hung before the icons, and a few chandeliers that had once adorned his parishioners' dining rooms were now suspended from the ceiling.

Entering the church, Bishop Raphael stood before the altar and offered prayers of thanksgiving for his safe travels. Turning to the congregation, he expressed how much he had been longing to visit Kearney again. The Syrians listened eagerly as he told them that his heart was inflamed with love every time he thought of the great distance between his home in New York and their little parish in Nebraska. He praised the congregation for their hard work and dedication in building up and preserving their church. Bishop Raphael then raised his hands and asked a heavenly blessing upon his beloved children in Christ.

Father Nicola stood beside the bishop and thanked him for making such a long and difficult journey to see his flock, adding that he hoped that the bishop's heart would be filled with joy from all that he would see during his stay. After his welcome, Father Nicola escorted Bishop Raphael and Archdeacon Emmanuel to his home and invited everyone to join them. The women in the community had been cooking all day, and a splendid reception awaited them. Packing into the Yanneys' small house, the people surrounded Bishop Raphael.

Father Nicola introduced John and Moses, who both stepped forward to kiss the bishop's hand. Bishop Raphael marveled that the two young boys he had baptized had grown into such handsome young men. As he told the boys the story of meeting their parents, others whom the bishop had married and baptized also came forward to reintroduce themselves and receive his blessing. Father Nicola sat at the bishop's side late into the night while the entire congregation stayed to speak with Bishop Raphael and listen to his teaching.

Over the next three days, the bishop continued to visit and pray with Father Nicola's family and his parishioners. On Sunday morning, he served the Divine Liturgy at Saint George. The church was overflowing. Syrians from across Nebraska had traveled to town for the weekend to meet the bishop. Members of the Kearney community also came to the service, having read about his visit in the local newspapers. Fascinated by Bishop Raphael, the Kearney press had already interviewed him several times. War had recently broken out in Europe, and the bishop told the reporters that he deplored the devastation it was causing and that he would be leading the congregation in prayers for world peace. He then invited the public to attend the Sunday services and promised to preach in English.

Near the end of the liturgy, Bishop Raphael stood before the congregation and their guests and gave an inspiring sermon. At first, he spoke about the divine love with which God loved them, giving His only Son for their sake. The bishop exhorted how they ought to respond to this immeasurable love in kind. Looking around the church, he then told them that they must also love God for the earthly treasures and material blessings that He had bestowed upon them, and that another aspect of their love for God was to care for God's house. Bishop Raphael ended by telling the congregation that they should build a new church. Their small, wood-frame building had served them well for the past decade, but now it was time for them to build a larger, more beautiful, and more permanent temple.

Though stirred by the bishop's words, many of the parishioners doubted whether such a task was possible. Their church was in financial trouble, and some were displeased that Father Nicola was away so often. Though he had planned to leave on Sunday after the service, Bishop Raphael decided to stay for four more days to continue encouraging the congregation. He also called a special parish meeting.

On the following evening, the parishioners gathered with Bishop Raphael and Father Nicola, and the bishop opened the meeting with prayer. He had an important plan that he wanted the church to implement alongside building their new temple. Before speaking of that, however, he needed to address an issue that was causing difficulties for both his priest and the congregation. Because a number of parishioners were not supporting the parish financially, Father Nicola was not getting paid the salary that had been agreed upon. There was also dissension due to his missionary journeys.

After convening the meeting, Bishop Raphael asked the treasurer how much money the church had on hand. The treasurer reported that while the church had over one hundred thirty dollars on their books, most of that money had been given out as loans to various parishioners. There were only sixteen dollars left in the church safe. The bishop then raised questions about the salary they had promised to pay Father Nicola. While the members of the parish council had previously agreed to pay him forty-five dollars per month, this was to come from parishioners' pledges and not from the church's savings. They had also agreed with Father Nicola that he would be out of town for two months every summer and every winter.

On hearing this, a number of parishioners expressed their resistance to paying pledges to cover their priest's salary. Tensions were high, and Bishop Raphael knew that he needed to help the congregation avoid a potential crisis. Having stayed with the Yanney family, he saw how humbly they lived. Because their father's salary was far less than even farmhands and laborers were paid, the boys had to work as well. Even still, many parishioners had not given their pledges, and the parish council had been trying to make up the difference by paying Father Nicola from the church's savings, which were now almost depleted.

After hearing their concerns and complaints, Bishop Raphael asked each person present if they would make a pledge to support their priest, collecting both the church's savings and their pledges into a single account. Moved by the bishop, many agreed and signed their names to a pledge list. In total, over thirty dollars was pledged. After further discussion, and in the presence of Bishop Raphael, the congregation again agreed to pay Father Nicola forty-five dollars each month, while still allowing him to be gone for four months out of the year.

With the contentious financial issue solved for the time being, Bishop Raphael shared with the parishioners an important vision he had regarding their children. Because most of the Syrians' children were attending local public schools, many were not learning to read and write Arabic. Even more important, however, was their need to study the basic principles of the Christian faith and the teachings of the Orthodox Church.

To accomplish this, Bishop Raphael proposed that the parish establish a church school. Along with the Arabic language, Father Nicola would teach the children religion classes for two hours every day. The bishop stipulated that the priest receive fifty cents per month for each child who attended. Those who could not afford this amount could pay twenty-five cents, while the poorest children could attend free of charge. Both Father Nicola and the parishioners agreed to the bishop's plan. While he wanted them to begin their church school immediately, Bishop Raphael and Father Nicola had already discussed where the school might find a permanent building. Once their new church was built, the congregation would remodel their existing building back into a schoolhouse. Everyone enthusiastically agreed.

After the meeting, the Syrians implored the bishop to stay and invited him to come and bless their homes. Accompanied by Father Nicola and Archdeacon Emmanuel, Bishop Raphael went from house to house over the next three days. After blessing their homes with holy water, he stayed to visit with the parishioners. Many still had doubts about the future of their church, and Bishop Raphael tried to answer their questions and assuage their fears. He also continued to offer spiritual guidance, teaching them at every opportunity.

On the morning before he was to finally leave town, Bishop Raphael was invited to bless a wedding. For the last time, the congregation gathered together with their bishop, as he, the archdeacon, and Father Nicola performed the service. It was an especially beautiful ceremony, after which Bishop Raphael said his farewells to many of the Syrians. All were sad to see him leave, including the many friends and admirers that he had made in the wider Kearney community.

That evening, Father Nicola said goodbye to his sons and joined the bishop and his secretary on the train as they departed for Iowa. As the train pulled out of the station, Bishop Raphael blessed the crowds and waved goodbye to those who had come to send him off. Before leaving, he had promised that he would to return to Nebraska to bless their new church as soon as they finished building it. Sadly, however, they would never see their bishop again.

On the next day, Bishop Raphael, Father Nicola, and

Archdeacon Emmanuel arrived in Cedar Rapids. The bishop was there to dedicate a new church building. Because Father Nicola had traveled there regularly and had functioned as the community's pastor for many years, Bishop Raphael had invited the priest to join him. The local Syrians greeted the bishop with excitement. They were also happy to see Father Nicola again, though he had been there two months earlier. The congregation in Cedar Rapids was comprised of only twenty-five families. For years, they had labored to raise funds, and at last they had collected enough to construct a large, handsome brick church. Though the parish still did not have a resident priest, the bishop was planning to assign one during his visit.

Father Nicola had reservations. He was close to the parishioners in Cedar Rapids and had served their community for the past decade. He was proud of their accomplishments and knew that they needed their own priest. The man that Bishop Raphael was planning to assign as their pastor, however, was the same man who had recently been in Ironwood—Father Elia Hamati. Earlier that summer, after only two years as their pastor, Father Elia had resigned his post, leaving Father Nicola's friends and relatives in Michigan without a pastor. The missionary priest feared that he would eventually do the same to the congregation in Cedar Rapids.

On Sunday morning, Bishop Raphael blessed the new building with Father Nicola and the archdeacon at his side. Though the interior was not quite finished, the bishop encouraged the parishioners to complete it and extolled them for their hard work and dedication in building such a beautiful church. The three clergymen stayed in the city for a week while the bishop visited and taught the local Syrians as he had in Kearney. Bishop Raphael even attended a citizenship class with a few of the parishioners and gave a brief sermon and led the attendees in prayers for peace in Europe.

At the end of their week in Cedar Rapids, the bishop invited Father Nicola to assist at a wedding. After the ceremony, the missionaries parted ways. Bishop Raphael and Archdeacon Emmanuel were continuing north to La Crosse. From Wisconsin, they planned to go to Illinois and Ohio before returning to New York. Father Nicola decided to head west to visit a few other communities in Iowa before returning home.

As they parted, the bishop commended his priest for his good work in Cedar Rapids over the years and all of his missionary labors. He also encouraged him to remain diligent with his parish in Kearney and to proceed with their plan. Once Father Nicola and his congregation built a large new temple—just as the Syrians in Cedar Rapids had—the bishop would return to Kearney to bless both their new church and their new school. Father Nicola kissed Bishop Raphael's hand with reverence and love and received his blessing. It was the last time he would see his beloved bishop alive.

Returning to a village in eastern Iowa where he had baptized two children only three weeks earlier, Father Nicola performed another baptism and visited with the Syrians living in the Sioux City area. He then traveled back to Kearney to implement the plans that Bishop Raphael and he had presented to the parish. Father Nicola hoped to proceed quickly.

Because their congregation had grown so much in the last decade, there was no longer enough room in their small church. At the bishop's suggestion, Father Nicola would begin raising funds for a new building. First, however, they needed a design. Father Nicola and his parishioners settled on a much larger floor plan for the new church, measuring 40 by 80 feet and having a full basement. Wanting it to be a beautiful and lasting building, they decided to construct it from concrete block and finish it in stucco. The interior would be finished in oak.

Father Nicola set about raising money. Once the funds were collected, the parish would first move the existing building to the adjacent lot. Then, the congregation could begin building their new church. Excited by the plan, Father Nicola hoped it would require only a few months to complete.

While home, the priest also considered another suggestion that the bishop had made. With his long beard and hair—still uncut since his ordination—Father Nicola looked like the Orthodox priests living in Syria, Greece, and Russia. In America, however, his traditional appearance was peculiar. Bishop Raphael had cut off his own long hair and trimmed his beard years earlier in order to appear like other American clergymen. During his visit, he persuaded his priest to do the same.

It was a difficult decision for Father Nicola, however, and his sons and parishioners were surprised to see him shorn. Deciding not to discard the pious custom entirely, the priest kept his cut locks and had them intricately woven into three long strands as a memento of his ordination. Taking them to a jeweler, he capped the ends and hung the small cross from his old chain on the cords of hair, making a new chain for his pocket watch.

Father Nicola's brief stay at home was interrupted by a trip to a western Nebraska town to perform several more baptisms and a marriage. By the end of the month, it was time for him to begin his winter travels. After spending two weeks in southern Colorado, he made a quick trip through North and South Dakota before traveling to Minnesota and Michigan. Since the congregations in Upper Michigan were again without a priest, Father Nicola spent two weeks in the communities of Ironwood and Iron

Mountain before returning to spend two more weeks between Saint Paul and La Crosse. Everywhere he went, he shared Bishop Raphael's plans for building a new church in Kearney.

Father Nicola returned to Saint George in time to celebrate Christmas with his family and his parishioners. Elias returned home for the holidays to the delight of his father. A few days later, Father Nicola baptized four infants. As he wrote down the last of their names in his record book, the missionary priest realized that he had performed exactly one hundred baptisms that year. Staying in town for Theophany, he departed immediately after the services, this time traveling south into Kansas and Oklahoma.

The Syrian community in Wichita was thriving, and during his week in the city Father Nicola performed ten baptisms in various homes, as well as serving a liturgy. From Wichita, he headed to two small villages southwest of the city, performing two baptisms and spending a day in each. From there, he traveled to several towns in Oklahoma. Having peddled for years, many of the Syrians in Oklahoma were opening dry goods stores in the towns springing up near the oil fields and mines in the eastern part of the state. Others living in the western and southern parts of the state made their living as farmers.

After spending a few days in a small Oklahoma town where he performed three baptisms, Father Nicola arrived in the village of Fargo one evening in early February. He was there to baptize the daughter of a local Syrian family the next morning. The dark skies overhead looked ominous. At dinnertime, a tornado suddenly appeared from a storm cloud and headed straight for the center of the village. All the people raced to their storm shelters. The twister soon passed, and Father Nicola and the residents of the town emerged unharmed. Though they had all been frightened, the tornado had been too high to do much damage.

After his time in Fargo, Father Nicola headed to the far southwestern corner of the state to a small depot that had sprung up along a railroad spur. Several Syrian families lived in the village of Brinkman and in another nearby town. Though they had received visits from another priest years earlier, Father Nicola had never called on them. Like the large colony in Wichita and the growing community in Oklahoma City, these families hailed from the town of Marjeyoun. During his brief visit, Father Nicola learned of a large reunion that was to take place later that year and was invited to return there in the fall.

Already mid-February, it was time for Father Nicola to head north. Before returning to Kearney, he stopped at several villages in western Nebraska to serve the liturgy and baptize four children. Though he had been away for a month, Father Nicola still felt confident that his congregation would begin construction on their new church in the next few months and remodel the old church into a schoolhouse.

When Father Nicola arrived home, he received unexpected and distressing news. Bishop Raphael was gravely ill again. The bishop had returned to Brooklyn only a month after leaving Kearney, utterly spent. His tour had exhausted the last of his strength, and over the next few months, his health had continued to deteriorate. By the end of December, he was confined to his bed, unable to rise. Bishop Raphael bore his illness with peace and tranquility, but by early February his condition was dire. Bishop Alexander, a Russian hierarch and colleague, sent out an urgent telegram to his clergy asking for prayers for his sick friend:

> Fathers and brothers, pray for the health of the ailing missionary Bishop Raphael deeply respected and warmly loved

> by all. Who among us does not know this great worker in the vineyard of Christ, who works not only among the Syrians who are related to him by blood, but also among the Russians? Who can forget his kind smile, which just like a ray of sunshine fills everything around with joy and warmth? Who can fail to find infinitely and precious even the outward, humble appearance of this bishop, who in the words of the Pentecostarion is always kind, merciful, condescending, yet infinitely strict with himself? Bishop Raphael is sick with exhaustion; he has given himself wholly and for all. His physical strength has failed.

Father Nicola prayed fervently for the man who had guided, encouraged, and ordained him—the man after whom he had patterned his own life of ministry—hoping for another miracle. Despite the entreaties of Father Nicola and clergy and faithful across the country, the bishop's condition grew worse. Five days after returning home, Father Nicola received a telegram one afternoon with devastating news: Bishop Raphael was dead.

Father Nicola, along with the entire congregation, was stunned. News of Bishop Raphael's death was printed in the local papers, reporting the profound sorrow among the Syrians and the sadness of the many admirers that the bishop had made in the Kearney community. Father Nicola served a memorial service for Bishop Raphael on the following day. His funeral was scheduled to be held in the Brooklyn cathedral a week later. Unsure if he would be able to attend, Father Nicola announced that he would hold a funeral service for the bishop in Kearney if he could not make it to New York.

Two days later, Father Nicola boarded a train for New York, having found funds to pay for the trip. By the time he arrived in

Brooklyn, Bishop Raphael's body had already been dressed in his episcopal vestments and placed in a mahogany coffin in the middle of the cathedral. Because Father Nicola had to travel the farthest, many of the Syrian priests had arrived before him. For five days, the Russian and Syrian clergy, together with the Russian hierarch, Bishop Alexander, had been serving the Divine Liturgy and memorial prayers in the cathedral. Entering into the church, Father Nicola reverently kissed the bishop's hand and took his place with the rest of the priests.

The cathedral was draped in black and decorated with flowers and candles. Father Nicola marveled at the splendid floral arrangements that surrounded Bishop Raphael's casket and filled the church. Some cost thousands of dollars apiece and had been sent by the many parishes and organizations throughout the diocese. Every morning and evening, the church was filled with people who had come for the services. Whenever Bishop Raphael's name was commemorated, both the clergy and the laity wept. In between the services, the priests took turns reading passages from the Gospels over the bishop's body, and they continued day and night.

Three days later, twenty-two priests and three deacons from the Syrian diocese gathered together with the Russian bishop and many of his clergy for the last Divine Liturgy before the funeral. A metropolitan visiting from Syria named Germanos Shehadi served together with Bishop Alexander. Metropolitan Germanos was a tall and striking figure and possessed a magnificent voice. Father Nicola had never met him, but the Syrian prelate was already well known to a number of his fellow priests.

More clergy arrived for the funeral service later that afternoon. The cathedral was overflowing, and many people stood outside in the snow in order to pay their respects to the departed bishop.

At the end of the funeral, everyone knelt and wept. The dean of the cathedral began extolling Bishop Raphael's many virtues and moved the crowd to tears once more. After several moving eulogies, Bishop Alexander spoke last, with Father Elia from Cedar Rapids translating his speech from Russian into Arabic. With the sermons finished, the funeral procession began. It was the most impressive sight that Father Nicola had ever seen.

Though it had snowed heavily the night before, city workers had cleared the streets early in the morning especially for the funeral. Three police officers on horseback—including the Brooklyn chief of police—led the procession. Three hundred other policeman lined the long route. A crowd of children dressed in white and carrying wreaths followed the mounted escort, behind whom walked the New York clergy and the various dignitaries and members of the many church organizations that had come. The altar boys carrying crosses and processional torches led Bishop Alexander and Metropolitan Germanos, followed by the priests bearing Bishop Raphael's coffin. A horse-drawn hearse came behind the priests. The entire funeral march was twenty blocks in length. After carrying their bishop for two blocks, the priests carefully placed his casket on the hearse. Bishop Raphael's family members walked behind the hearse, and at the end of the parade came the thousands of mourners. Astonished by the size of the crowd, Father Nicola was told that there were eight thousand people in the procession.

The funeral procession eventually turned back toward the church and came to a stop at a crypt outside of the east wall of the cathedral. It had been specially prepared for Bishop Raphael so that he might be buried beneath the altar. Bishop Alexander gave a farewell address to his departed friend as the ornate floral arrangements were placed inside the crypt. The Syrian clergy surrounded Bishop Raphael's casket as it was carefully lowered into a bronze vault. Before the lid was closed, Metropolitan Germanos spoke. His words were eloquent as he repeated what other eulogizers had already said of the bishop's sanctity:

> Receive now, O Church, your master and builder. Receive him, O Church, as a holy relic and a holy shrine which will help your people remember the efforts of the saint and his examples of piety. Farewell, O reverend master. Farewell, O Bishop Raphael. Soar in your spirit towards your Lord and receive from Him your crown. Leave for us your body as a holy relic and a precious treasure, and trust that we will keep your covenant forever, remember your tenderness always, and commemorate you with fragrance until we meet you in the day of eternity and peace.

As the priests and the crowd of mourners watched, the lid was finally closed. The orphaned Syrians began to weep and wail as the Russian bishop and the Syrian metropolitan placed earth over the vault. Following his fellow priests, Father Nicola stepped forward. Grief-stricken, he cast a handful of dirt on Bishop Raphael's grave and wondered how they would all fare without their beloved shepherd to guide them.

CHAPTER TWELVE

Founders and Benefactors

MARCH 1915 TO OCTOBER 1916

THE WHISPERS BEGAN BEFORE THE funeral service had even ended. Clergy and laity alike were all wondering who might succeed Bishop Raphael. Father Nicola knew few of his peers. Three of the twenty-six Syrian priests were from Koura, and one was from his home village of Fi'eh. Father Nicola had met a few of the others over the years. To most, however, he was known only by reputation as the priest from Nebraska. Yet, though he was isolated on the furthest edge of the diocese and many of his fellow clergy were strangers to him, even Father Nicola had been privy to the hushed and anxious rumors that had passed through their ranks.

Bishop Raphael had never indicated a successor, and there were few celibate priests among the Syrian clergy from which to choose. The senior-ranking clergyman was a young man named Aftimios Ofiesh. Though they had a sometimes-strained relationship, Bishop Raphael had elevated Father Aftimios to archimandrite a year before his death. When Ofiesh had first come to America, he had served as Bishop Raphael's assistant, but he was now pastoring one of the congregations in Montreal. Though respected, Archimandrite Aftimios was known to have an intense and polarizing personality.

Other clergy spoke of consecrating Archdeacon Emmanuel as the bishop's successor. He had been Bishop Raphael's secretary for years and was familiar with both the Russian hierarchy and the administrative affairs of their own diocese. The archdeacon also knew all of the Syrian clergy, having traveled with Bishop Raphael to their parishes. He was only twenty-five years old, however, and many considered him too young. Nonetheless, the dean of the cathedral, himself an adversary of Aftimios, was throwing his support behind Emmanuel and had already begun quietly gauging the support of his fellow priests.

Still others wondered about the visiting bishop from Syria. Several of the clergy were unsure of Metropolitan Germanos

Fr. Nicola with Metropolitan Germanos and parish, October 1916

Shehadi. The rest, however, were glad for his presence at the funeral and had been inspired by his chanting and his eulogy. Over six feet tall, the metropolitan was an imposing figure. He spoke eloquently and had a beautiful singing voice. Though a high-ranking bishop in the Church of Antioch with his own diocese in Syria, Germanos had fled at the outbreak of the First World War. Originally destined for Odessa, he had switched ships and headed for the United States when he had learned of Austria's impending declaration of war. Publicly, the metropolitan claimed to have come to America on a fundraising tour.

As the rumors swirled, Father Nicola started for home. He had dearly loved Bishop Raphael, as had all of the Syrian clergy. The Russian bishop and his priests held him in very high esteem as well. Father Nicola had seen their reverence and love in the way they had mourned and prayed over the prelate during the memorial services and the funeral. The Russians had always supported the Syrians, both in their homeland and in America. They had even consecrated Bishop Raphael to lead their diocese and had supported the Syrians' fledgling congregations.

Father Nicola looked at his gold watch and remembered the holy vessels, icons, and vestments that he had brought back to Kearney after his ordination—gifts from the Russian hierarchy on behalf of the tsar. Yet Father Nicola was also a Syrian and a son of the Church of Antioch. He felt conflicted, but thought of Bishop Raphael who himself had worked for many years to free their patriarchate from two centuries of Greek domination. Though the Russians had never oppressed them, some of his fellow priests were beginning to speak of returning to Antioch rather than remaining under the foreign hierarchs. Father Nicola's work lay fifteen hundred miles from Brooklyn, however, and he was glad to return to his missionary labors.

Though Holy Week and Pascha were only a few weeks away, Father Nicola took the opportunity to visit a few communities on his way back to Kearney. From Brooklyn, he traveled to a small town in upstate New York to confess and serve the liturgy for a small group of Syrians that he knew. He also stopped to visit his sister and her family in Pennsylvania. It had been years since Father Nicola had seen Anna. The siblings' reunion was brief, though joyous. The priest encouraged his older sister in her hardship. Anna's husband had died several years earlier, and she had struggled to make ends meet while raising her five children. Father Nicola invited them to visit Kearney and promised to return to Pennsylvania again.

A consummate missionary, Father Nicola had brought his container of Holy Chrism with him on his trip to New York, ready for any opportunity to do his priestly work. Traveling from his sister's home to another town fifty miles away where several acquaintances from Koura had settled, he chrismated two Syrian teenagers who wanted to convert to the Orthodox faith. From there, he traveled to visit the large Syrian community located in Pittsburgh. The congregation had been without a priest for six months. Father Nicola ministered to them and spoke about Bishop Raphael's passing and funeral.

By the time Father Nicola returned to Kearney, he had been away for almost four weeks. The priest arrived home on the morning of Lazarus Saturday, and news of his return quickly spread throughout the neighborhood. Father Nicola greeted his sons, unpacked his bags, and attended to the parishioners who began arriving at his doorstep. One Syrian family had a small child that they wanted to baptize, and Father Nicola decided to perform the baptism in conjunction with the Palm Sunday services. On Saturday evening, the church bell that had been silent for almost a month rang out to announce the first of the weekend's services.

On the morning of Palm Sunday, the parishioners gathered to celebrate the feast. They had been without services for most of Lent, but Father Nicola had returned in time for Holy Week. Near the end of the liturgy, the packed church emptied as the congregation processed around the building, bearing palms and branches. Later, Father Nicola recounted the details of Bishop Raphael's funeral. He described the many priests and thousands of faithful who attended, the beautiful floral arrangements in the church, the grand procession with the police escort, and the heartrending eulogies. He also told the congregation about meeting the metropolitan from Syria and brought greetings from their distant friends that he had visited after the funeral.

For a brief moment, Father Nicola recalled his own ordination. It had been eleven years ago on the feast of Palm Sunday that the newly consecrated Bishop Raphael had ordained Father Nicola his first priest. Then, the Syrian diocese was just beginning in earnest with only a handful of parishes. Now, under their bishop's guidance, thirty congregations had been established, and many more communities were gathered that might someday become churches. Bishop Raphael was gone, however, and the future was uncertain.

With the busy schedule of Holy Week, Father Nicola spent much of the next week in church. Outside of the services, he visited his parishioners and heard their confessions. After Pascha, Father Nicola once again turned his attention to his missionary flock, continuing to build on the foundations that Bishop Raphael had laid. The bishop's plan to erect a church in every region of the diocese was bearing significant fruit. Father Nicola's parish of Saint George had served as a missionary center for more than a decade, and after years of labor, other full-fledged congregations were springing up across the plains.

Before leaving home on a longer missionary journey, Father Nicola made a brief trip to Sioux City, where he performed two baptisms. The local Syrians were still excitedly discussing the possibility of building their own church. For almost two years, the missionary priest had been encouraging them to erect a building in which to worship. As many of the Syrian farmers in North Dakota were selling their homesteaded land and moving back to Iowa and Minnesota, the congregation in Sioux City was growing. Although the group was still too small to accomplish the task on its own, Father Nicola had appealed to the local newspaper that a church might be built with help from the wider community.

From Sioux City, Father Nicola returned home for another month before leaving to visit the communities in the far eastern portion of his territory. He had not been to Ironwood for several months. Since their first resident priest had resigned, Father Nicola was once again responsible for the congregation. Over the years, with much prayer and dedication, and with the encouragement of their missionary priest, the local Syrians had built a small church named after Fi'eh's patron, Saint Simeon. For the past four years, the congregation had had their own place to worship. With more hard work and sacrifice, they had eventually been able to procure a full-time pastor. Father Elia had stayed for only two years, and his resignation had been a great disappointment. Though Father Nicola would continue to serve the parishioners of Saint Simeon, he knew that his friends in Ironwood needed their own priest.

Bishop Raphael's untimely death had placed such fledgling parishes in a difficult situation. Without their own bishop, the

Syrian churches now relied on Bishop Alexander and the Russian hierarchy to ordain and assign their pastors. Like the community in Ironwood, the congregation in La Crosse was facing similar hardships. Father Nicola made his way to Wisconsin from Michigan and, as usual, found the small but energetic community making bold plans.

A few years earlier, the local families had built their own church, which Bishop Raphael had blessed them to name after the Prophet Elias.[7] When Father Nicola arrived in town for his latest visit, he heard of their plans to start a church school similar to the one he was founding in Kearney. They hoped to teach forty students. A spiritual son of Father Nicola named Elias Sady headed up the local Sunday School program and was to be the school's superintendent. In their enthusiasm, the congregation had even voted to raise the building off its foundation in order to add a finished basement to use as classrooms for the school. During the three years since the official founding of their parish, however, they had been without a priest.

The parishioners of Saint Elias had discussed the problem with Bishop Raphael during his visit to La Crosse several months before his death. Though the local Syrians were devoted to Father Nicola and had relied on his frequent visits for a decade, they too desired to have their own priest. The parishioners had recently requested that Bishop Alexander send them a pastor, promising to pay a monthly salary. However, they shared with Father Nicola that they had yet to receive any response from the Russian hierarch.

As usual, Father Nicola was planning to spend two weeks in La Crosse. He was scheduled to baptize four children over the weekend. Before he could perform the services, however, he

7 The Prophet Elijah.

received an urgent call to Cedar Rapids and had to postpone the baptisms. Father Nicola feared a crisis. Like the congregations in La Crosse and Michigan, the parishioners in Cedar Rapids were devout and dedicated. Not only had they erected a beautiful brick church placed under the patronage of Saint George, but they had also built a rectory for a priest and his family and had purchased a cemetery.

Though he had once visited them frequently and pastored them from a distance, Father Nicola had not been to Cedar Rapids since accompanying Bishop Raphael and his deacon to the dedication service. At that time, the bishop had installed Father Elia Hamati as the parish's first resident priest—who only months before had resigned his pastorate in Ironwood. A Russophile, Father Elia was erudite and had been chosen to deliver a sermon in Russian during Bishop Raphael's funeral services. The Palestinian priest, however, struggled pastoring the congregations to which he had been assigned. As Father Nicola traveled to Cedar Rapids to help address the difficulties in the parish, the missionary priest suspected that he might soon be regularly visiting the congregation once again.

In the past few years, Father Nicola's labors in the northeast had lessened. With Father Elia first serving in Michigan and then in Iowa, Father Nicola's missionary duties in the region were now shared. Another clergyman, Father Seraphim Nassar, had been serving as an itinerant priest out of Chicago and also provided regular visitations to communities like La Crosse, Ironwood, and Iron Mountain. With the continued immigration, however, Father Nicola was busy as ever as more Syrians were settling in Nebraska and across the southern plains.

Offering what counsel he could in Cedar Rapids, Father Nicola returned to La Crosse a few days later to perform the postponed baptisms and pastor his flock. Turning west, he spent the next month visiting communities in Iowa, South Dakota, and Nebraska. After a short stay at home, the missionary priest traveled south, first stopping in Wichita. The city's Syrian community was continuing to flourish, and more peddlers were trading in their packs and horse-drawn carts to open small shops, groceries, and specialty stores. Although the local families were now being occasionally visited by a priest who had immigrated to New York from their hometown of Marjeyoun, Father Nicola still traveled to Wichita regularly. Due to their wealth and growing numbers, he began encouraging the community to build or buy a church in which to hold services.

Because of the success of their loved ones, more Syrians were immigrating to America from Marjeyoun. Some were settling in Kansas. Others, however, were joining their friends in Oklahoma. Traveling to the far southwestern corner of the state as he had promised months earlier, the missionary priest returned to the tiny village of Brinkman. Several families lived in the area, but a much larger number were gathering there for a reunion.

Though it was early fall, heavy rains hampered the work of the local Syrian farmers. The unseasonable weather did not dampen their spirits, however. Father Nicola labored among them for the next two weeks. Between the festivities and the services that he led, the priest was busy with baptisms. Sixteen of the families who had come to the reunion had children who had never been christened. One family alone—that of Michael Shadid, a well-known physician—had eight children who needed to be baptized. Each day, as more families arrived, Father Nicola baptized one or two children, and sometimes as many as six or seven. Near the end of his time in Brinkman, he had performed thirty-eight baptisms.

As he was preparing to travel to other towns and villages

in the state, Father Nicola received a telegram from home. A young Syrian farmer in Colorado had been trampled to death by his horses. The family was shipping his body to Kearney for the funeral. Promising to return to Oklahoma after the burial, Father Nicola caught the next train and began his long trip back to Nebraska. Three days later, he performed the young man's funeral. The Kearney community marveled at the thousand-mile round trip that the priest had made to bury one of his parishioners, only to immediately return to his missionary duties.

A month later, Father Nicola was visiting his communities in Iowa again, then traveled for three weeks between the various settlements in North Dakota. Making stops in Minnesota, Iowa, and rural Nebraska, he returned home in time to celebrate Christmas. After the feast, he visited a few families who had moved away from Kearney.

Over the years, a number of his parishioners had relocated to small towns throughout Nebraska to open stores or start farms. Though they occasionally traveled back to Kearney for major feast days, Father Nicola also regularly paid them visits. Many times, he would take others with him. John Shada, Mike Hayek, and others traveled with their priest to stand as godparents when Father Nicola was called to perform a baptism on an outlying farmstead. The visits also helped the priest maintain close ties with members of the Kearney community who had moved several hours away.

When Father Nicola returned home for Theophany, he filled out his annual sacramental registry. The year had begun and ended with traveling and had been especially marked by the death of Bishop Raphael and his own unexpected month-long journey to the East Coast. As he filled in his records, he noticed that he had performed even more baptisms than the previous year.

Despite his busy schedule, Father Nicola kept abreast of news throughout the diocese. Besides the diocesan journal that Bishop Raphael had founded, Father Nicola also read the Arabic newspapers that were printed in New York. No one had yet been chosen to succeed Bishop Raphael, nor had any election been announced. Tensions were rising. Combative editorials had begun appearing in the different Syrian papers—some calling for the parishes to acknowledge Antioch as their only ecclesiastical authority, while others expressed their loyalty to the Russians.

In the midst of the rising tensions, Metropolitan Germanos continued visiting parishes throughout the diocese and voicing his support for Antioch. He also began presenting himself as an official representative of the patriarch, quietly putting himself forward as a potential successor to Bishop Raphael. Unbeknownst to the Syrian clergy, the metropolitan's claims were false. Over the coming years, the Antiochian patriarch would call Germanos to return to his own diocese in Syria, a call which the charismatic hierarch would long ignore.

Archimandrite Aftimios and Archdeacon Emmanuel—the two other candidates who might succeed Bishop Raphael—had both remained loyal to the Russian hierarchy. Political machinations had continued, however, and there was no clarity as to which of the two would become the holy hierarch's successor. As editor of the diocesan journal, Archdeacon Emmanuel began writing against Metropolitan Germanos and making a case for the Syrian congregations to remain under Russian authority. In the midst of the growing dissension, Father Nicola returned to his pastoral and missionary work.

After performing half a dozen baptisms in his congregation, Father Nicola traveled to Sioux City to marry a young couple. While there, he was encouraged to hear that the local Syrians had formed a church society and were planning to buy a small church building to refurbish, just as he had been encouraging them to do for several years. Called back to Nebraska to perform two funerals, he soon returned to Iowa to continue his visitations. As he had feared, Father Elia had recently left the parish in Cedar Rapids for another congregation. Father Nicola spent two weeks in the city, then traveled home to Kearney for the beginning of Lent.

One week later, Bishop Alexander and the dean of the Syrian cathedral in Brooklyn arrived in Cedar Rapids to ordain a young man and assign him as the congregation's new priest. Father Nicola knew the candidate. Joseph Kacere had lived and worked for several years in a packing house in Sioux City before moving to Cedar Rapids. When Father Elia had resigned, the parish had petitioned that Joseph be ordained to the priesthood. Though he would serve faithfully for many years to come, he was being ordained by the Russian hierarchy. The only other nearby Syrian clergyman was the itinerant priest from Chicago, Father Seraphim, who was a fervent supporter of both Antioch and Metropolitan Germanos. Father Nicola, Father Seraphim, and the newly ordained Father Joseph were all responsible for the smaller Syrian settlements throughout the region, and their ministrations often overlapped. Sadly, Father Nicola realized that the growing dissension in the diocese was no longer a distant problem, but might soon divide communities across the Great Plains.

A week after Pascha, the missionary priest began another season of travel, visiting Syrians in South Dakota, Iowa, and elsewhere. With Elias's recent return to Kearney, all of Father Nicola's boys were once again living at home. Another son, however, was soon to leave. Moses was still in high school, but John had graduated. After working for a year, he had decided to enlist in the army. When word came for John to report to basic training, Father Nicola returned home to spend a few weeks with his son and to say goodbye. Though proud of his son, he was concerned about the war in Europe. The United States had not yet entered into the conflict, but the priest was nonetheless worried for his son's safety.

A few weeks before John's enlistment, troubling news had begun to reach the Syrians living in America. The war had been raging for two years, and almost all communication from Syria had stopped during the conflict. Father Nicola and his fellow countrymen knew that with each passing month, life grew more desperate for their loved ones stranded in their homeland. Now, in newspapers across the country, they read of even greater calamity. Under the Ottomans, both the Armenian and Syrian Christians were suffering terribly. According to the reports, one million were living in utter destitution. Though the Christians might relieve their plight by converting to the Muslim faith of their oppressors, they were choosing to suffer instead, even eating grass when the Ottoman government prevented them from supporting themselves by any means.

With an international appeal being made for Syrian and Armenian relief, Father Nicola wondered how he might help as he returned home again late that summer. His plans for the parish had been frustrated, both by Bishop Raphael's death a year and a half earlier and by his own extended missionary work. He still hoped to begin construction on the new church soon, but decided to delay it until the coming year. In the meantime, with the Americans' growing awareness of the horrific plight taking place in Syria, the priest poured his attention into raising funds to help his fellow Christians.

Reports soon began circulating that three-quarters of a million

Armenians had been killed, and many more Armenians and Syrians were close to starving to death. As a national relief campaign began in earnest, Father Nicola led the local fundraising drive in Kearney. For a month, the priest worked to raise awareness among the local community and to collect donations from his own parishioners. The Kearney mayor and other local ministers took interest as the Syrian priest asked for the public's support in the face of the humanitarian crisis.

Local churches began to take special collections, businesses were solicited, and the town held a fundraiser by selling carnations door to door. When the campaign was finished, several hundred dollars had been raised. Father Nicola publicly thanked everyone who participated in the fundraising and generously contributed, stating that he and his parishioners were very pleased. Through their own hard work, the congregation of Saint George had contributed half of the total amount raised throughout the entire community.

With the fundraising campaign winding down, Father Nicola returned his attention to his immediate pastoral duties. A growing number of his parishioners were concerned about the situation in the diocese. They had noted that the editorials in the rival Arabic newspapers were becoming more heated, and the archdeacon's diocesan journal had largely become a diatribe against Metropolitan Germanos.

The metropolitan himself was exacerbating the situation. He had continued touring the diocese, claiming that his purpose was to raise funds for an agricultural school in his diocese in Syria, all the while calling for the Syrian churches in America to come under Antioch. Though he had settled in New York, he was not only attending to the large Syrian communities on the East Coast but was also visiting small congregations like Ironwood and La

Crosse. Feeling neglected by the Russian hierarchy, the Syrians there welcomed him with open arms. Metropolitan Germanos was even planning on touring North Dakota and stopping in the town of Williston, the settlement at the far northwestern corner of Father Nicola's missionary territory.

Though grateful for the support of the Russian Church for the past twenty years, most of the communities that Father Nicola had served desired to be under the Church of Antioch. Several congregations wanted to remain with the Russians, however, and still others were being torn in two by the strife. Even individual families were becoming bitterly divided. Whatever the future would bring, Father Nicola knew that a fierce storm was brewing that threatened to engulf them all.

CHAPTER THIRTEEN

Russia or Antioch

OCTOBER 1916 TO APRIL 1918

ALTHOUGH THE SITUATION IN THE Syrian diocese was continuing to deteriorate, Father Nicola had an even more pressing concern—his eldest son. Elias had grown into a fine young man. He was exceptionally bright and had good prospects. Finishing his studies in Omaha, he had returned to Kearney a year earlier and had gone into partnership with his uncle George. They had opened a grocery store together. The venture was successful so far, though George was sometimes overly generous, letting his customers carry too much on credit without paying. Elias, however, had keen business sense. He had always been very good with numbers, and Father Nicola knew that his son would do well if he chose to pursue another career rather than follow in his father's footsteps.

Many people commented on how similar the two were even in appearance. Elias had long grown accustomed to hearing how much he resembled his father. Though Elias was shorter and not quite as thin as Father Nicola had been at his age, they did bear a striking resemblance. Some even expected Elias to become a priest. In his youth, he had considered it. However, he knew firsthand how difficult life could be for a priest and his family.

Elias's father had poured his whole life into the church. His travels took him away for months at a time, and even when he was home, he had little time to himself or to spend with Elias and his brothers. People were constantly calling on him with their problems and seeking his advice to settle family squabbles or heal larger divisions within the Syrian community. When counsel was given, Elias knew that it often went unheeded. Father Nicola deeply loved his people and anguished over their welfare. They, in turn, trusted him. Yet, Elias sometimes wondered whether his father was more highly respected by those he visited on his missionary journeys than by his own parishioners in Kearney.

Elias was not bitter; yet he knew that for all of his father's sacrifices, there was little to show for them. Though Father Nicola taught the parishioners' children when he was home in Kearney, the church school brought in little extra money. During the late Bishop Raphael's visit, the parish had agreed to pay Father Nicola forty-five dollars a month, yet they still only gave him thirty-five dollars. Many members paid their church dues with chickens, eggs, and produce instead of money. All their offerings were graciously accepted, but with little income, Father Nicola had a difficult time making ends meet. Elias knew that he carried debt. Their house and property were heavily mortgaged, and try as he might, his father only barely managed to make the interest payment every month, and he was never able to pay down much of the principal itself.

Father Nicola, too, had long noticed the similarities between his eldest son and himself. Unlike his father, however, Elias was almost twenty-three years old and still unmarried. Father Nicola had been nineteen when he wed Martha. Now that Elias was establishing himself as a respected businessman, his father felt that it was time for his son to marry. As a priest, he had helped to arrange marriages in the many communities he visited. Father Nicola would do no less for his own son, and he already had a particular young woman in mind.

Her name was Mary Abraham, the daughter of his niece Mineshi. Father Nicola had seen Mary often on his trips to Ironwood and knew her family well. A close relative of the Yanneys, Mineshi was the daughter of Father Nicola's oldest sister, Nour, who had remained in Koura and after whom he had named his infant daughter. Because of the close relation and Mary's disposition, Father Nicola felt that she would be a good wife for Elias. Mary's parents agreed, especially her mother.

The boys' American friends sometimes dated different young women, then chose one that they wanted to marry when the time came for them to settle down and start a family. Even some in the Syrian community had begun doing this, though their elders frowned upon the practice. As the priest's son, however, Elias's marriage would be arranged, just as Father Nicola's marriage had been by his father. Though Elias had never met or even seen Mary, he obediently accepted his father's decision.

Preparations began, despite the initial hesitance of Mary's father. Habeeb Abraham knew and respected Father Nicola, but he dearly loved his daughter and did not want her to move away to Nebraska. Even more, he wanted her to be able to choose whom she wanted to marry. Mary was only sixteen and still had time to finish her education. Mineshi, however, had insisted that her daughter stop her schooling after eighth grade. The tradition of arranged marriages was still strong in the Syrian community, and it would be an honor to marry the priest's son. Mineshi was especially insistent about the wedding and soon prevailed, despite her husband's hesitation and Mary's own misgivings.

With Elias's situation decided, Father Nicola turned his attention to his younger sons. Moses, the youngest, was in his final years of high school. Sixteen years old, he was well liked and gregarious. John was still in the army, having worked as a laborer and cook in a local hotel before enlisting. Father Nicola was sometimes concerned about his middle son. Moses was outgoing, and Elias, though serious, was quick witted. John, however, was introverted and less ambitious than his brothers.

Besides his sons, Father Nicola had other concerns. The family's large mortgage was always on his mind. The struggle of pastoring so many people—both in Kearney and in the communities he visited—was constant. A potential crisis was looming, however, and it threatened to divide every congregation that the late Bishop Raphael had founded, along with every smaller community that Father Nicola served.

The Russian hierarchy had yet to choose either Archdeacon Emmanuel or Father Aftimios to succeed Bishop Raphael, deciding to bide their time in hopes of maintaining unity among the Syrians. Although Emmanuel continued to manage the daily operations of the Syrian diocese and had others campaigning on his behalf, because of Aftimios's age and rank, the archimandrite was slowly emerging as the candidate most likely to be chosen by the Russians. In the meantime, Metropolitan Germanos's popularity was growing.

The Syrian hierarch had made a striking impression when he had served Bishop Raphael's funeral and preached at his burial. He had arrived in America several months before the bishop's death—on the very same day that Bishop Raphael had arrived in Kearney. The visiting prelate had received a blessing to tour the country to raise funds for an agricultural school he was planning to build in his diocese. During his visits to the Syrian parishes, he began questioning their relationship to the Russian hierarchy and openly spoke of them belonging to the Church of Antioch. Hearing that Metropolitan Germanos was stirring up trouble in his congregations, Bishop Raphael had chastised him. Sadly, he had died only a short time later.

In the year and a half since the saintly bishop's death, Metropolitan Germanos had continued to visit communities throughout North America. Before Germanos's arrival, a few of Bishop Raphael's priests had been outspoken in their allegiance to Antioch, disavowing their affiliation with the Russian Church. One clergyman had even been disciplined for spreading his contentious views. The metropolitan's presence now emboldened those who wanted closer ties to Antioch as he himself traveled from parish to parish and used Bishop Raphael's own words to support his cause.

During his entire time in America, Bishop Raphael had served under the authority of the Russian Church. All the while, he had maintained close relations with his mother church in Antioch. At the time of his consecration to the episcopacy, the Antiochian patriarch had sent his blessing to Archbishop Tikhon and the Russian hierarchy to proceed. The patriarch even stated that Bishop Raphael was to be considered as a member of the Antiochian synod of bishops.

Bishop Raphael returned the sentiment. When the Patriarch of Antioch died several years later, the bishop had him commemorated throughout his diocese and, because the primate had blessed his own consecration, listed himself among those that the patriarch had personally elevated to the episcopacy. Bishop Raphael even went so far as to state that his diocese belonged to the Church of Antioch, though in name it was under the Russian Church.

Such sentiments were printed in the monthly diocesan journal for the Syrians to read, yet caused no dissension. While encouraging warm affection and close relations with the Church of Antioch for the sake of his flock, Bishop Raphael displayed perfect obedience to the Russian ecclesiastical authorities. Throughout his twenty years of service, he was both personally and professionally close to all of the Russian hierarchs. They, in turn, deeply loved and respected him. Guided by Bishop Raphael's selfless character, deep piety, and unwavering devotion, the Syrian diocese had flourished—in spiritual unity with the Church of Antioch while operating under the authority and with the financial support of the Russian Church.

After Bishop Raphael's death, seeing that a large portion of the Syrians longed for a closer relationship with Antioch, Metropolitan Germanos reminded them of the departed bishop's words and played on his seemingly ambiguous stance toward the Russian hierarchs. Without Bishop Raphael to guide them, many began to be persuaded by Germanos's arguments. Some were resentful because of the Russians' inaction to appoint Bishop Raphael's successor or assign clergy to their struggling parishes. Others distrusted both of the presumed successors Aftimios and Emmanuel. Rumors that Archimandrite Aftimios was secretly a Mason had been circulating for years. Though the accusations were unsubstantiated, the archdeacon had also been rumored of having ties to the organization. One outspoken American priest who had worked closely with Bishop Raphael published a letter in the New York newspapers stating that any past or present affiliation with the Masonic order must lead to an automatic disqualification from being a candidate for the episcopacy.

Amid the growing turmoil, Father Nicola received a message from Metropolitan Germanos, offering to visit the church in Kearney for a few days. Father Nicola gladly accepted. The priest and his congregation were ramping up their fundraising efforts for the Armenian and Syrian relief, and they looked forward to hearing a report from the metropolitan about the current conditions in their homeland. Father Nicola was also keen to discuss the situation in the diocese.

The priest and his congregation arranged a grand reception for Metropolitan Germanos, as they had for Bishop Raphael two years earlier. When he arrived in Kearney, the visiting hierarch was met by a local band and a number of prominent townsfolk, including the mayor, who delivered a welcome address on behalf of the entire community. The mayor then escorted Father Nicola and the metropolitan on a tour of the city in his automobile, after which he delivered the two clergymen to the priest's home.

The entire congregation and the members of the community who had gathered at the depot were invited to Father Nicola's house for a reception in honor of Metropolitan Germanos. Several local reporters attended. Along with many other townsfolk, they were enamored with the foreign prelate. Though the metropolitan himself knew no English, they spoke of his spiritual demeanor, his impressive countenance, and his melodious voice.

Father Nicola invited the public to the Sunday morning liturgy. Many guests came, and the small church was overcrowded. Father Nicola translated as the metropolitan spoke to the crowd of the desperate situation in their homeland. Still purportedly raising funds to build a large school in his diocese, he told them that he hoped to go to South America before returning home. He was now planning on a five-year tour. Encouraging the congregation in their own efforts to send aid to their brethren suffering in Syria, Metropolitan Germanos related that eight of his fellow bishops had been killed since the beginning of the conflict. He also spoke eloquently of patriotism, believing that America would ultimately bring a resolution to the conflict.

Three days after his arrival, Germanos left for Omaha, having made a significant impression on the Kearney community and the local congregation. Hearing of Elias's upcoming marriage, he also promised Father Nicola that he would attend and officiate at the service, as was the custom. In their homeland, the weddings of a priest's children were often conducted by a bishop. Father Nicola had not dared to hope for such an honor with Bishop Raphael gone and the diocese in disarray. He and his family were deeply grateful for Germanos's offer.

Three weeks after the metropolitan's visit, Father Nicola was on the road again, this time heading to Wisconsin. Though he had to tend to his missionary communities there, he had arranged for his oldest son to meet him in Ironwood a few weeks later. When the time came, Elias traveled alone, leaving Moses at home in the care of other family members. As the train sped toward Michigan, he wondered what it would be like to be married. In a week, he would be twenty-three years old. Elias had never dated other girls, nor ever seen his bride-to-be. Mary was also restless as she awaited the day of the wedding. The prospect of marrying a stranger and moving so far away from her home and her family upset her. She was only sixteen years old. Though she was unhappy, she remained quiet and obedient to her mother's wishes.

Learning of Mary's impending nuptials, a local admirer threatened to show up at the train depot with a group of his friends to scare Elias away. When he finally arrived in Ironwood, the nervous bridegroom mistakenly got off of the train on the wrong side of the platform, missing the confrontation with Mary's would-be suitor and the ruffians. Meeting his father at the station, Elias went with him to meet the Abrahams.

Elias and Mary were sheepish at their first meeting and throughout the subsequent wedding festivities. When the time for the ceremony came, the small church of Saint Simeon was filled as Father Nicola, Metropolitan Germanos, and another priest who had been invited to help with the service gathered with the bride's family and the local congregation. After the ceremony, Mary's parents hosted a lavish dinner in their home. Elias and Mary were showered with gifts, and many speeches and poems that had been written for the occasion were recited in honor of the newlyweds. The poets also praised their most esteemed guest, Metropolitan Germanos, and especially the proud father of the groom, who had faithfully served their community for so many years.

Wedding of Fr. Nicola's son Elias in Ironwood, Michigan

Elias and Mary stayed with her family for three days after the wedding, then left for Nebraska. Mary tearfully bid farewell to her parents. The metropolitan departed to visit the Syrians living in Saint Louis, and Father Nicola continued the missionary trip that he had begun a few weeks earlier, making his way west to North Dakota. When the newlyweds arrived in Kearney a few days later, they were enthusiastically greeted by the local Syrians. George and Rebecca hosted a reception for their nephew and his bride, welcoming Mary to the community and their family.

Father Nicola had another month of visitations to make before Christmas. Nonetheless, he returned home from North Dakota to first see how Elias and Mary were settling into the family home and their new life together. Greeting the newlyweds, the priest saw that his daughter-in-law was unhappy and missed home. Mary had to adjust not only to marriage but also to living with Father Nicola and Moses, and cooking and cleaning for the entire household.

After a few days with his family, Father Nicola returned to Wisconsin for his semiannual stay in La Crosse. Afterward, he headed south to Kansas. The Syrians in Wichita had once again invited Father Nicola for Western Christmas. Staying in the city for a week, he performed six baptisms and held the festal services for one hundred Syrians in a local Episcopal church they had arranged to use.

Father Nicola stopped in Omaha before returning to Kearney to celebrate Christmas with his family and parishioners. When he arrived home, the young couple seemed more at ease. Besides adjusting to married life, Elias was busy with George running their store. Their business was successful enough that the nephew and uncle had moved into a newly remodeled storefront. Getting their customers to pay their bills on time, however, continued to be a struggle.

After two months in Kearney, Mary was growing more comfortable. She often communicated with her parents, and the Abrahams began talking about moving to Kearney to be closer to their eldest daughter. Mary was constantly busy with housework, and she now had a large hand in hosting the customary Sunday dinners for out-of-town guests and parishioners whenever her father-in-law was in town.

A month after Christmas, Father Nicola was traveling again, visiting several settlements in rural Nebraska and Minnesota. The large Syrian community in Saint Paul was no longer meeting above the wealthy merchant's storefront, but had purchased a beautiful Episcopal church. Though Metropolitan Germanos had consecrated the building a year earlier, the congregation still did not have their own priest. Father Nicola enjoyed visiting them again before continuing to Colorado, Iowa, and Michigan. Having spent most of Lent traveling, he returned to Kearney in time to celebrate Holy Week and Pascha.

During Father Nicola's missionary travels, the situation in the Syrian diocese had continued to unravel. Archdeacon Emmanuel had withdrawn his candidacy to succeed Bishop Raphael, and support had quickly coalesced around Archimandrite Aftimios. With Aftimios's consecration almost guaranteed, the opposing factions became openly hostile. Those who supported the Russians pressed the Russian hierarchy to make Aftimios their bishop immediately in hopes of preventing more parishes from defecting to Germanos. Those who wanted to be directly under Antioch, however, petitioned the Russians to delay elevating Aftimios. Each side hoped to avoid an outright schism, but the divisions were too deep.

Only a week after Pascha, fearing Aftimios's inevitable consecration, a Syrian congregation in Massachusetts became the first to publicly split from the Russians and openly proclaim their loyalty to the Church of Antioch. Other parishes quickly began to do the same. Because the Antiochian parties did not have their own bishop in America, they asked Metropolitan Germanos to serve as their interim hierarch. The visiting metropolitan gladly accepted, even founding a parish for his supporters in Brooklyn not far from the cathedral that Bishop Raphael had founded.

A week after the situation in the diocese had come to a head, Father Nicola and several of his parishioners were visiting two isolated Syrian families who had moved to a village several hours from Kearney. When he returned home a few days later, a telegram was waiting for him. Though he had long been isolated from the hierarchy and his fellow clergy, the vast distance between the East Coast and the Great Plains no longer sheltered him. Father Nicola faced a monumental decision.

Archimandrite Aftimios's elevation to the episcopacy had been scheduled, and Bishop Alexander had sent Father Nicola a message, asking him to attend the upcoming consecration service in New York. Father Nicola had followed the arguments in the Arabic papers and the diocesan journal for a year. He also knew both Aftimios Ofiesh and Emmanuel Abo-Hatab. Beyond any personal concerns, however, the priest felt a loyalty to Antioch. Bishop Raphael himself had done the greatest work in helping free the Antiochian Church from foreign rule. Father Nicola also knew the guidelines by which the Patriarchate of Antioch elected its bishops, and he questioned Bishop Alexander about the manner of Aftimios's election. Receiving no response, he gathered his parishioners for a special meeting and told them that the Russian hierarchy was planning to consecrate Bishop Raphael's successor.

After explaining the situation, Father Nicola's parishioners refused to support Archimandrite Aftimios's installation as their bishop, instead desiring to follow the parishes that had aligned themselves with Antioch under Metropolitan Germanos. Immediately after the parish meeting, Father Nicola sent a message to the Russian primate, then drafted a letter on behalf of himself and his congregation. The isolated missionary priest and his parishioners had chosen a side. Their letter was soon published in one of the Arabic newspapers:

> From the Priest of Nebraska and His Congregation
> Refusing Ofiesh and Welcoming Antioch
>
> I received a telegram from the Russian Bishop Alexander asking me to come to the consecration of Ofiesh, so I answered him with a telegram asking him how he was elected. Was it by a majority of the congregations and the clergy? I never received an answer. Then I explained to my congregation what the Russians are planning to do. The whole congregation's answer was that we do not care whom they elect—we are all from Lebanon and Koura, and we have to follow Antioch. We are not here to lift anybody from the clergy to be in power unless it is from the Antiochian Patriarchate. Then when we knew that Germanos had been elected to head the Antiochians, we were so happy and accepted him with pleasure. We sent a telegram to [the Russian archbishop] Evdokim that we do not agree, and that we are refusing the elevation of Ofiesh. This was the same answer of the Priest Makarios al-Safy and the Priest Seraphim Nassar. God bless everyone.
>
> Father Nicola Yanney, priest of Saint George Syrian Orthodox Church, Nebraska.

Father Nicola's letter was one of many. In the weeks leading up to Aftimios Ofiesh's consecration, telegrams sent from fifty communities across the country begged the Russian hierarchy not to consecrate him. Despite their pleas, Ofiesh was made a bishop a few days after Father Nicola issued his letter on behalf of his congregation. The consecration was done by the hands of two Russian bishops at the Russian cathedral in New York. It had been almost two and a half years since Bishop Raphael's death, and his diocese was now rent in two. The deep division would not be completely healed for another seventy years.

The subsequent weeks and months were difficult ones for Orthodox Syrians across America. Messages protesting both Germanos and Aftimios continued to fill the Arabic newspapers. Bishop Aftimios eventually issued an edict refusing Holy Communion to anyone who sided with Germanos, while Archdeacon Emmanuel wrote articles in the diocesan journal, decrying the ordinations that Germanos had performed as uncanonical and stating that no clergy could serve with or receive sacraments from the metropolitan. The former rivals were now working closely together to keep the parishes still in their diocese from defecting to Germanos.

Syrian communities across the country became openly divided in their loyalties, creating a further difficulty for Father Nicola in his missionary work. Most still called upon the services of the missionary priest, but some families distanced themselves from him because he had sided with the Church of Antioch.

In the midst of the ecclesiastical turmoil, Father Nicola's son John returned home from the army. Though America had officially entered into the war, and John had voluntarily enlisted, now that troops were being sent to fight in Europe, he was honorably discharged. Undeployable because of his malformed feet,

John returned to Kearney and moved back into the crowded house with his father, brothers, and sister-in-law. Though John was disappointed, Father Nicola was proud of his son and happy to have him home safe.

A month after Bishop Aftimios's consecration, Metropolitan Germanos called for a meeting at his newly founded parish in Brooklyn, now a self-proclaimed cathedral. The priests and parish representatives that had wanted to be under the Church of Antioch and had refused to acknowledge Bishop Aftimios were asked to attend. Father Nicola left for New York, once again deciding to make a missionary journey out of the long trip. Stopping off in Ironwood, he visited with the Abrahams and was happy to hear that they were making their final arrangements to move to Kearney within the next few weeks. The priest also visited a childhood friend named John Saba who had emigrated from Fi'eh a few years earlier. The congregation in Ironwood was still in need of a priest, and Father Nicola's friend was being considered as a candidate.

Tensions were high when Father Nicola finally arrived in the Syrian neighborhood in New York. Germanos's church was only a few blocks from the Syrians' original cathedral, where Bishop Aftimios was now headquartered. Over the next two days, the clergy and parish representatives gathered in their new cathedral to discuss their situation. The metropolitan encouraged them to remain faithful to the Antiochian patriarchate and not to accept Ofiesh.

During one of their meetings, the names of all the Syrian clergy were written down, and those in attendance were asked to sign beside their names whether they sided with the Russian hierarchy or Antioch. When his turn came, Father Michael Husson, a prominent priest from Worcester, reminded the others that

Archbishop Tikhon had sought the permission of the Antiochian patriarch to consecrate Bishop Raphael, and claimed that the Russian bishop had always admitted that he had no spiritual authority over the Syrians. When Father Nicola's name was called, he stepped forward and signed his support for Antioch.

On the following day, the discussions moved to electing a bishop according to the rules of the Church of Antioch. Though the priests supported Germanos's leadership for the time being, they wanted all of the clergy and faithful in their congregations to elect three candidates, then submit the names so that the patriarchal synod might choose one. The participants were happy with their deliberations, and the meeting was adjourned.

The supporters of Bishop Aftimios were well aware of the proceedings taking place in the opposition's cathedral. On the very first day of the meeting with Germanos, the Russian faction began filing lawsuits in a Brooklyn court against the Syrian clergy who were siding with the metropolitan. Summons were delivered to an apartment in the Syrian neighborhood where Germanos was living with relatives. Father Nicola's name was included as one of the defendants in the lawsuits.

Desperate to prevent the metropolitan from gaining control of the Syrian parishes, Bishop Aftimios and Archdeacon Emmanuel had each decided to sue Germanos's supporters on behalf of their diocese, hoping to gain control of their churches. Emmanuel had filed the suit against the priest from Nebraska. Before leaving New York, Father Nicola knew that he was being sued. However, Metropolitan Germanos promised to hire a local attorney so that Father Nicola and the other defendants would not have to return all the way to Brooklyn for the court date.

From New York, the missionary priest traveled to Pennsylvania and visited his sister and her family. He continued west and eventually far to the south, when he was called to a Syrian community in Alabama that he had never visited. Father Nicola then turned north, stopping in several settlements along the Mississippi River as he made his way back to Nebraska. When he returned home, the priest informed his family and parishioners of the meeting and told them of the archdeacon's pending lawsuit.

Near the end of the summer, Metropolitan Germanos made a trip to La Crosse, answering the local congregation's pleas by finally ordaining a priest for their community. Elias Sady—the young man who had headed the local church school—was chosen to be their priest. Two weeks after his ordination, Father Elias traveled to Kearney to study with his mentor and spiritual father. Returning from La Crosse, Metropolitan Germanos stopped in Ironwood. Interviewing Father Nicola's friend from Fi'eh, he promised to return soon. Three weeks later, the metropolitan came back to Michigan, ordaining John Saba and installing him as the pastor of the congregation of Saint Simeon.

Meanwhile, having finished training the newly ordained Father Elias, Father Nicola left Kearney for his annual trip to the northern region of his missionary territory. He spent the next month and a half visiting communities in Wisconsin, North Dakota, and Minnesota, baptizing a dozen children and ministering to scattered farmers and families, as well as the congregation in Saint Paul. While his father was traveling, Elias was at home working with the local city leaders, continuing the efforts that Father Nicola had spearheaded a year earlier to raise funds for the Syrian and Armenian relief.

Father Nicola continued his travels, returning in time to celebrate Christmas with his family. He was relieved to see that his daughter-in-law was happy. Her parents had settled in a house down the street from the Yanney home. Moses had graduated from high school and was now employed as a store clerk, while John was working as a section man for the Union Pacific railroad. Elias and George were busy at their store. Father Nicola had still received no word from Brooklyn about the lawsuit.

A week after the holiday, Father Nicola's congregation suffered a tragic loss. Julia George, a young Syrian woman who had been a classmate of Moses, died suddenly of heart trouble. She had worked in her father's downtown store and was well known throughout Kearney. Julia had also been instrumental in helping organize the parish's relief efforts. Hundreds gathered for her funeral, and the small church was filled with flowers offered by the many mourners from the community. Father Nicola tried to console Julia's large family and her many friends. Members of the men's group that Elias led helped with the funeral and served as pallbearers.

A few weeks later, the congregation met to elect its parish council members. Father Nicola was proud that his eldest son had been one of those chosen. Though only twenty-four years old, Elias was already recognized as a leader within the local community. A few weeks later, Father Nicola communicated with Metropolitan Germanos, asking for his blessing to install the newest council members. At the same time, he received bad news from Brooklyn.

Eight months after Emmanuel had filed his complaint on behalf of the diocese, the court had rendered a verdict. Though the archdeacon had hoped to regain control of the churches that had sided with Germanos, the Kearney congregation had not lost their church property. However, a judgment had been rendered against Father Nicola for one hundred and twenty dollars, plus court expenses. The damages amounted to the church dues lost to the diocese since Father Nicola and his congregation had sided with the Antiochian faction.

Father Nicola found the entire affair deplorable and had been surprised that a conflict within the Syrian diocese had been taken to the American courts. Living in borderline poverty, the priest had no immediate way to pay the damages. The judgment had been rendered in New York, however, and Father Nicola wondered if the relatively small damages would be considered a defeat by the bishop and the archdeacon, who had sought to gain control of the church. Hoping that the conflict was over and that the matter might be dropped, Father Nicola continued his missionary and pastoral duties. Home for the beginning of Lent, he poured himself into the prayers and church services.

Two weeks before Pascha, however, Father Nicola was proven wrong. Answering a knock at his front door, the priest had expected a parishioner. He was met instead by a deputy sheriff. The officer recognized the priest and spoke to him briefly, explaining the reason for his visit. He then handed Father Nicola a summons. Archdeacon Emmanuel had hired a local lawyer and was taking him to court again—this time, in Kearney.

CHAPTER FOURTEEN

A Christian Ending

APRIL TO NOVEMBER 1918

THE JUDGE WAS SURPRISED WHEN he looked at his schedule. On the docket for the morning was a case against a local clergyman. He recognized the name. The defendant pastored the Syrian church located only a mile from the courthouse. The judge had often seen the bearded man strolling through town, dressed in his black priestly garb. The Reverend Yanney was held in high regard in the city of Kearney. His wide-ranging travels were often reported in the local newspapers, and he had recently led a local fundraising campaign to aid his countrymen starving in Turkey. The priest had even been a visitor to the courtroom over the years. When cases involved his parishioners, he sometimes showed up to act as a translator or simply to offer encouragement. Sadly, he was the one now being summoned.

As he checked his notes, the judge saw that the plaintiff was a resident of New York named Emmanuel Abo-Hatab, another clergyman of the same religious organization. The judge remembered reading an article in the local paper about a visiting prelate a few years earlier. Apparently, there were divisions among the Syrian congregations over who was in charge of their churches.

The judge reviewed the case. A suit had been brought against Father Yanney in a Brooklyn court, and damages had been awarded for money on contract. According to the plaintiff, the congregation rightfully belonged to his organization. Father Yanney had not been present at the time of the trial, but had been represented by an attorney. The verdict had been rendered in favor of Abo-Hatab two months ago. Though the damages plus interest only came to one hundred and forty dollars, the plaintiff had not received his money yet and had hired a local attorney to sue for payment in the county court located in Kearney.

The plaintiff's attorney stood before the judge, waiting. The case was straightforward. Damages had already been awarded by the Brooklyn court, and the judge wondered why the defendant had not paid. He would have asked that very question, but surprisingly, the defendant had yet not arrived. The judge confirmed with the sheriff that a deputy had personally delivered the summons to the Reverend Yanney five days earlier. The judge waited for an hour, but the priest never showed. Judgment was rendered to the plaintiff by default.

The lawsuit brought against Father Nicola in Brooklyn was one of several. Desperate to keep the Syrian parishes under the Russian Church, Bishop Aftimios and Archdeacon Emmanuel spent months going from city to city and court to court, suing the priests and congregations who had publicly sided with Metropolitan Germanos. Though neither of them would travel as far as Nebraska, and Father Nicola had little to his name but his heavily mortgaged property, the priest feared that they were even willing to take his home.

Though Father Nicola had received the summons, he refused

to attend. Since the case had already been decided in New York, he knew the inevitable outcome. Neither the ruling in Brooklyn nor the one in Kearney changed the fact that he could not pay. Though the damages awarded to Archdeacon Emmanuel seemed small, the amount was more than one-third of his annual salary. Father Nicola was poor. His parish struggled to pay him even thirty-five dollars a month.

In order to survive, Father Nicola had taken out a fifteen-hundred-dollar mortgage on the family's house and land, and was barely managing to pay the interest on the loan. Worried about the initial lawsuit, Father Nicola had made a decision months before the Brooklyn court's ruling. Knowing that the indebted property was the only thing of worth he possessed, and fearing that Aftimios and Emmanuel might press their claim against him because he and his parish had sided with Germanos, he had deeded his house and land to his sons, Elias, John, and Moses.

Father Nicola dearly loved his boys. When he gave them his house and the surrounding property, he had the notary write on the deed that his sons' payment to him was to be one dollar and their love and affection. As a father, he knew that his priesthood had cost his boys a great deal. A poor priest, he had little of earthly value to give them. The house and the land would be their only inheritance, and Father Nicola had hoped to leave it to them someday without any debt. Ever since hearing that Emmanuel was trying to sue him, however, he feared that even the boys' home might be taken from them.

Three weeks after the county court's decision, a deputy appeared at the Yanneys' door once again, this time delivering a document with the court's decision that Father Nicola pay the specified damages to Archdeacon Emmanuel. Two days later, the sheriff reported back to the court that the defendant was unable to make the payment due to lack of goods. Father Nicola did not have the money to pay the damages, nor would he beg or borrow from his parishioners to pay off the archdeacon and his bishop. Emmanuel's attorney immediately filed a lawsuit against both the priest and his sons—this time in the district court—petitioning that Elias, John, and Moses deed the house and land back to their father, and that the property then be sold to make payment. The attorney also served a summons to the Nebraska State Building and Loan Association, where Father Nicola had procured his mortgage loan. The priest's worst fears had come true.

One of the local papers printed a brief announcement about the new lawsuit against the Yanneys. Father Nicola was shamed by the publicity. Even more, he was worried that the very home in which he and his sons and daughter-in-law lived might be taken away. A month after Emmanuel's petition, the district court decided in the archdeacon's favor. Obedient in defeat, Father Nicola had his sons deed the property back to their father.

Father Nicola's legal troubles had come at an inopportune time, right before Holy Week. The temptations and distractions during the penitential services were a particularly heavy cross for him to bear. The ongoing lawsuit had also prevented Father Nicola from leaving on his usual missionary journey immediately after Pascha. Many congregations were divided in their allegiance, leaving a number of splintered communities that had sided with Germanos without the services of a priest. Because Father Nicola knew all of the Syrians living across the Great Plains from his many years as a circuit-riding priest, the metropolitan had charged him with serving them. Yet, until his legal matters were resolved, the priest had not been able to leave town.

With the final court decision made, Father Nicola began his preparations to undertake a belated missionary journey. Though the prospect of losing the family home weighed heavily on him, another event filled his heart with joy. Elias and Mary had begun making their own preparations—Mary was pregnant with her first child. The child was due in the fall, and the entire family was abuzz with excitement. Habeeb and Mineshi were overjoyed and helped their daughter prepare for the baby's arrival.

Both Elias and Father Nicola were especially happy that Mary's parents were close at hand during her pregnancy. With the war still raging in Europe, Elias had recently been called up in the draft. With his imminent military service, he knew that he would no longer be able to manage the store, and he and George had been forced to sell their business. Because Elias was especially gifted with numbers and had studied accounting, he had been assigned to the accounting department of the Union Pacific railroad, which was being administered by the government during the war. By early summer, he was commuting to their offices in Omaha and was often away from home. With his older brother living in Omaha during the week, Moses also decided to move there, finding work as a clerk in a department store and enrolling in classes at a local college. With both Elias and Moses gone, and Father Nicola often away because of his pastoral and missionary duties, the family was relieved that Mineshi and Habeeb lived only a few blocks away to keep watch over Mary.

Though he had been delayed in starting, Father Nicola finally left on another missionary journey, visiting communities on the plains that were still without their own priest. His travels, however, were cut short. Hearing that Metropolitan Germanos was making a tour of his parishes and planned to visit Kearney, the priest returned home to make preparations.

In the midst of making final arrangements for the hierarch's visit, Father Nicola received a telegram that Germanos was arriving unexpectedly early and rushed to meet the bishop at the train station. When the metropolitan arrived late one afternoon near the end of September, the mayor and a local school band were there to meet him again, as well as the Syrians that Father Nicola had mustered on short notice. Father Nicola invited the public to attend the Sunday morning services at which Metropolitan Germanos would preside, and promised that they would be conducted partly in English.

After receiving him at the depot, Father Nicola and his parishioners accompanied the metropolitan to the Yanneys' home and honored him with a large reception. Germanos held church services on the next morning for the Feast of the Elevation of the Cross. Though it was a weekday, many of the Syrians attended and excused their children from school so that they could take part in the services. Near the end of the Divine Liturgy, the children and their parents joined the metropolitan and Father Nicola for a procession around the church.

On Sunday, the church was again filled with parishioners and guests who had come to meet the visiting hierarch. Father Nicola translated the metropolitan's sermon into English as he spoke with impassioned patriotism about the ongoing conflict in Europe. Entreating all able-bodied Syrian men to enlist, he called those who would not fight cowards and traitors. He continued, telling the congregation that fighting for America meant the salvation of the entire oppressed world and freedom for their homeland. After three days in Kearney, Metropolitan Germanos left town, making his way back to New York.

After the metropolitan's departure, Father Nicola left home for the southern states in his missionary territory. During his travels, he began to hear alarming news. A second wave of influenza was spreading across the country, even more potent than the epidemic that had hit in the early spring. The first wave had started in Kansas. Several hundred soldiers stationed at Camp Funston—two hundred miles southeast of Kearney—had been stricken with severe symptoms. Dozens had died.

By October, as the war was beginning to wind down and the Allies' victory seemed assured, a new strain of the disease that the press was calling the Spanish flu had emerged and was quickly spreading across the country. By the time Father Nicola arrived in Wichita, a citywide quarantine had been enacted. Even the churches had been closed, and the priest was unable to serve in the new church that the local Syrian community had finally been able to purchase.

As Father Nicola visited parishioners across the city, many were beginning to come down with the illness. He anointed them and prayed with them. Sadly, a sixteen-year-old girl died during his visit. Because of the quarantine, Father Nicola held the funeral at one of the local funeral parlors, trying to console the small group of family and friends who had gathered for the service. Not long after the girl's funeral, Father Nicola headed north to visit several congregations in Nebraska before returning to Kearney.

The influenza outbreak worried the priest. He was especially concerned for his sons in Omaha. Elias sent his father a letter, reassuring him that both he and Moses were well. Elias, however, was terribly worried about his father and his wife. Threatened with losing the house, Father Nicola had been forced to turn to his eldest son for money. Unable to help due to his own debts, Elias promised to assist when he could. Because of the family's difficult financial situation, he had disagreed when his father had undertaken another expensive missionary journey. Even more, he feared for his father's health, traveling among so many people during the widespread sickness.

Father Nicola initially ignored his son's protests and continued to visit his flock as the public began to panic. When Elias made a plea for his wife's sake, however, Father Nicola changed his plans. Mary was scared about her pregnancy and the upcoming delivery. Though her parents were close at hand, Mineshi and Habeeb were busy with three young children of their own at home. With John away working on the railroad, Mary was alone in the house. To ease Elias and Mary's fears, Father Nicola started for home. As he did, troubling news reached him. The influenza had spread to Kearney and many of his parishioners were beginning to get sick.

When Father Nicola arrived home, he tried to reassure Mary. However, he found the situation in Kearney very much changed since he had been gone. As in Wichita, a citywide quarantine had been enacted, shutting down schools, theaters, churches, and any places of business where crowds might congregate. Public gatherings were banned, and children were prohibited from playing outside. One day later, a similar quarantine was enacted across the entire state of Nebraska. With their places of work closed, Elias and Moses returned from Omaha. Father Nicola immediately began gathering news of the sick and visiting his parishioners, though he himself was beginning to feel ill.

Taking the reserve sacrament from the church, the priest went from door to door throughout the neighborhood. Though many of the Syrians were sick with influenza, it was the normally young and healthy adults who seemed to be the worst afflicted. Father Nicola heard their confessions, anointed them with oil, and gave them Holy Communion. The first death came not long after he had arrived home. After a few days of sickness, one of John Shada's nephews died. Only twenty-five years old, he was a married father with three young children himself. Father Nicola tolled the church bell and the community mourned as news of the young man's death spread. On the next day, the bell tolled again. This time, a toddler had died—the youngest son of another Shada brother.

Although feeling worse himself, Father Nicola served the two funerals on the following day. More and more parishioners came down with the flu, and reports of fatalities across the city were rising dramatically. Many of the Syrians grew anxious, fearing that the church bell would toll again at any moment. In the midst of their fears, Father Nicola continued to minister to the sick. As the epidemic hit the Hayek home, John Shada's family, and others in the congregation, the exhausted priest diligently made his rounds, encouraging his friends and parishioners and attending to them as best as he could.

Compounding their suffering, a cold front swept across the Great Plains, dumping four inches of snow. A message came to Father Nicola that two of John Shada's children were sick. The next night, one of his eldest boys—whom Bishop Raphael had baptized during his first visit to Kearney—was close to death. Fearing for his son's life, John wandered outside in despair, dressed only in his long underwear. Kneeling in the dark in the cold and snow, he prayed that his boy might be spared. The morning dawned sunny and clear, John's son still alive. Father Nicola made his way to his best friend's house through the slush and snow to pray for and commune the young man.

With the sickness touching every household, Father Nicola had others in the neighborhood to see. Having made the last of his visitations, he finally returned home late in the day. His boys were distressed at the sight of their father and helped him as he fell exhausted into bed. Father Nicola had known that he would likely contract influenza at some point, exposed as he had been to so many afflicted with the disease. From the aches and fatigue that he felt, he knew that he had been sick for days. The more distressing signs that he now bore were the same he had seen at the bedsides of the dying. The telltale dark blotches had appeared on his face, and he was unable to catch his breath.

Though he had been tending to his parishioners only hours earlier, Father Nicola was confined to bed—unable to rise, his strength gone. By late that night, he knew that he was dying and had little time left. Motioning weakly, he beckoned his sons to his side. He had left them on their own so many times, and now he was leaving them once more. Calling Elias, John, and Moses close, Father Nicola said goodbye as he struggled for breath. As they leaned over their father, he gave them a final word by which he himself had tried to live, whispering, "Keep your hands and your heart clean."

Speaking soon became impossible. Knowing that God would watch over his boys, and that Elias would take care of his brothers as he always had, Father Nicola fell unconscious. The boys stayed at their father's bedside. Over the next hour, his breathing grew slow and shallow until he drew his last breath and was gone.

Even in the middle of the night, news of Father Nicola's death spread quickly through the neighborhood. Someone ran to the church and began tolling the bell. Though it was past midnight, several of the Syrians came running out of their houses to find out who had died. They returned to their homes shocked to hear that it was their priest; he had just been among them visiting the sick that very afternoon.

In the morning, the boys sent telegrams to Metropolitan Germanos and several other clergy, as well as their loved ones in Fi'eh. Though still afraid because of the quarantine, parishioners began coming to the Yanney house to pay their respects. When the wider community learned of the Syrian priest's death, reporters contacted the family and began printing moving obituaries,[8] showing the esteem in which the entire community held Father Nicola, extolling his dedication to his congregation and marveling at the vast missionary territory that he had served.

Metropolitan Germanos responded to the family's telegram. He was grieved by the news and sent the family his condolences, telling them that he would return to Kearney to serve their father's funeral. He also published an announcement in one of the Arabic newspapers, expressing his great sadness at Father Nicola's death and praising his missionary and pastoral labors. Germanos also asked that all the Syrian clergy pray for their departed brother.

As they awaited the metropolitan's arrival, there were many arrangements for the family to make and many mourners to receive. In a quiet moment, however, Elias went into his father's room and found his thick, worn Bible and his father's precious pocket watch and chain. Since Elias was the oldest son, both would pass down to him. Handling the watch, he saw his father's name inscribed on the face plate along with the date of his ordination. The braids of his father's hair still connected the pocket watch to the fine gold cross. His father had carried them with him wherever he went.

Elias opened the Bible and turned to the pages near the back. There, he saw where his father's familiar handwriting had recorded Elias's birth and baptism, along with that of his brothers and his sister Anna. Also recorded were the deaths of his uncles Michael and Simon. He read of his mother's repose and her burial, and remembered how those terrible days had changed their lives. Beneath the entry for his mother was the record of the birth and death of his infant sister, Nour, and of her

8 See appendix.

burial alongside their mother in the cemetery north of their old homestead.

Turning the pages, he read a description of his parents' crowning by the village priests in Koura, a place Elias had never seen. Between the records of births and deaths, he read what his father had written about his own ordination as a deacon by the hands of Bishop Raphael and, one week later, of his elevation to the holy priesthood. Among a list of deaths, he glanced to the place where Father Nicola had recorded that of his own parents. Finally, Elias came to a blank page. Moved by his grief and affectionate memories, he picked up a pen and wrote in the family Bible for the first time in the Arabic letters that his father had taught him as a child:

> The translation of the faithful servant to the heavenly chamber; my tender and loving father, the beatified and ever-memorable Priest Nicola Yanney on Monday evening at twenty minutes before midnight on the 28th of October 1918 in Kearney, Nebraska, United States of America, passed away from the Spanish flu at forty-four years of age. He was ordained to the priesthood by the beatified and ever-memorable Bishop Raphael Hawaweeny in 1904 for the parish in Kearney, Nebraska which he served until the hour of his death, by God's mercy. Amen.[9]

After Father Nicola's body was washed and prepared, it was placed in the church. With the influenza cases receding, the quarantine was lifted three days after his death. Parishioners gathered to pay their respects and to pray for their departed priest. The family received word that two of Father Nicola's

9 Father Nicola was actually forty-five years old when he died.

protégés—Father Elias Sady from La Crosse and Father John Saba from Ironwood—would be assisting Metropolitan Germanos with the funeral. Elias and his brothers, however, were still waiting for the metropolitan to come so that the time of the service could be announced.

When Metropolitan Germanos finally arrived at the end of the week, the funeral was set for Monday, a full week after Father Nicola had died. The metropolitan, together with the visiting priests, served the Divine Liturgy on Sunday morning as Syrians flocked into town for the funeral. Inside the small church, the icons and hanging lamps were draped in black ribbon. Father Nicola lay vested in an open casket in the middle of the church, surrounded by floral arrangements that had been offered by family and friends.

On Monday morning, the congregation gathered for another Divine Liturgy, followed by a special funeral service for a priest.

Fr. Nicola's funeral on November 4, 1918

The services lasted for three hours. After a meal offered in Father Nicola's memory, another funeral service began at two o'clock. The church was overflowing. Elias and his brothers stood beside their uncle George, their cousin Michael, and other family and loved ones. Parishioners from Kearney and all around Nebraska pressed together with other spiritual children of Father Nicola who had traveled from afar to pay their respects. A large number of townspeople also came to reverence the man who had worked so long and so faithfully in their community.

Metropolitan Germanos, Father John, and Father Elias all spoke during the services, offering words of consolation and comfort to Father Nicola's grieving family and flock. The metropolitan related his great sorrow at hearing the news of the missionary priest's death, and praised him for his dedication in spreading the Faith and for his wholehearted efforts in building up their local congregation. The visiting clergy shared their memories of Father Nicola's visits to their own communities and how he had encouraged and preserved them in their faith during the many years when they had no churches or priests of their own.

At the end of the funeral service, the congregation and visitors were invited to kiss Father Nicola's hand. The mourners wailed as they looked on his face for the last time. The family stepped forward—weeping before their beloved father, brother, and uncle—and said their final goodbyes. The metropolitan then anointed Father Nicola's body with ashes and the holy oil that the priest himself had used during his last days at the bedsides of the sick and the dying.

Loading the coffin onto a wagon, the clergy led the crowd as they processed to the cemetery two miles north of the church. Because the gravediggers were busy opening graves for so many victims of the Spanish flu, they buried Father Nicola in the fresh grave that had been dug for the young Shada child two weeks earlier. After the last prayers and hymns were sung, the casket was lowered into the ground. Father Nicola's spiritual children shared their memories and read poems written in honor of the great missionary. At the conclusion of the service, Elias thanked the metropolitan and the priests on behalf of the family and parish. The crowd slowly dispersed, still weeping. Seeing the clergy and guests off at the train depot, the family finally returned home to rest after the long and wearying week.

Throughout the epidemic, Elias had been worried about Mary and their unborn child, and was grateful that his wife was still healthy. His father's death and the time leading up to the funeral had been a stressful ordeal. Elias would have to return to Omaha soon, but with the war ending and the baby coming soon, he hoped to find work again in Kearney.

On the morning after the funeral, Mary felt strange and asked Elias to fetch her mother. Mineshi came quickly. Examining her daughter, she told the young couple that Mary was fine but was going to have the baby soon. Other women from the neighborhood gathered at the home while Elias and his brothers waited with Mary's father. Mary's pains grew steadily worse throughout the day, and later that night she went into labor. Elias prayed as he paced anxiously, eager for news. Finally, at eleven o'clock, his mother-in-law sent a message for him to come.

Elias found his wife resting in bed with an infant swaddled at her side. Despite her fears, Mary and the baby were both healthy. Elias thanked God as he smiled at his wife and peered into the tiny face of the sleeping child. Mary had given birth to a little girl. As he raised her into his arms and held her gently, Elias decided to name his daughter Martha.

CHAPTER FIFTEEN

Memory Eternal

NOVEMBER 1918 TO TODAY

IN THE DAYS AFTER THE funeral, the plague that had taken the lives of so many mysteriously disappeared. At the very same time, the Great War came to an end. Though the world reeled at the sixteen million soldiers and civilians who had lost their lives in the four years of fighting, it would be decades before an even grimmer statistic came to light. In less than a year, fifty million people around the world had died from the Spanish flu.

As those around them celebrated the end of the war, the Yanney family and the congregation of Saint George continued to mourn. Two weeks after Father Nicola's death, the flu claimed a last victim from their community. The young man was only twenty-one years old. Every family in the parish had now lost a relative or close friend in the influenza epidemic. All of the victims were either very young or in the prime of life, making their deaths all the more tragic.

Returning to New York after the funeral, Metropolitan Germanos pondered over what to do in Kearney. The majority of

Syrian Orthodox churches were still under Bishop Aftimios. The parish in Kearney was a sizable congregation. More importantly, due to the late Father Nicola's labors, it was a hub from which the metropolitan could reach many smaller communities.

Having no spare priests to send, Metropolitan Germanos began searching for a layman that he might ordain and send to Nebraska. He soon found the perfect candidate—one of the Hamaty brothers whom Father Nicola had visited for years during his missionary journeys. Elias Hamaty was a pious young man living with his family in southeast Missouri. He, too, had grown up in Koura, and his home village of Aafsdiq was close to both Fi'eh and the Balamand monastery. Like Father Nicola, he had been educated at the monastery's school and had even been a seminarian before coming to America. Elias had first immigrated to Boston, but had later opened a restaurant in Poplar Bluffs, Missouri, one of the places that Father Nicola had regularly visited. Whenever the missionary priest arrived in the area to serve the liturgy or perform a baptism, Elias would assist him.

Five months after the funeral, Metropolitan Germanos returned to Nebraska along with Father John Saba. They planned to pray at and erect a headstone over Father Nicola's grave. During his weeklong visit, the metropolitan would also ordain Elias Hamaty and install him as the pastor of the congregation of Saint George. Germanos believed that his roots in Koura and his acquaintance with Father Nicola would make him a good fit for the local church.

Two days after arriving in Kearney, the metropolitan and Father John gathered with Elias, John, and Moses at their father's grave, along with their family and fellow parishioners. Metropolitan Germanos once again led the prayers as he and Father John chanted the funeral hymns and petitions on behalf of the departed priest. After the memorial prayers, both men spoke to the group of mourners, encouraging them and extolling Father Nicola's zealous character and his many years of selfless service. Laying flowers on the grave, the crowd departed. Although the metropolitan had helped raise funds and even designed a gravestone for his priest, the planned monument was never erected. The site of Father Nicola's burial would remain unmarked for another fifty-five years.

On the following weekend, Syrians from around the region packed into their small church. Metropolitan Germanos contacted the local newspaper and invited the general public to attend. On Saturday morning, he ordained Elias Hamaty as a deacon, and on Sunday morning—the Sunday of the Adoration of the Cross—Metropolitan Germanos ordained him to the priesthood. At the conclusion of the service, he presented Father Elias to the congregation as their new pastor.

The parish of Saint George was happy with their new priest, especially given his connection to Koura. That evening, a reception was held in Father Elias's honor. The event was hosted by the recently established Sunday school. Though the small church school had been closed after Father Nicola's death, two months later, several parishioners began a program to teach the children on Sunday mornings. Father Nicola's nephew Michael had taken the initiative in the effort and was appointed as the Sunday school's superintendent.

Father Elias moved his family to Kearney and began settling into his new vocation. He was well received, and by the end of 1919 the congregation returned to the subject of building a new church. It had been five years since the first attempt. Like Bishop Raphael's death, the loss of Father Nicola had delayed the project. A committee was again formed to proceed with planning and fundraising, but it would ultimately take five more years before construction would begin in earnest.

Not long after his ordination, Father Elias was given the task of serving as a missionary priest. Although taking up his predecessor's mantle and visiting numerous communities, Father Elias's responsibilities were significantly smaller. During Father Nicola's tenure, several parishes had been formed throughout the region. The resident priests now serving in La Crosse, Ironwood, Cedar Rapids, Saint Paul, and Sioux City all divided Father Nicola's original missionary territory between them. No Syrian Orthodox priest in America would ever again tend such a vast area as Father Nicola once had.

While a number of the communities that Father Nicola had cared for developed into parishes, many did not. The settlements in southeastern Colorado and those near the Mississippi River in Missouri, Kentucky, Tennessee, Arkansas, and Illinois would never mature into full-fledged churches. The Syrians living there would eventually move to larger communities or join local Protestant congregations. While a significant Orthodox population remained in the Dakotas, most who had originally homesteaded on the northern plains were already moving back to be near their loved ones in Cedar Rapids, Sioux City, and Saint Paul.

The large Syrian community in Wichita was especially well organized and prosperous. With Father Nicola's encouragement, they had purchased their own church building only months before his death. Their close kin scattered across southern Oklahoma were already migrating to Oklahoma City. They would eventually send for their hometown priest in Syria. Coming to America from Marjeyoun in 1920, he would pastor the congregations in both Wichita and Oklahoma City for years to come.

Father John Saba and the congregation in Ironwood,

Michigan, would also serve those living in Iron Mountain for several years. Abraham Khoury and his friends, however, would eventually purchase property and found a church in Iron Mountain as well. The Syrian families living in Omaha would attend a local Greek church for many decades until—their numbers bolstered by loved ones moving to the city from Sioux City, Cedar Rapids, and Kearney—they formed their own parish fifty years after Father Nicola's death.

With other missionary priests soon ministering from Kearney, Cedar Rapids, Sioux City, Saint Paul, Ironwood, Oklahoma City, and Wichita, the communities that Father Nicola had pastored in their infancy would give rise to numerous other churches and missions. Sadly, the division between the two Syrian factions would continue. Communities far and wide had been caught up in the conflict and were divided in their loyalties between Bishop Aftimios and Metropolitan Germanos. The scattered settlements in Father Nicola's former missionary territory would often be served by competing priests.

Father Elias and his family stayed in Kearney for only three years. With Orthodox priests still scarce and in great demand, he was soon called away. With a vacancy in one of his much larger parishes, Metropolitan Germanos sent Father Elias to pastor his congregation in Boston. Father John Saba was sent to Kearney, but left after a short time. The church in Kearney was again without a pastor, sadly foreshadowing the trials that the community would experience in the coming decades.

Conspiring as they had for Father Nicola's ordination, the parishioners of Saint George contacted Metropolitan Germanos, asking that he ordain once again one of their own to serve as their priest. Father Nicola's nephew Michael had continued to be a leader in the community. Another Yanney who had been raised and educated at the Balamand monastery, he was seen by many as Father Nicola's true successor. Though Michael had to be convinced by his friends and family, he finally accepted the calling and was put forward as a candidate for the priesthood.

Returning to Kearney for the last time, Metropolitan Germanos ordained Father Michael Yanney in 1923. During his years at Saint George church, Father Michael finally fulfilled Bishop Raphael and his uncle's vision by overseeing the construction of a new church. Built largely by the parishioners themselves, the new temple was erected on the lot next to the original church. The remodeled schoolhouse that Father Nicola had intended to reconvert into a parish school had to be sold to help pay off the congregation's debts. After seven years in Kearney, Father Michael Yanney moved to Sioux City, Iowa, to pastor the church of Saint Thomas. There, he served for over three decades and used his experience of building the church in Kearney to eventually oversee the construction of a large, new temple for his congregation in Sioux City.

Following Father Michael's pastorate, the church in Kearney was often without a priest. Because other parishes in the region had grown much larger than the congregation of Saint George and there was still a demand for priests, resident pastors became less frequent in the small Nebraska community. Those who were sent to Kearney often stayed only a few years, and sometimes less, before being moved or requesting a transfer. It would be many years after Father Nicola's repose before his parish would finally begin to have a continuous line of resident pastors.

With Father Nicola's death, the lawsuit against him by Archdeacon Emanuel came to an end. Because Father Nicola had no will, ownership of the house and property was divided between his three sons. Elias, John, and Moses also inherited the large mortgage on the land. As the eldest son, Elias received Father Nicola's most precious possessions—the family Bible and the gold pocket watch that Bishop Raphael had given his father at his ordination, along with the braided chain made of his father's hair.

Elias was given guardianship of his youngest brother until Moses came of legal age. For several years after his father's death, John worked as a laborer. He signed away any claim to his portion of the property, but continued to live in the house with Elias, Mary, and Moses.

Elias and Mary stayed in the family home another decade, struggling but never managing to pay down the large mortgage. After a falling out with his brothers, John decided to leave Kearney and confided to his aunt Rebecca that he would never return. He never did. Moses lived with Elias and Mary until his mid-twenties, when he met and married a young Syrian woman named Wadia. He and his new wife soon moved into their own home. After the birth of their daughter Martha, Elias and Mary eventually had eight more children. When their small house became too crowded, they moved to a larger home on the other side of Kearney, near the Hayek family.

Elias and Mary's new home continued to be a gathering place not only for their extended family but also for many parishioners. The Yanneys kept the Sunday dinner tradition that Father Nicola had started, serving as lavish a meal as they could afford to anyone who came. Out-of-town guests who traveled to Kearney to attend church always found lodging and hospitality with the Yanneys.

Though during his youth Elias had considered following in his father's footsteps, he never sought ordination. He knew too well the sacrifice that came with being a priest and the hardships that such a life would cause his family. With nine children, they could not survive on a meager priest's salary. Elias did, however, continue his deep commitment to the church, serving on the parish council over many years and teaching the adult Sunday school class. Like his father, he was also involved in the education of the parish's children and became superintendent of their burgeoning Sunday school program.

As Father Nicola's eldest son, Elias continued to hold a place of honor in the parish. Nine years after his father's death, Elias's godfather John Shada died from a gunshot wound while trying to make peace with a group of local ruffians who had come to disrupt a baptismal reception. After John's murder, Elias came to be seen as the community's elder. He supported the priests who were sent to their church and helped keep the church going when no priest could be found to serve them. Elias's guidance and direction were sought during difficult times in the congregation as he helped resolve disputes both within the parish and between families. When parishioners fell on hard times—whether personal, legal, or financial—Elias was always there to help, continuing his father's ministry in his own way.

Though for years he had sacrificed his own education to care for his brothers while their father traveled on his missionary journeys, Elias's brilliance with numbers eventually landed him a successful career as an Internal Revenue Service agent. Like Father Nicola, Elias's job required him to work long hours and often took him away from home during the week. Nonetheless, he tried to return to Kearney every weekend to be with his family, teach Sunday school, and tend to church matters. Meanwhile, Mary raised the children and fed the family from the large garden which they had continued to keep.

The extraordinary work ethic that Elias had learned from his father drove him to place his family's well-being above his own health. Due in large part to his intense work schedule, Elias suffered a debilitating stroke at the age of forty-nine. Though he eventually recovered, he returned to work against his doctor's advice. Suffering a second stroke, Elias died on Christmas Eve of 1944 at the age of fifty-one. His funeral was held at his beloved Saint George church, where he was lauded as a true gentleman—highly intelligent, well respected, and compassionate to all.

After Elias's death, Mary Yanney never remarried. Several children remained at home, and, struggling without her husband's income, she often relied on the produce from her large garden both to feed the family and to make ends meet. She lived another twenty-five years after Elias, succumbing to a stroke herself in 1970 at seventy years of age. Mary died as she had lived—serving others—in the very act of helping Mike Hayek's daughter, her ailing friend and neighbor.

After Moses and his wife, Wadia, moved out of the family home shortly after their wedding, he continued working as a clerk in a local general store for several years. Later, the couple moved to the nearby town of Lexington, where they ran a café and began their large family. Always warm and gregarious, Moses stayed active at Saint George church. He and Elias remained close, their families visiting and staying with each other over the holidays. Moses and his family eventually moved to Lincoln, Nebraska, where they became members of the local Greek Orthodox parish. There, he and Wadia opened a café and had their seventh and last child.

A few months after Elias's premature death, Moses' own health began to rapidly decline. The once lively and jovial man who loved to play pranks on his friends and children was forced to turn his business over to his two eldest sons. After suffering for a year, he died on June 6, 1946, at only forty-six years old. His cousin, Father Michael Yanney, came down from Sioux City to serve Moses' funeral at the Greek church in Lincoln. Tragically, Moses' wife Wadia died in an automobile accident not long after her husband, leaving their seven children orphaned.

When Elias's and Moses' brother John first left Kearney, he moved to Ironwood, Michigan, where he worked and lived with family acquaintances. Later, he made his way to the large Syrian community in Wilkes-Barre, Pennsylvania, where several loved ones from Fi'eh were also living. John found work in a soda-bottling factory. He never married and remained there until his death.

Near the end of his life, John reached out to his sister-in-law Mary and expressed a desire to return to Kearney to see his family. Sadly, it was too late. By that time, both Elias and Moses had already died. John was soon diagnosed with cancer, and his arm and shoulder were amputated to stall the spread of the disease. He died several months later on January 25, 1953, at fifty-five years of age. His funeral was held at Saint Mary Orthodox Church in Wilkes-Barre, which he had attended while living in Pennsylvania. John was remembered as a soft-spoken and humble man who was deeply respectful to the clergy.

Father Nicola's brother George continued to help serve the congregation in Kearney. He and Rebecca raised nine children. George's ventures prospered for a time, but during the Great Depression, he eventually lost his business. In the face of financial turmoil and an unsure future, the rest of the family decided to move to Omaha in hopes of finding work. Reluctant to leave the community that had been his home for almost forty years, and suffering from a severe bout of depression, George tragically took his own life. Rebecca moved to Omaha with her children, with young ones still to raise. She lived another thirty-four years. Her final wish was to be returned to Kearney and buried next to her husband.

In the months following Father Nicola's death, Metropolitan Germanos could no longer present himself as a refugee who was unable to return to his diocese in Syria because of the war. With the conflict ended, so had his original justification for remaining in the United States. Though the Patriarch of Antioch would attempt to recall him several times, Germanos remained in North America, continuing to proclaim himself as an official representative of the patriarchate in order to win more parishes.

At the onset of the Russian-Antiochian split, the majority of the Syrian parishes had remained under Bishop Aftimios. Together with Emmanuel, Aftimios continued to write letters to the Antiochian patriarchate and to use litigation in his attempt to bring Germanos's parishes back under his authority. Rifts in the Syrian communities deepened. Recognized for his loyalty and service to the Russian hierarchy, Aftimios was eventually elevated to archbishop.

In the years following the split, a few parishes changed allegiance to Metropolitan Germanos. In 1923, seeing the division of the Syrians in America and the growing chaos in the Russian Church in the aftermath of the Bolshevik Revolution, the Patriarch of Antioch announced his intention to establish an official presence in North America. A year later, he had Archimandrite Victor Abo-Assaly consecrated as the Archbishop of New York. Both Aftimios and Germanos vigorously protested, with Aftimios publicly denouncing the Antiochian patriarch.

Archbishop Victor's presence in North America paradoxically

both simplified and complicated the situation for the Syrian Orthodox Christians living there. A gentle, pastoral, and even saintly man, Abo-Assaly labored in the spirit of Bishop Raphael. Most of Aftimios's parishes remained loyal to him for several more years. However, several of the communities under Metropolitan Germanos—including the congregation of Saint George in Kearney—quickly came under Archbishop Victor's jurisdiction, realizing his legitimacy as the true representative of the Church of Antioch.

The Antiochian parishes were now able to be under the direct authority of their mother church, something they had desired since the death of their beloved Bishop Raphael. Though providing them an authentic and canonical relationship to the patriarchate, Archbishop Victor's presence also added to the already chaotic situation, effectively creating three separate and competing Syrian Orthodox dioceses. Aftimios and Emmanuel were incensed that the Church of Antioch had sent a further challenge to their authority, and Germanos continued to lurk, refusing to return to Syria.

Fifteen years after Father Nicola's repose, the situation providentially rectified itself. A few years after Archbishop Victor's arrival, Aftimios was tasked by the local Russian hierarchy with creating an indigenous American Orthodox Church. Consecrating Emmanuel as his vicar bishop, the visionary Aftimios set about organizing a new entity that would be autonomous, not bound or beholden to any mother church in the Old World.

Due to his increasingly erratic behavior, however, Archbishop Aftimios eventually estranged himself from his fellow bishops. Bishop Emmanuel asked to be released back to the Russians and returned to Brooklyn to shepherd the remnant of the original Syrian diocese. In an act that challenged the Orthodox

Church's universal practice of mandatory celibacy for its bishops, Archbishop Aftimios married a young woman whom he had met while serving at one of his parishes. The marriage brought an immediate end to any recognition of his episcopal authority. Aftimios lived with his family in semi-reclusion for the rest of his life, dying in 1966.

Meanwhile, Bishop Emmanuel, seeing the growing turmoil and schisms in the Russian Church in the aftermath of the Bolshevik Revolution, began quietly working to bring his flock directly under the Church of Antioch. Stricken with cancer, Emmanuel died before the canonical release of the churches under his jurisdiction was granted. Nonetheless, his final earthly act helped to bring about the long-desired unity of the Syrian Orthodox churches in America. Ironically, Bishop Emmanuel's longtime adversary Metropolitan Germanos served his funeral, eulogizing eloquently about his departed rival.

With little support left in America, Metropolitan Germanos finally heeded the repeated calls to return to his diocese in Syria after an absence of almost twenty years. He died shortly thereafter. Within a matter of months, the painful divisions had come to an end, with all the Syrian parishes in North America unified under Archbishop Victor's diocese. Sadly, a year later in 1934, the gentle archbishop, who had also been afflicted with cancer, passed away. The unity that the Syrian parishes had experienced under Archbishop Victor would prove to be all too brief. When the time came to elevate his successor, two competing bishops were consecrated for the Syrian diocese on the very same day, creating another division that would not be healed for forty more years.

The administrative chaos that threatened to envelop Orthodox Christians in North America had started in the years immediately prior to Father Nicola's death. The subsequent pandemonium would take decades to resolve, and much that had happened in the earliest years of Orthodoxy in America would be forgotten in its wake. Nonetheless, the Orthodox congregations on the Great Plains and throughout America would continue to flourish despite the jurisdictional turmoil. While many parishes grew as the original immigrants continued to have large families, Father Nicola's parish in Kearney declined in prominence. Gone were the days when it served as a missionary center and mother parish for the entire region. With the premature deaths of his sons, little of Father Nicola's story was passed down even within his own family. Beyond the small church that he had helped to found, the legacy of the priest from Nebraska was largely forgotten.

Yet the testimony of that legacy remains to this day, even a century after Father Nicola's righteous repose. In the earliest years of the Syrian diocese—now known as the Antiochian Archdiocese of North America—Father Nicola was responsible for baptizing almost one thousand souls. Through his constant missionary journeys across the plains, he ministered to many thousands more. The communities that he pastored in their infancy developed into thriving parishes that nurtured other congregations. One hundred years after Father Nicola's ordination, a diocese was born, due in part to the missionary priest's labors.

A century ago, Father Nicola's spiritual sons who followed him in the priesthood found in the missionary priest a true father, mentor, and good shepherd. The thousands of lives that he touched as he served his enormous flock, in turn, passed down the Faith of Jesus Christ that they received from him even to the present generation. The legacy of Father Nicola Yanney continues to this day in the Diocese of Wichita and Mid-America, in the Antiochian Archdiocese of North America, across the Great Plains, and beyond. For in him we see a worthy model of the Christian life—one who was faithful in adversity, steadfast in suffering, zealous in evangelism, and selfless in serving others. Through the daily sacrifice of his priesthood, Father Nicola laid down his life for his friends in imitation of his Master. Truly, "unless a grain of wheat falls into the ground and dies, it remains alone; but if it dies, it produces much fruit" (John 12:24).

May Father Nicola's legacy be remembered and may his memory be eternal!

AFTERWORD

The Legacy of Father Nicola

BY MATTHEW NAMEE

THE END OF THIS STORY seems like a bit of a downer—Father Nicola's sacrificial death was followed by the decline of his community and troubles in his family, leaving him an almost-forgotten footnote in history. Yes, his missionary travels as a circuit-riding priest were impressive, but there were a lot of those priests in American Orthodox history. Yes, he was the first priest ordained by St. Raphael, but of course, *someone* had to be the first. He's important to members of the Antiochian Diocese of Wichita and Mid-America, but beyond that, what's his significance? Why does he matter for the rest of us?

NICOLA DID NOT SEEK THE PRIESTHOOD, and by accepting the call to it, he knew that he was giving up the farm life that he loved, and time with his children, and the possibility of remarriage. Young widowhood, single parenting—these are involuntary crosses that Nicola bore well. To these he added the cross of a missionary priesthood. It's exhausting to read about Fr. Nicola's missionary travels—the months-long trips away from his children; the journeys across vast areas of land, mostly by train and sometimes by horse and buggy; the nights spent in all manner of uncomfortable and makeshift beds; cold, heat, loneliness, discomforts of every sort.

Fr. Nicola was a homebody, happy to spend months on end working diligently on his little farm. His correspondence with his children reveals how deeply he loved them. He was not some kind of escapist who wanted to be away from home to avoid family life. He wanted to be with his children, farming the land, but he sacrificed that for the sake of his ministry, to bring the sacraments to Syrian immigrants who otherwise would starve spiritually.

All this would have been sacrifice enough, but then—in an episode that calls to mind the long-suffering Job—Fr. Nicola, on a mission trip serving sheep of Christ's flock, got word that his eleven-year-old daughter was gravely ill. He rushed home, but it was too late to say goodbye. An event like this would have broken some men—his service to Christ meant that he wasn't there for his daughter as she lay dying. But, like Job, Fr. Nicola did not curse God or abandon his post.

It would have been completely understandable if Fr. Nicola had canceled his long missionary journey at this point. His daughter was dead, his sons needed him, and his parish in Kearney needed him, as they too mourned the loss of Anna. How could you blame him for staying home for a long while? But no—Fr. Nicola remained in Kearney for only two or three weeks, and then he was back on the road, back to seeking out those scattered Antiochians, serving liturgies and baptisms and weddings and funerals. His duty to his God came before all else.

Fr. Nicola endured immense tragedy. He also suffered injustice.

After St. Raphael's death, his priests were divided about whether they should be under the Church of Russia or the Patriarchate of Antioch. Fr. Nicola was totally removed from church politics, trying to make the best decision in an impossible situation, with two really poor options. He suffered for his choice: at the time of his death, Fr. Nicola was on the verge of losing his house—fallout from the lawsuit filed against him. And then the Spanish flu pandemic hit.

He probably first heard about this new wave of the flu during his travels, in early October. He made it back to Kearney in late October, just in time for the flu outbreak to hit the town. The local and state governments imposed a quarantine. But he did not rest. I wonder if it even occurred to him to rest—would it have even been a temptation to a priest who had already so crucified his own will, his own self-interest, for the sake of Christ and his flock? A lesser man—a normal man, really—could have rationalized the need for rest. After all, he had great responsibilities—his parishioners needed him, as did all the other Syrians throughout mid-America. His grandchild would be born any day. His family needed him. But Fr. Nicola did not stop visiting his people, anointing them, giving them communion, helping them either to heal or to prepare for death.

This, in fact, was his own preparation for death. He ministered to his people until he physically could not continue and literally collapsed. This calls to mind the Lord Himself, whom Fr. Nicola imitated and served—having loved his own, he loved them to the end (John 13:1).

In the middle of the third century, a terrible epidemic beset the great city of Alexandria, in Egypt. The pagans of the city deserted the sick and dying and tried to protect themselves.

The Christians did the opposite. In the words of St. Dionysius the Great of Alexandria:

> Most of our brother-Christians showed unbounded love and loyalty, never sparing themselves and thinking only of one another. Heedless of the danger, they took charge of the sick, attending to their every need and ministering to them in Christ, and with them departed this life serenely happy; for they were infected by others with the disease, drawing on themselves the sickness of their neighbors and cheerfully accepting their pains. Many, in nursing and curing others, transferred their death to themselves and died in their stead, turning the common formula that is normally an empty courtesy into a reality: 'Your humble servant bids you good-bye.'
>
> The best of our brothers lost their lives in this manner, a number of presbyters, deacons, and laymen winning high commendation, so that death in this form, the result of great piety and strong faith, seems in every way the equal of martyrdom.

WHAT, THEN, IS THE LEGACY of Fr. Nicola? It is not merely that of a pioneering priest, a founder of parishes, the first ordination by St. Raphael. No, the legacy of Fr. Nicola is much more than that—it is a legacy of martyrdom. By the choices he made in his life, culminating in his self-emptying death, he bore witness to the reality of the Gospel. No man of little faith could have endured such suffering and accepted such tribulation. No man of little faith could have so disregarded his own self-interest to care for the sick and dying.

By his life, and most especially by his death, Fr. Nicola declares to us loudly that Christ is indeed risen, that it is all true, that the Lord reigns and is coming again. Like the long-suffering Apostle Paul, Fr. Nicola cries out to us with his death,

> Yet indeed I also count all things loss for the excellence of the knowledge of Christ Jesus my Lord, for whom I have suffered the loss of all things, and count them as rubbish, that I may gain Christ and be found in Him . . . that I may know Him and the power of His resurrection, and the fellowship of His sufferings, being conformed to His death, if, by any means, I may attain to the resurrection from the dead. (Phil. 3:8–11)

And so in the end, like all the martyrs and saints, Fr. Nicola draws our attention not to himself, but to the One whom he serves, who has revealed Fr. Nicola to us in these recent years, whose Gospel Fr. Nicola continues to preach even now, this very day, through his life and his death and his prayers before the Throne of God.

APPENDIX

Obituaries

REV. N. E. YANNEY DEAD

Passes Away at His Home in This City Tuesday Morning

For the past twenty years Rev. N. E. Yanney has been a most familiar figure on the streets of Kearney. During that time many noble and worthy deeds can be placed on the proper side of his ledger. But such is to be no more, as death claimed him on Tuesday morning, October 29.

Coming to this city twenty years ago he at once set about in the organization of a Syrian colony, and later established the Syrian Orthodox church. From that time on until death he lived and worked for his people and church, doing good wherever he went.

None who knew him spoke other than good of him. He held his people in his confidence and never missed an opportunity to speak to them, encourage them and help them.

During the present quarantine for Spanish influenza several of his people were afflicted, and although not feeling well himself, he called upon them to encourage them in their affliction and giving them what attention he could. This work he continued until death called him Tuesday morning.

That his people will miss him and that his familiar figure will be missed upon our streets is certain.

At the time of death he was forty-four years of age, and is survived by three sons, one a resident of Omaha, while another is in the service of Uncle Sam and another a resident of this city.

—printed in *The Kearney Democrat*, October 31, 1918, p. 1

REV. N. E. YANNEY IS VICTIM OF THE FLU

Syrian Pastor Worked With His Parish Members to Last.

Rev. Nicola E. Yanney, pastor of the Syrian Orthodox church in Kearney, passed away at his home here on Tuesday morning, a victim of pneumonia following an attack of the Spanish influenza. Rev. Yanney was forty-four and had been a resident of Kearney for about twenty years. He is survived by three sons, E. K. Yanney being married and located in Omaha. Arrangements for the funeral are to be announced later and it is highly probable that Archbishop Germanos will be called from Brooklyn and officiate at the service.

During the past week Rev. Yanney worked faithfully among his parish members here, many of them being stricken with the influenza. Considerable exposure to the disease was inevitable and although he had complained of not being in the best of health he continued his work uninterrupted until the last.

Rev. Yanney, since coming to Kearney, won the love of all of his people and esteem and admiration of all in the community. He organized the Syrian colony here and established the local church. In recent years he was assigned a large missionary district, extending from Canada to the Gulf and from the Mississippi to the Rockies. Regular visitations within the bounds of this district resulted in his developing a wide acquaintance and thousands of loyal devoted followers. He did much in the way of community development work while stationed in Kearney and his untimely death is deplored by the entire municipality.

—printed in *The Kearney Daily Hub*, October 29, 1918, p. 2

MEMORY ETERNAL

Even as everyone was celebrating the Allies' victory and that our country Syria was freed, we lost so many young people because of the Spanish flu. We received news that our beloved priest Nicola Yanney passed away in Kearney, Nebraska. This adds all the more to our sadness.

He was a faithful priest and beloved son of the church community in Kearney. He spent very much time spreading the faith and serving the church and the people there. With the deepest sadness, we offer our sympathy to his family and parishioners, and to his relatives and friends in Fi'eh al-Koura.

We ask God to give sympathy to his family and friends, and we ask God to give him a place in heaven with all the saints. We are traveling tomorrow to pay our respects. The funeral will be held on November 4th in Kearney, and we ask all the priests to say a prayer in his name.

This was written on Oct 30th, 1918 by Metropolitan Germanos.

It was the worst hour when we received the telegram from the children of Father Nicola. They told us that we had lost him because he was always the first to serve the people and the congregation. We wept bitterly and we offer our condolences to our Metropolitan Germanos and to the congregation in Kearney, Nebraska, and to all of his family in the old country.

—printed in the Brooklyn Arabic newspaper
Al-Nasr (The Eagle), October 31, 1918, p. 3

CRY THEE THE PATRIOT

Cry Thee Antiochian Homage

The sun had barely set on Tuesday 29th of October 1918 when we received a telegram carrying unbearable news. We were in shock, our hearts burning, our eyes crying, our limbs in pain for the news was the death of a man of great piety, religious patriotism, and loyalty—Khoury Nicola Yanney—the priest of Kearney's church, and one of the great fighters in holy service and patriotism for Antioch and the Syrian people.

This was how the bad news arrived:

> From Kearney Nebraska on the 29th of October 1918. To Najeeb Gergi Badran in New York. Our dear father Khoury Nicola Yanney passed away at 12:00 midnight.
> —Elias Khoury Yanney and brothers

We were shocked by the news and the extent of this tragic event. It had a big impact on our hearts and souls. Who will hear of such news and not be in pain and agony? . . . By losing him, we lost a cornerstone of our patriotic foundations and a major support of our [Syrian] nation. We lost a father that was fighting for his nation and the principles of liberty and democracy. We lost a priest who was a leader among those who announced their preservation of their original spiritual reference. Our loss is immense. So, cry thee the patriot. Cry thee Antiochian Homage.

The Father that was very humble, kind, and gentle has died today. The church is sad, the congregation is grieving, and so is all the Syrian community. Every single one of his congregations knew him as a trustworthy and faithful friend.

When we started with our national project, the voice of

Khoury Nicola Yanney was that of patriotism and reverence to the head of the Antiochian Archdiocese. . . . [H]e stood faithful to these principles without paying attention to criticisms because he saw that a true servant of God and truth is one who endures all the agony and pain as did the prophets before him.

Those who were untruthful to their fathers' church tried to sway his position, yet he never gave in. They threatened him, yet he did not blink. They did all they could to antagonize him, yet he was just like his great master in patience, loyalty, and persistence. . . . He was very principled in his religious values, a free man in his national work, and a fighter in all spiritual responsibilities. May God rest his pure soul that has departed and left us to sadness and sorrow.

"The Eagle" is so sad for your departure and so are the Eagle's supporters. We mourn your loss and the loss of your pure hands and all that you have done for the congregation, the church, and this newspaper. We will remember you till eternity.

So long thee loyal friend, kind Father, and patriot who never waned in his responsibilities and duties. So long thee the priest of the Almighty.

To you our blessed Metropolitan Germanos, we send our sincerest sympathies. And to you our Syrian nation in North America, we send our sorrow for this tragic event. And to the family of the deceased, the congregation and all children of our nation, this loss is as big for us as it is a big loss for you.

May God grant us patience. May God bestow his mercy on our Father. May God keep you safe and sound. Amen.

—printed in the Brooklyn Arabic newspaper
Al-Nasr (The Eagle), November 1, 1918, p. 4

Bibliography

Letters and Personal Records

Letter to Elias K. Yanney on his wedding, November 12, 1916. Author unknown. Collection of Rocky Steinbrink, Kearney, NE.

Shehadi, Germanos. Letters to Elias K. Yanney, December 3, 1918, and January 19, 1919. Collection of Rocky Steinbrink, Kearney, NE.

Yanney, Awad Michael. Letter to Father Nicola Yanney, November 6, 1904. Collection of Rocky Steinbrink, Kearney, NE.

Yanney, Elias. Letter to his son Father Nicola Yanney, August 10, 1907. Collection of Rocky Steinbrink, Kearney, NE.

Yanney, Elias K. Letter to Father Nicola Yanney, October 21, 1918. Collection of Rocky Steinbrink, Kearney, NE.

Yanney, Nicola. Letter to Elias K. Yanney, July 10, 1914. Collection of Rocky Steinbrink, Kearney, NE.

Yanney, Nicola. Notes from special parish meeting, September 21, 1914. Collection of Saint George Orthodox Church, Kearney, NE.

Yanney, Nicola. Sacramental records for baptisms, weddings, and funerals performed by the Reverend Nicola Yanney. 1904–1918. Collection of Rocky Steinbrink, Kearney, NE.

Yanney, Nicola, and Elias K. Yanney. Notes in the Yanney family Bible. 1899–1918. Collection of Rocky Steinbrink, Kearney, NE.

County, State, and Federal Records

1910 United States Census. City of Kearney, Buffalo County, Nebraska, April 15, 1910.

1900 United States Census. Valley Township, Buffalo County, Nebraska, June 11, 1900.

Mortgage Records. Nicola Yanney to Abood Abood. Buffalo County, Nebraska, January 5, 1905.

Mortgage Records. Nicola Yanney to Campbell Abood. Buffalo County, Nebraska, December 29, 1905.

Mortgage Records. Nicola Yanney to Dan Morris. Buffalo County, Nebraska, November 11, 1910, and January 11, 1913.

Mortgage Records. Nicola Yanney to the Nebraska State Building and Loan Association. Buffalo County, Nebraska, November 30, 1917.

Quit Claim Deed Record. C. M. Hull and wife to Nicola Yanney. Buffalo County, Nebraska, June 9, 1906.

Quit Claim Deed Record. John K. Yanney to Elias K. Yanney. Buffalo County, Nebraska, August 5, 1919.

Quit Claim Deed Record. Phoebe S. Switz to Nicola Yanney. Buffalo County, Nebraska, June 9, 1906.

Release of Mortgage. Campbell Abood to Nicola Yanney. Buffalo County, Nebraska, November 10, 1917.

Release of Mortgage. Dan Morris to Nicola Yanney. Buffalo County, Nebraska, November 11, 1917, and December 14, 1917.

Release of Mortgage. Nebraska State Building and Loan Association to Rev. Nicola E. Yanney. Buffalo County, Nebraska, December 2, 1930.

Standard Certificate of Death for Nicola E. Yanney. State of Nebraska, October 29, 1918.

Treasurer Tax Deed Record. M. N. Troufie to Nicola Yanney. Buffalo County, Nebraska, December 13, 1906.

United States War Department. *Final Statement of John K. Yanney.* National Personnel Records Center, Saint Louis, MO, June 18, 1917.

Warranty Deed Record. Elias Yanney and wife, et. al., to Nicola E. Yanney. Buffalo County, Nebraska, June 26, 1918.

Warranty Deed Record. Nicola Yanney to Elias Yanney, et. al. Buffalo County, Nebraska, April 8, 1918.

Warranty of Deeds. D. S. Ingram and wife to Nicola Yanney. Buffalo County, Nebraska, February 21, 1905.

Articles, Books, and Theses

Abo-Hatab, Archdeacon Emmanuel. "General Assessment of the Orthodox Syrian Diocese of the Year 1914." Translated by Adnan Trabulsi. *The Word* 59, no. 6 (June 2015): 11–18.

Abood, Roy. "History of the Orthodox Church of Kearney by Roy Abood." Collection of Saint George Orthodox Church, Kearney, NE, 1978.

Barry, John M. "Journal of the Plague Year: 1918 Outbreak." *Smithsonian* 48, no. 7 (November 2017): 34–43.

Booshada, Elizabeth. *Arab-American Faces and Voices: The Origins of an Immigrant Community.* Austin: University of Texas Press, 2003.

Couri, Randy. "The Itoo Immigrants: My Heritage." *Arab American Institute (blog),* November 26, 2010. www.aaiusa.org/the-itoo-immigrants-my-heritage/.

Damick, Andrew S. "*The Archbishop's Wife: Archbishop Aftimios Ofiesh of Brooklyn, the American Orthodox Catholic Church, and the Founding of the Antiochian Archdiocese.*" MDiv Thesis, St. Tikhon's Orthodox Theological Seminary, 2007.

Damick, Andrew S. "The Many-Stranded Cord: The Separation of the Syrians from the Russian Orthodox Archdiocese and the Formation of the Antiochian Archdiocese (1904–1975)." Collection of Andrew S. Damick, Emmaus, PA, 2011.

"Disease Quarantine of Inbound Vessels." *The Gjenvick-Gjønvik Archives*. Accessed January 15, 2015. www.gjenvick.com/Immigration/Medical-Mental-InspectionOfImmigrants/1892-06-BarriesAgainstInvisibleFoes-DiseaseQuarantine.html/.

Essey, Bishop Basil. "Address Delivered by His Grace Basil on the Occasion of His Enthronement as Bishop of Wichita and Mid-America." Speech given at Saint George Orthodox Christian Cathedral, Wichita, KS, December 15, 2004. ww1.antiochian.org/bishop-basil-enthronement-address/.

Essey, William. "The 'Antacky-Russy' Dilemma." *The Word 20, no. 9* (September 1976): 7–9.

Fehr, Alma Shada. "The History of the Family of John and Mary Shada." Collection of Bob and Marci Duryea, Glen Ellyn, IL, 1974–1994.

Fehr, Alma Shada. "The Story of the John Shada Family." Collection of Bob and Marci Duryea, Glen Ellyn, IL, 1974–1994.

Ferguson, Timothy. "Calling to Remembrance: Archimandrite Elias Simon Hamaty." *Message from Fr. Timothy (blog)*. St. George Orthodox Church of Boston, June 2015. stgeorgeofboston.org/news/message-frtimothy/archives/messages-2015/frtimmessagejune2015/.

Gabriel, Antony. "A Retrospective: One Hundred Years of Antiochian Orthodoxy in North America." In *The First One Hundred Years: A Centennial Anthology Celebrating Antiochian Orthodoxy in North America*, edited by George S. Corey, Peter E. Gillquist, Anne Glynn Mackoul, Jean Sam, and Paul Schneirla. Ligonier, PA: Antakya Press, 1995.

Gabriel, Antony. *The Ancient Church on New Shores: Antioch in North America*. San Bernardino, CA: St. Willibrord's Press, 1996.

Garret, Paul D. "The Life and Legacy of Bishop Raphael Hawaweeny." In *The First One Hundred Years: A Centennial Anthology Celebrating Antiochian Orthodoxy in North America*, edited by George S. Corey, Peter E. Gillquist, Anne Glynn Mackoul, Jean Sam, and Paul Schneirla. Ligonier, PA: Antakya Press, 1995.

Gualtieri, Sarah M. A. *Between Arab and White: Race and Ethnicity in the Early American Diaspora.* Berkeley: University of California Press, 2009.

Hapgood, Isabel F. "Weeping Syrians Join in Procession in Streets and Stirring Ceremonies at Burial of Bishop." *New York Tribune,* March 8, 1915, 4.

Heaton, Eliza Putnam. "A Sham Immigrant's Voyage in Steerage." *The Gjenvick-Gjønvik Archives.* Accessed January 15, 2015. www.gjenvick.com/Steerage/1888-ShamImmigrantsVoyage/index.html/.

Hitti, Philip K. *The Syrians in America.* Piscataway, NJ: Gorgias Press, 2005.

Issa, Andre. "*The Life of Raphael Hawaweeny, Bishop of Brooklyn: 1860–1915.*" MDiv Thesis, St. Vladimir's Orthodox Theological Seminary, 1991.

Issa, Andre, and John Mack. *Our Father among the Saints Raphael Bishop of Brooklyn. Ligonier, PA:* Antakya Press, 2000.

Jacob, John. "On the Fiftieth Anniversary of the Lebanese Syrian Church, Kearney, Nebraska, The United States of America." Collection of Saint George Orthodox Church, Kearney, NE, 1953.

Jesch, Aaron D. "*A Peddler's Progress: Assimilation and Americanization in Kearney, Nebraska from 1890–1920.*" MA Thesis, University of Nebraska at Kearney, 2008.

"Journey in the Steerage—1890." *The Gjenvick-Gjønvik Archives.* Accessed January 15, 2015. www.gjenvick.com/Steerage/1890-LifeInSteerage-ATransatlanticVoyage.html/.

Kayal, Philip M., and Joseph M. Kayal. *The Syrian-Lebanese in America: A Study in Religion and Assimilation.* New York: Twayne Publishers, 1975.

Miller, Deborah L. "Middle Easterners: Syrians, Lebanese, Armenians, Egyptians, Iranians, Palestinians, Turks, Afghans." In *They Chose Minnesota: A Survey of the State's Ethnic Groups*, edited by June Drenning Holmquist. St. Paul: Minnesota Historical Society Press, 1981.

Moreno, Barry. *Images of America: Ellis Island.* New York: Arcadia Publishing, 2003.

Naff, Alixa. *Becoming American: The Early Arab Immigrant Experience.* Carbondale: Southern Illinois Univeristy Press, 1985.

Naff, Alixa. "The Arab Immigrant Experience." In *The First One Hundred Years: A Centennial Anthology Celebrating Antiochian Orthodoxy in North America,* edited by George S. Corey, Peter E. Gillquist, Anne Glynn Mackoul, Jean Sam, and Paul Schneirla. Ligonier, PA: Antakya Press, 1995.

Namee, Matthew. "Cassocks or Collars?" *The Society for Orthodox Christian History in the Americas,* December 7, 2009. orthodoxhistory.org/2009/12/07/cassocks-or-collars/.

Namee, Matthew. "Free Masonry in American Orthodox History." *The Society for Orthodox Christian History in the Americas,* November 20, 2012. orthodoxhistory.org/2012/11/20/freemasonry-in-american-orthodox-history/.

Namee, Matthew. "Hanna v. Malick: the Russy-Antacky Schism in the Michigan Supreme Court." *The Society for Orthodox Christian History in the Americas,* June 9, 2011. orthodoxhistory.org/2011/06/09/hanna-v-malick-the-russy-antacky-schism-in-the-michigan-supreme-court/.

Namee, Matthew. "Some Thoughts on the Russy-Antacky Schism." *The Society for Orthodox Christian History in the Americas,* April 24, 2012. orthodoxhistory.org/2012/04/24/some-thoughts-on-the-russy-antacky-schism/.

Namee, Matthew. "Who Was St. Raphael under—Antioch or Russia?" *The Society for Orthodox Christian History in the Americas,* October 8, 2014. orthodoxhistory.org/2014/10/08/raphael-antioch-russia/.

Nassif, Mary. *A Centennial History: St. George Antiochian Orthodox Church, Cedar Rapids, Iowa, 1914–2014.* Cedar Rapids: Eagle Book Bindery Publishing Company, 2014.

"Renewal of the Parish Council of Saint George in Kearney, Nebraska." *Al-Kalimat [The Word]* (October 1914): 611–612.

Report of the Superintendent of the Coast and Geodetic Survey Showing the Progress of the Work from July 1, 1900, to June 30, 1901. Washington, DC: Government Printing Office, 1902.

Reports of weddings, baptisms, and marriages. *Al-Kalimat [The Word]* (Annual volumes, 1905–1917).

Saliba, Najib E. "Arab Immigration to North America." In *The First One Hundred Years: A Centennial Anthology Celebrating Antiochian Orthodoxy in North America,* edited by George S. Corey, Peter E. Gillquist, Anne Glynn Mackoul, Jean Sam, and Paul Schneirla. Ligonier, PA: Antakya Press, 1995.

Shadid, Anthony. *House of Stone: A Memoir of Home, Family, and a Lost Middle East. Boston:* Houghton Mifflin Harcourt, 2012.

Shadid, Michael A. *A Doctor for the People: The Autobiography of the Founder of America's First Co-operative Hospital. 2nd ed. New York:* Vanguard Press, 1939.

Sherman, William C., and Playford V. Thorson, eds. *Plains Folk: North Dakota's Ethnic History.* Fargo: North Dakota Institute for Regional Studies at North Dakota State University, 1988.

Sherman, William, et. al. *Prairie Peddlers: The Syrian-Lebanese in North Dakota.* Bismarck, ND: University of Mary Press, 2003.

Steinbrink, Minnette Yanney. "St. George Orthodox Church, Kearney, Nebraska." Collection of Saint George Orthodox Church, Kearney, NE, 1990.

Steinbrink, Minnette Yanney. "The Lebanese in Kearney Part 1." *Buffalo Tales* 9, no. 4. Buffalo County Historical Society, Kearney, NE, April 1986.

Steinbrink, Minnette Yanney. "The Lebanese in Kearney Part 2." *Buffalo Tales* 9, no. 5. Buffalo County Historical Society, Kearney, NE, May 1986.

Yanney, Michael B., and Lisa Roskens. *No Small Plans: The Heritage of Elias K. and Mary A. Yanney.* Self-published, 2006.

Yanney, Murrish. "A Brief Biography and Genealogy of the Yanney Family Heritage 1850-1983." Collection of Rocky Steinbrink,

Kearney, NE, 1983.

Yanney, Murrish. "Elias Khoury Yanney." Collection of Rocky Steinbrink, Kearney, NE, 1930.

Newspapers and Periodicals

Aberdeen Daily American (Aberdeen, SD), March 26, 1912.

Akron Register Tribune (Akron, IA), September 19, 1918.

Al-Nasr [The Eagle] (Brooklyn, NY), May 7, 1917–October 31, 1918.

Anaconda Standard (Anaconda, MT), February 13, 1912.

Burden Times (Burden, KS), February 1, 1912.

Cedar Rapids Evening Gazette (Cedar Rapids, IA), May 22, 1911–October 5, 1914.

Cedar Rapids Republican (Cedar Rapids, IA), March 12, 1916.

Fargo Republican (Ellis County, OK), January 29, 1914–February 11, 1915.

Gibbon Reporter (Gibbon, NE), January 14, 1904.

Gothenburg Independent (Gothenburg, NE), January 25, 1917.

Ironwood Times (Ironwood, MI), December 10, 1904–October 13, 1917.

Kearney Daily Hub (Kearney, NE), September 27, 1899–December 26, 1944.

Kearney Democrat (Kearney, NE), October 31, 1918.

Kearney Morning Times (Kearney, NE), September 18, 1914–October 8, 1916.

La Crosse Tribune (La Crosse, WI), September 29, 1907–August 24, 1918.

Mir'āt al-Gharb [Mirror of the West] (Brooklyn, NY), May 14–June 30, 1917.

New-Era Standard (Kearney, NE), July 11, 1907–January 16, 1909.

New York Times, September 15, 1895.

Omaha Daily Bee (Omaha, NE), May 1, 1906–March 14, 1915.

Omaha Herald (Omaha, NE), February 18, 1895–July 30, 1914.

Ottumwa Tri-Weekly Courier (Ottumwa, IA), May 20, 1911–April 15, 1913.

Rock County Leader (Bassett, NE), February 18, 1915.

Russian-American Orthodox Messenger, March 15, 1900.

Saint Louis Republic (Saint Louis, MO), July 25–27, 1904.

Sioux City Daily Tribune (Sioux City, IA), March 17, 1914.

Sioux City Journal (Sioux City, IA), May 11, 1911.

Topeka Daily Capital (Topeka, KS), May 11–July 9, 1906.

Tryon Graphic (Tryon, NE), January 20, 1916–May 10, 1917.

Wichita Beacon (Wichita, KS), October 15, 1918.

Wichita Daily Beacon (Wichita, KS), May 16–July 9, 1906.

Wichita Daily Eagle (Wichita, KS), March 18, 1904–December 15, 1916.

Wichita Eagle (Wichita, KS), July 8, 1906–October 14, 1918.

Williston Graphic (Williston, ND), July 27–August 10, 1916.

Court Records

County Court of Buffalo County, Nebraska. *Emmanuel Abo Hatab v. Nicola Yanney*. April 25, 1918.

District Court of Buffalo County, Nebraska. *Emmanuel Abo Hatab v. Nicola Yanney, Elias Yanney, John Yanney, Moses Yanney, and the Nebraska State Building and Loan Association.* May 18 and 27, 1918.

Personal Correspondence and Interviews

Karam, Georges. "Re: Late Fr. Yanni House and Fih Photos." Received on February 8–13, 2015.

Naff, Alixa. Interview with Arab-American Immigrant George Maloley of Lexington, NE. 1962.

Saba, Rafaat. "Re: questions about Yanni family and Fih." Received on March 3, 2015.

Yanney, Michael B. Personal Interview. June 22, 2013.

Yanney, Wayne. Personal Interview. June 22, 2013.

Ancient Faith Publishing hopes you have enjoyed and benefited from this book. The proceeds from the sales of our books only partially cover the costs of operating our nonprofit ministry—which includes both the work of **Ancient Faith Publishing** and the work of **Ancient Faith Radio**. Your financial support makes it possible to continue this ministry both in print and online. Donations are tax-deductible and can be made at **www.ancientfaith.com.**

To view our other publications,
please visit our website: **store.ancientfaith.com**

Bringing you Orthodox Christian music, readings, prayers, teaching, and podcasts 24 hours a day since 2004 at **www.ancientfaith.com**